ON A SHOESTRING TO COORG

Other books by Dervla Murphy published by the Overlook Press:
FULL TILT: *Ireland to India with a Bicycle*
EIGHT FEET IN THE ANDES
THE WAITING LAND: *A Spell in Nepal*
MUDDLING THROUGH IN MADAGASCAR

ON A SHOESTRING TO COORG
An experience of southern India

a travel memoir by
Dervla Murphy

The Overlook Press
Woodstock, New York

First published in 1989 by
The Overlook Press
Lewis Hollow Road
Woodstock, New York 12498

Library of Congress Cataloging-in-Publication Data

Murphy, Dervla. 1931-
On a shoestring to Coorg / Dervla Murphy.
p.   cm.
Reprint. Originally published: London: Murray, © 1976.
Bibliography: p.
Includes index.
1. India, South—Description and travel. 2. Kodagu (India)—
Description and travel. 3. Murphy, Dervla. 1931-
—Journeys—India, South. I. Title.
DS484.2.M87   1989
915.4'8045—dc20   89-8830   CIP
ISBN 0-87951-372-1

*To Rachel and her father
with love and gratitude*

It may yet be found that the traveller who tosses up at every cross-roads will arrive first at the goal.

from *The Thoughts of Wi Wong*
by Arland Ussher

Contents

Acknowledgements

My thanks must go in many directions: to A. C. Thimmiah and Dr Chengappa of Virajpet, who made it possible for us to settle in Coorg; to the Bernstorffs of New Ross, who had us to stay for three months while I was writing this book and created a perfect background atmosphere of sympathetic encouragement; to Alison Mills and Karen Davenport who gallantly typed from an almost illegible manuscript without error or complaint; to Diana Murray who tactfully but relentlessly de-purpled many passages, and provided endless inspiration and comfort during the darkest hours of Revision; to Jane Boulenger and John Gibbins who helped prepare a chaotic typescript for the printer; to Patsy Truell who helped with the index and with correcting the proofs and to the editors of *Blackwood's Magazine* and *The Lish Times* in which some extracts first appeared.

ON A SHOESTRING TO COORG

Prologue

In August 1973 it was exactly five years since I had been outside Europe. Therefore feet and pen were equally itchy and I decided that this was the moment – before schooling started in earnest – to share with my daughter Rachel the stimulation of a non-European journey. Already she had twice proved, on European testing-grounds, that she could enjoy short bouts of travelling rough: but I did realise that no 5-year-old could be expected to proceed as speedily as my faithful bicycle or as sturdily as my Ethiopian mule.

A period of happy dithering followed; I consulted the atlas almost hourly and received much conflicting advice. One friend, a political journalist, thought International Harmony badly needed a book on China by D. M. and urged me to write to the Chinese Embassy in London. I obeyed, ingratiatingly quoting a pro-Mao passage from my book on Nepal, but there was no reply. From Australia, another friend who works in god-forsaken mines wrote that the outback has much more to it than Europeans imagine; that the animal life and landscapes are fantastic; that if I avoided all cities I would adore the place and could write a pornographic classic about the mining sub-culture. From Kuala Lumpur, a friend's daughter who had been teaching in Malaysia for two years almost succeeded in persuading me that it is the *only* country worth an intelligent person's attention; and another friend was adamant that anybody who has neglected to walk through the Pindus mountains knows nothing of the more sublime joys of travel.

Most tempting of all, however, were the letters from a charmingly eccentric millionaire who repeatedly invited us out to explore the mountains of Central Mexico. His Mexican estate is embedded in primeval jungle and the nearest town of any size is many miles away. I liked the sound of all this, and one does not have to be a nasty calculating bitch to appreciate the advantages of a tame millionaire in the background.

Meanwhile, my publisher (who is Rachel's godfather and

takes his duties seriously) was expressing the opinion that for me there is a book in Scotland. And left to myself I rather fancied Madagascar or New Guinea – though neither, I realised, is the ideal country in which to blood a 5-year-old.

In the end I settled for Mexico, under the influence of the superb photographs that arrived in the post at least once a month. Included were views of a Gothic-style temple recently built in the middle of a mountain torrent for a colony of tame ducks who had found the surrounding terrain uncomfortable. One day I showed these pictures to an imaginative friend who said, 'If that's what he's built for his ducks, what will he build for you?'

Everybody was suitably impressed/censorious/envious/incredulous when I announced that soon I was going to Mexico to live with a millionaire in a jungle. But then a friend came to stay, who had just returned from India, and as we talked a most delightful feeling took possession of me.

I recognised it at once, though some years had passed since I last felt it. It was an excitement amounting almost to intoxication, a surging impatience that quickened the pulse. It was a delicious restlessness, a stirring of the imagination, a longing of the heart, a thirst of the spirit. It meant that I did not want to go to Thailand, Greece, Kenya, Australia, Malaysia, Dhagestan, Tanzania, Scotland, Madagascar, New Guinea, Mexico or anywhere other than India. It was absurd – and, at that stage of my planning, downright inconvenient. But I welcomed it.

My choice of Mexico had been quite arbitrary. All the other possibilities had seemed equally attractive and just as likely to bear readable fruit; and this detachment had been, I now realised, a bad omen. If travel is to be more than a relaxing break, or a fascinating job, the traveller's interest, enthusiasm and curiosity must be reinforced by an emotional conviction that at present there is only one place worth visiting.

Initially I felt bewildered by this effervescence of what must have been fermenting for years in hidden corners of my mind. Far from having fallen in love with India during previous visits I had been repelled by some aspects of Hindu life, irritated by others, uneasily baffled by most and consciously attracted by very few. On balance I had found the Indians less easy to get on with than the Pakistanis and Nepalese – to say nothing of the

Afghans and Tibetans – and by making this fact too plain in my first book I had deeply offended a number of people.

Why, then, my compulsion to go back? I had no quasi-mystical ambition to improve my soul by contact with Hindu spirituality, nor had I forgotten the grim details of everyday Indian life – the dehumanising poverty, the often deliberately maimed beggars, the prevaricating petty officials, the heat, the flies, the dust, the stinks, the pilfering. Is it, perhaps, that at a certain level we are more attracted by complexities and evasions, secrets and subtleties, enigmas and paradoxes, unpredictability and apparent chaos, than by simplicity, straightforwardness, dependability and apparent order? It may be that in the former qualities we intuitively recognise reality, and in the latter that degree of artificiality which is essential for the smooth running of a rationalistic, materialistic society.

Certainly I had always been aware – without always being prepared to admit it – that my more unsympathetic responses to Hindu culture exposed a personal limitation rather than the defects of Indian civilisation. In other words, India represented a challenge that I, like countless other Europeans, had run away from. However, unlike the impregnably self-assured Victorian imperialists I could not convince myself that a failure to appreciate India was a mark of virtue. So perhaps it is not really surprising that as the time-gap widened between India and me the pull to return to the scene of my defeat and try again operated like an undertow in the unconscious – growing steadily stronger until, on that September evening, it took command.

By next day, however, my euphoria had ebbed slightly and I was seeing this return to India as a dual challenge. Apart from the subtle, impersonal challenge of India itself, there would be the personal challenge posed by trying to achieve a successful fusion of two roles: mother and traveller. It seemed those roles must inevitably clash and at moments I doubted if they could ever be made to dovetail. Then I realised that from the outset one role had to be given precedence: otherwise the whole experience would be flawed, for both of us, by my inner conflicts. So I decided to organise our journey as Rachel's apprenticeship to serious travelling.

In effect, this decision meant not organising it; we would fly to Bombay and slowly wander south to Cape Comorin, planning our route on a day-to-day basis. As things turned out, these inconsequential ramblings had the happiest results. In South-West India, between the Malabar coast and the Carnatic, we both fell in love with the little-known province of Coorg. And there we stayed for two months.

At Heathrow there was a cheerful man behind the weighing-machine and I felt rather smug when he said – 'So you're off to India for a short week-end?'

I think I can claim to have perfected the art of travelling light. Neither my medium-sized rucksack nor Rachel's mini-rucksack was quite full, yet no essential had been left behind. We were even carrying some luxuries; seven minute rubber animals in a tin box: crayons and felt pens: a favourite furry squirrel: one story-book (a Rupert Bear annual – not my choice) and half a dozen school-books. For four months in South India one needs much less kit than for four weeks in Europe. From November to March the weather is warm and dry, and light clothing costs so little in the bazaars that our wardrobe consisted only of a change of underwear. Rachel's pack held *Squirrel Nutkin*, our sponge-bag and our first-aid kit, water-purifying pills, antiseptic ointment, Band-Aids, multi-vitamin capsules and anti-dysentery tablets. My pack held a bathing-costume, our sleeping-bags, books, notebooks and maps.

As our plane took off Rachel plunged into conversation with an amused gentleman from Kerala and I suddenly became conscious of having embarked on an adventure that would demand mental rather than physical stamina. This was to be my first long journey with a human travelling-companion, and I am a person who needs solitude. Yet there were obvious compensations. I regard other adults – however congenial – as a form of insulation against the immediate impact of travelling experiences; but small children form links, not barriers. And I was enjoying a delightful 'holiday feeling', knowing this to be the start not of an endurance test but of a carefree journey 'as the spirit moved us'.

Initiation in Bombay

16 November.   Y.W.C.A. Hostel, Bombay.

Somewhere Apa Pant has remarked that air-travellers arrive in two instalments and for me this is Disembodied Day, that dreamlike interval before the mind has caught up with the body; and because a natural parsimony compels me to eat all the meals served *en route* the body in question feels so overfed I wish it could have been left behind, too.

Oddly enough, Rachel seems immune to jet-lag, despite having had less than three hours' sleep. I chose to stay in this hostel for her sake, thinking it would serve as a not too unfamiliar half-way house between Europe and Asia. But such solicitude was soon proved needless and I last saw her disappearing up the street with two new-found Indian friends. It seems she has gone to lunch with someone; I felt too exhausted to find out exactly with whom or where.

Of course even I was buoyed up, for the first few hours after our landing at 7.00 a.m., by the simple fact of being back in India. Emerging from the cool plane into warm, dense air (72 °F., according to official information) I was instantly overwhelmed by that celebrated odour of India which I had last smelt many hundreds of miles away, in Delhi. It seemed to symbolise the profound – if not always apparent – unity of this country. And it is not inappropriate that one's first response to India should involve that sensual experience least amenable to analysis or description.

Outside the airport buildings the scores of waiting taxi-wallahs made little effort to capture us – no doubt they understand by now the financial implications of a rucksack – and with the roar of jets in the background we walked for the next forty minutes through scenes of poverty, filth and squalor which make exaggeration impossible. On flat stretches of wasteland dozens of men were performing their morning duty, unselfconsciously squatting, with rusty tins of water to hand and sometimes a hopeful pig in the background. The Hindu opening his bowels must be the world's greatest mass-manifestation of the ostrich-mentality. Your average Hindu is an extremely modest man, but because he can't see you, having his gaze fixed on the ground, he will serenely evacuate while hundreds of people pass to and fro near by.

So we proceeded, with bougainvillaea gloriously flourishing on one side of the highway and the stench of fresh excrement drifting to us from the other. All around were uncountable thousands of homes – many no bigger than small tents – constructed of bamboo matting, or driftwood, or beaten kerosene tins. Between and in these shelters people seethed like so many ants, and diseased pi-dogs nosed through stinking muck, and shrivelled-looking cattle were being driven on to the dusty, grey-green wasteland to eat Shiva-alone-knows what. After some time Rachel observed dispassionately, 'I must say this place seems rather shattered' – a tolerably graphic description of the outskirts of Bombay. Yet I was not overcome by that nauseated depression which similar scenes induced ten years ago. Perhaps I am no longer quite sure that India's dire poverty is worse than the dire affluence through which we had been driving twelve hours earlier in London.

Outside one sagging bamboo shelter at the edge of the road a graceful, dark-skinned young woman was washing her feet, using water taken from a stagnant, reeking pond with a lid of bright green scum. She looked up as we passed, and met my eyes, and smiled at us: and her smile had a quality rarely found in modern Europe. It recalled something I had read on the plane, in Dr Radhakrishnan's essay on 'Ethics'. 'When the soul is at peace, the greatest sorrows are borne lightly. Life becomes more natural and confident. Changes in outer conditions do not disturb. We let our life flow of itself as the sea heaves or the flower blooms.'

Presently a taxi slowed beside us and the driver suggested – 'You go Gateway of India for only Rs.40?'* He dropped abruptly and unashamedly to Rs.10 on realising I was no newcomer to India. Then, when I still shook my head, he looked sympathetic and advised us to board an approaching city-bound

* One rupee equals 5 pence and there are 100 paise to the rupee.

bus. The fare, he said, would be only 40 paise for me and 20 paise for 'the baby'.

The bus was crammed and we were nowhere near a scheduled stop. Yet the driver obligingly halted and the conductor curtly ordered a barefooted youth with dirty, matted hair – probably a tribal outcaste – to give up his seat to the foreigners. The youth obeyed at once, but sullenly; and his resentful glare so embarrassed me that I remained standing beside him while Rachel sat down. Then another young man, weedy-looking but neatly dressed, offered me his seat, told me his name was Ram and asked, 'Where is your native place?' He thought Glasgow was the capital of Ireland but claimed to be a *Times of India* staff reporter.

A cool breeze freshened the windowless bus as we slowly jolted through mile after mile of slums, semi-slums and swarming bazaars. Rachel was fascinated to see bananas growing on trees, cows lying on city pavements and a crow boldly swooping down to steal a piece of toast off a street-vendor's stall. And I was relieved to feel myself rejoicing. On the plane it had suddenly occurred to me that this return could prove a dreadful mistake. But now, looking affectionately out at India's least attractive urban-slum aspect, I knew it was no such thing.

Ram followed us off the bus and spent over two hours – 'It is my duty . . .' – helping us to locate this hostel. I can never come to terms with his type of doggedly helpful but obtuse Indian. To us such people seem too self-consciously altruistic as they offer help or hospitality, though in fact this is a gross misinterpretation of their state of mind. Nevertheless, the *mleccha* – the foreigner – is usually helped by Indians like Ram not because the Indian cares about the individual's fate but because he regards the needful stranger as an incidental source of religious merit, a messenger from the gods who, if given aid, will act as a channel for valuable blessings. Granted, this is a nice idea: but from the *mleccha's* point of view it tends to stunt many of his relationships with Indians. Few Westerners enjoy being discounted as individuals; and most travellers like to be able to feel that each new acquaintance is potentially a new friend.

This morning I would have much preferred to find my own way and we might well have got there sooner without a guide who refused to admit that we were repeatedly being sent astray. Every one of whom we sought assistance gave us a different set of wrong directions with complete assurance. I had forgotten the Indians' propensity for being ultra-dogmatic when in fact they haven't a clue; and on a hot day in a big city with a small child after a sleepless night I found it excessively trying. Moreover, because Ram meant so well, and yet was being so stupid and obstinate, I felt increasingly irritated and ungrateful and therefore guilty. It is on such trivia that everyday Indo-European relations most often founder.

When at last we arrived here Ram held out his hand to say a Western-style good-bye and fixed his gaze on a box of cigars sticking out of my bush-shirt pocket. 'Give me those cigars', he requested, in an oddly peremptory tone. I stared at him, nonplussed by the strength of my disinclination to reward him for all his efforts. Then I opened the box and handed him one cigar. He could see there were four others, but he seemed not to resent my meanness. Turning away from him I realised something was out of alignment, though I couldn't quite determine what. Perhaps because of this being Disembodied Day, the whole incident made me just a little apprehensive. It seemed to conceal a warning of some sort, possibly to the effect that it is perilously easy for Indians and Europeans to bring out the worst in each other.

It is now 2 p.m., so Rachel should be back soon from her luncheon party. I had planned to sleep while she was out, but I seem to have reached that point of exhaustion at which sleep eludes one. Why do people regard flying as an *easy* way to travel?

Later. My philosophical acceptance of Indian destitution did not survive this afternoon's stroll around Bombay. Men with no legs and/or arms were heaped in corners or somehow propelling themselves along pavements; lepers waved their stumps in our faces or indicated the areas where their noses had been; deformed children frantically pleaded for paise and hung on to my ankles so that, as I tried to move away, their featherweight bodies were dragged along the ground; and – in a way worst of all – perfectly formed children, who could be like Rachel, sat slumped against walls or lay motionless in gutters, too far beyond hope even to beg. One pot-bellied, naked toddler stood quite alone, leaning against the pillar of a shopping arcade with a terrible expression of resignation, and mature awareness of misery, on his pinched, mucus-streaked face. Should he survive he will doubtless end up resembling the next wreck we passed – an ancient, armless man, wearing only a token loin-cloth and sitting cross-legged beneath the arcade, his shaven head moving all the time slightly to and fro, like a mechanical toy, and his hardened, sightless eyeballs rolling grotesquely.

Around the next corner we came on a small girl who had festering scurvy sores all over both legs and was sitting on the edge of the pavement with her baby brother (I suppose) in her lap. He lay gasping, his mouth wide open, looking as if about to expire. He weighed perhaps ten or twelve pounds but, judging by his teeth, must have been at least a year old. Near by, a young woman with the dry, lined skin of the permanently hungry lay stretched full length in the shadow of a wall. Her skeletal torso and flaccid breasts were only half-covered by a filthy cotton wrap and her eyes were partially open though she seemed to be asleep. She may have been the children's mother. None of the passers-by took any notice of her. One 5 paise piece lay in the tin begging-bowl by her side and a small glass of tea now costs at least 20 paise. As I dropped 50 paise into the bowl I was ravaged by the futility of the gesture. Of course one has seen it all before, and read about it, and heard about it, and despairingly thought about it. Perhaps it is too commonplace, too 'overdone', to be worth talking or writing about again. Perhaps the tragedy of poverty has lost its news-value. Yet it has not lost the power to shatter, when one comes face to face with fellow-humans who never have known and never will know what it feels like to eat enough.

This evening I find another of Dr Radhakrishnan's comments more pertinent than the one I quoted earlier. 'There was never in India a national ideal of poverty or squalor. Spiritual life finds full scope only in communities of a certain degree of freedom from sordidness. Lives that are strained and starved cannot be religious except in a rudimentary way. Economic insecurity and individual freedom do not go together.'

In the bed next to mine is an Iraqi woman journalist who

also arrived today to report on India's reaction to the oil-crisis. She admitted just now to feeling no less shattered than I am, though during the 1960s she worked in Bombay for four years. 'One forgets,' she said, 'because one doesn't want to remember.' 'And *why* doesn't one want to remember?' I wondered. She shrugged. 'It serves no purpose to clutter the mind with insoluble problems. Tonight, as you say, we are shattered. And in what way does that help anybody? It simply boosts our own egos, allowing us to imagine we have some vestige of social conscience. It's only when the Mother Teresas feel shattered that things get done. Now I must sleep. Good-night.'

A forceful lady – and a realist.

17 November. Y.W.C.A. Hostel, Bombay.

Most of the young women here seem to be Christians from Kerala or Goa. They speak intelligible though not fluent English and work as teachers, secretaries, clerks, receptionists or shop-assistants. By our standards the majority are outstandingly good-looking, though too many have bewilderment, loneliness – and sometimes disillusion – behind their eyes. Transplanted from sheltered, gregarious homes to this vast and callous city of 6 million people, their lives must be dreary enough. Overprotected upbringings will have done nothing to prepare them to make the most of their stay in what is – much as I dislike the place – India's premier city and an important centre of every sort of social and cultural activity.

None of those to whom I have spoken has any relative or friend in Bombay: if they had they would not be staying in a hostel. Yet they consider themselves lucky to have got into the Y.W.C.A. and one can see their point; the place is clean and spacious, though gloomy with the endemic gloom of institutions, and the charges are reasonable. We are paying only Rs. 25 per day for four meals each – as much as one can eat – and two beds in a six-bed, rat-infested dormitory. To Rachel's delight, pigeons nest in the dormitory rafters (hence the rats, who appreciate pigeon eggs) and cheeky sparrows by the dozen hop merrily around the floor. The walls are decorated with large, violently coloured photographs of the girls' favourite film stars and four ceiling fans keep the temperature comfortable.

In India the establishment of even the simplest facts can take several hours and it was lunch-time today before I could feel reasonably certain that tomorrow at 8 a.m. we may board a steamer to Panaji (Goa) from the Ballard Pier. However, our misdirected wanderings in search of this information were enjoyable enough and at one stage took us through the narrow, twisting streets and lanes of the old city, where many of the Gujarati houses have carved wooden façades, recalling Kathmandu. Rachel was thrilled to see craftsmen at work behind their stalls – sandalwood carvers, tortoise-shell carvers, brass-smiths, coppersmiths – and when we passed the unexciting eighteenth-century Mombadevi Temple she said she wanted to 'explore' it. But a rather truculent priest demanded Rs.10 as an entrance 'offering' so I suggested she postpone her study of Hindu architecture until we reached some more spiritual region.

In the enormous, high-ceilinged hostel refectory we lunched at the matron's table by an open window and, as we ate our rice and curried fish, watched a kite eating a rat (ex-dormitory?) in the topmost branches of a nearby fig-tree. Then Rachel got into conversation with two friendly Peace Corps girls, on their way home from Ethiopia, who invited her to accompany them to Juhu beach. She accepted delightedly and, as an afterthought, suggested that I might come, too.

Juhu is only ten miles from the city centre but it took us two hours to get there. Today Bombay's taxis are on strike, in protest against the government's suggestion that auto-rick-shaws should be introduced into the city to conserve fuel, so the buses were impossibly crowded and we had to walk to the rail-way station.

Even when the suburban train was moving, agile urchins constantly leaped in and out of our carriage, hawking a wide variety of objects, edible or decorative. The little girls were no less daring and strident than the little boys and Rachel became quite distressed lest one of them might fall under the train. (She herself is by nature extremely cautious, with a tendency to pessimism which can be exasperating: but at least it means I need never worry about her doing reckless deeds.) There is an enormous difference between the children of the truly destitute, who are past trying, and these ragged but enterprising youngsters with their mischievous eyes, wide grins and flashing teeth.

Juhu beach is lined with tall palms, expensive hotels and the homes of the rich. Where we approached it, through a gap between the sea-front buildings, a large notice said 'Danger! Bathing Forbidden!' The sand stretched for miles and was unexpectedly deserted, apart from a few servants of the rich exercising a few dogs of the rich, yet within seconds of our beginning to undress a score of youths had materialised to stand and stare.

The Americans decided simply to sunbathe, because of the above-ground sewage pipes we had passed on the way from the station, and to avoid whatever the danger might be I kept close to the shore, where the water was shallow, tepid and rather nasty. I couldn't even feel that I was being cleaned, since my own pure sweat was obviously being replaced by something far less desirable. I soon got out but Rachel refused to emerge until the huge red balloon of the sun had drifted below the horizon.

Back on the road, we stopped at a foodstall to buy deliciously crisp, spiced potato-cakes, stuffed with onions and freshly cooked over a charcoal fire that flared beautifully in the dusk. Then we stood at a bus stop for thirty-five minutes, during which time seven alarmingly overcrowded buses lurched past without halting. The eighth and ninth did stop, but took on only the more belligerent members of the assembled mob, so before the tenth appeared I requested the girls to fight their way on, take Rachel from me and, if I got left behind, cherish her until we were reunited. In fact neither the tenth nor the eleventh stopped, but we successfully assaulted the twelfth.

The narrow streets of the Ville Parle bazaar were lit by a golden glow from hundreds of oil-lamps hanging over stalls heaped with every sort of merchandise: bales of shining silks and vividly patterned cottons, stacks of gleaming copper pots and stainless steel ware, round towers of glittering glass bangles, pyramids of repulsively Technicolored sweetmeats, acres of fresh fruit and vegetables, mountains of coconuts, molehills of cashew-nuts, hillocks of melons, forests of sugar-cane and gracefully overflowing baskets of jasmine-blossom. Mingling with the dreamy richness of the jasmine was that most character-istic of all Indian evening smells – incense being burned in countless homes to honour the household gods. (Foul gutters and festering sores, jasmine and incense: India in a nutshell?)

Through the jostling, noisy crowd – uninhibitedly abusing, joking, arguing, gossiping, chiding, haggling: no sign here of Hindu inertia – through this pulsating crowd moved creaking ox-carts and hooting buses, chanting sadhus and yelling balloon-sellers, thoughtful-looking cows and overloaded hand-carts, cursing cyclists and battered trucks, hoarse lottery-ticket sellers and faceless Muslim housewives carrying so many purchases beneath their burkahs that they looked pregnant in the wrong places. 'It's fun here,' said Rachel, 'but you must be careful not to lose me.' She fell asleep on the train and had to be given a piggy-back home from Churchgate Station.

2

Hippies in Goa

18 November. At sea between Bombay and Panaji.

The deck-area of our steamer is not too crowded and after Bombay one appreciates sea-breezes, even when adulterated by clouds of hash; forty or so of our fellow deck-passengers are hippies on their annual migration from Nepal, or the north of India, to Goa.

In affluent Europe I find it easy enough to understand an individual hippy's point of view, but on seeing them massed against an Indian background of involuntary poverty I quickly lose patience. Several of those within sight at this moment are emaciated wrecks – the out-and-outers, travelling alone, carrying no possessions of any kind, clad only in tattered loin-cloths, their long sadhu-style hair matted and filthy, their bare feet calloused and cracked, their legs pitted with open scurvy sores, their ribs and shoulder-blades seeming about to cut through their pallid skins, their eyes glazed with over-indulgence in Kali-knows-what and their ability or will to communicate long since atrophied. This is dropping-out carried to its terrible conclusion – but dropping into what, and why? Certainly these wrecks will soon drop into a nameless grave, and for their own sakes I can only feel the sooner the better. One agrees when hippies criticise the essential destructive-ness of a materialist society, but what are they offering in its place?

All day we sailed south under a cobalt sky, within sight of the mountainous Maharashtrian coast, past dark-sailed fishing-boats that scarcely have changed since pre-Aryan times. The deck, shaded by a vast tarpaulin, never became too hot and now the night breezes feel deliciously cool.

This afternoon, while Rachel was bossing three shy little Goan boys into playing her sort of game, I was talked at by a young engineer from Poona who proved to be a compulsive statistics quoter. He told me that Maharashtra makes up one-tenth of India's territory, that two out of every five industrial workers employed in India are Maharashtrians, that the Indian film industry, most of the defence factories and two-thirds of the textile and pharmaceutical industries are in Maharashtra, that that State contributes more than one-third of India's revenues and that its *per capita* consumption of electricity is more than twice the all-India average.

At this point the plump, amiable young Goan who was sitting on my other side – father of Rachel's current boy-friends – remarked thoughtfully, 'And in the capital of Maharashtra more than a lakh people sleep on pavements every night.'

The Maharashtrian glared. 'At Nhava Sheva a second Bombay is to be built soon,' he said coldly.

'How soon?' wondered the Goan mildly, his eyes on the Western Ghats.

'Sooner than anything is likely to be built in Goa!' snapped the Maharashtrian.

The Goan continued to gaze at the mountains. 'But I don't think we *need* new buildings,' he said. 'Not many, anyhow. We are content.'

'*Content!*' sneered the Maharashtrian. 'Do you not know that after 450 years of the the Portuguese ruling not one village had electricity? Now after eleven years of the Indians' ruling, most villages have it.'

The Goan looked from the mountains to me and smiled very slightly. 'But for a lot of those 450 years no village anywhere had electricity,' he observed.

Then he and I stood up and went to make sure our respective offspring had not flung each other overboard.

At about five-thirty we altered course, making for Ratnagiri harbour, and the sun was swiftly sinking as we sailed between high headlands, covered with long red-gold grass that glowed like copper in the slanting light. A romantically ruined fort and a small white temple crowned the cliffs to starboard – lonely against the sky, looking out to sea. 'It is a very holy temple,' my Roman Catholic Goan friend told me. A civilised respect for all religions has rubbed off on to many Indian Christians from their Hindu neighbours.

In Ratnagiri's wide lagoon little craft sped towards us like water-beetles and briefly the western sky was a flaring expanse of scarlet and purple, orange and violet. Then the sun was gone, but still I stood enchanted, gazing across the dark green waters of the bay to where distant flecks of firelight marked the many thatched huts on the lower slopes of the steep encircling hills.

A steamer puts in at Ratnagiri every evening, except during the monsoon, yet our arrival caused such excitement we might have been calling at Pitcairn. The unloading and loading of passengers and cargo took over an hour, but unfortunately Rachel missed the fun – having gone to sleep, almost literally on her feet, at four o'clock. A Spartanish upbringing is now paying off: she thinks nothing of lying down on a filthy deck amidst scores of talking, eating, praying or copulating Indians. Yet she cannot – positively cannot, without retching – tolerate the deck-class loo and I have had to show her the way to the first-class lavatories. No amount of Spartan brainwashing can reasonably be expected to eradicate this sort of inherent fastidiousness.

A hazard I had overlooked was the degree of spoiling to which a small child would be exposed in India. During these first few days it has perhaps helped to give Rachel confidence in relation to her new surroundings, but I hate to think what four months of it will do to her.

Indian reactions to the very young can be most trying from a European's point of view. While we were unloading at Rat-nagiri Rachel slept deeply, undisturbed by hundreds of people – passengers, crew and coolies – running, leaping and shouting all around her. Yet, despite her being so obviously exhausted, at least a dozen women had to be physically restrained from trying to fondle, play with and talk to her. I fear a few of them misunderstood my motive and fancied I was operating some *mleccha* caste taboo. In a country of overcrowded joint-family dwellings there can be no conception of a child's need for long hours of unbroken sleep. In other respects, too, the tendency is to treat Rachel as an animated toy rather than a human being. Most of the Indians we have met so far are complimentary about her in her presence, recklessly provoke her to show off (little provocation is needed) and allow her to interrupt their conversations with impunity. All this naturally aggravates her bumptiousness, which trait seems to me the chief distinguishing mark of small female humans. But perhaps I should have said 'Western humans', since most Indian children are evidently immune to it. The Indian tradition discourages the development of a child's self-reliance and no doubt counteracts what to us is 'spoiling'. One can afford to be tolerant of bad manners and constant demands for attention, and effusive about a child's allegedly winning ways, if one has no real regard for him as a unique human personality.

Another minor problem at present is how to take Rachel's occasional harsh criticisms of the behaviour of certain Indians. For instance, early this morning our half-empty bus twice sped away from bus stops, leaving several would-be passengers behind, and she asked, 'Why didn't the driver give these people time to get on? He's being cruel.'

Not wishing her to become the sort of habitually condemnatory traveller one too often meets in India, I muttered something about 'thoughtlessness rather than cruelty'; but I could see she was not impressed by this. Our bus-driver's behaviour was most probably a result of his enjoyment of power, but it would have been both absurd and unwise to try to explain to Rachel that recently urbanised young Indians, in positions of petty authority, often become bullies for complex reasons connected with the structure of the Hindu family. Therefore, to avoid confirming her deduction that many Indians are callous louts, I had fallen back on the sort of waffling she so rightly scorns. The snag is that small children have their own black and white code and to try to make them focus on the grey areas too soon would impose an unfair strain. Against one's own cultural background one manages this situation without even thinking about it, but given the added complication of an alien set of values it can become decidedly awkward.

I have been advised that the best and cheapest place to relax in Goa is Colva beach, where the hippy colony is small, the beach long and the absence of man-eating insects makes sleeping out feasible. Although Goa has a lot to offer I don't plan to explore: we are pausing there solely to give Rachel a few days' rest while she completes her adjustment to the time-change.

19 November. Colva Beach.
We berthed at Panaji two and half hours late; I'm not sure
why, but who cares anyway? Today I have been quite overcome by Indian fatalism plus European sybaritism. This beach
really is everyman's dream of a tropical paradise.

Our night on the boat was imperfectly restful; during the
small hours we stopped twice at obscure ports and the usual
pandemonium ensued by the light of the moon and a few Tilly
lamps. Soon after five o'clock both Rachel and I gave up the
attempt to sleep and sat looking over the side at the tender
beauty of moonlight on water. Then gradually came a dove-
greyness to the east; and then a lake of bronze-green light
widening behind the Western Ghats; and finally a sudden
reddening and a radiant arc above the night-blue mass of the
hills. That was a sunrise to remember.

We sailed up the palmy, balmy Aquada estuary through
schools of frolicking porpoises, yet despite its lovely setting I was
not impressed by Panaji which is being developed with more
haste than taste.

Goa has traditionally enjoyed a standard of living higher than
the Indian average, but recently new industries fostered by
Delhi have attracted thousands of landless peasants, from
Andhra Pradesh, U.P. and Mysore, and many have been unable to get the jobs they hoped for. Therefore the scene as we
berthed was not quite what the tourist literature leads one to
expect of dreamy, easy-going, old-world Goa. Some fifty or
sixty porters were grouped on the quay and they fought each
other like tigers for access to the boat and an opportunity to
earn the equivalent of two and a half pence. In some places
such *mêlées* are no more than a local sport; here the frantic
desperation on these men's faces made one realise that carrying
a load could mean the difference between a meal and no meal.

Panaji's best buildings line the quay – the Old Fort, Government House and the Palace of the Archbishop, who is Primate
of the Roman Catholic Church in India. (Since reading
Desmond Morris I cannot use that phrase without visualising a
gorilla in cardinal's robes.) Having strolled past these and other
handsome façades we spent half an hour wandering through the
narrow but astonishingly neat and clean lanes of the old,

Iberian-flavoured quarter of Fontainhas. During Portuguese times every urban householder was compelled by law to paint the outside of his house annually, after the monsoon, and it seems the Goans have not yet abandoned this habit.

From Panaji one can take a motor-launch to Rachol, *en route* for Colva beach, but wishing to glimpse the countryside we went by bus – a roundabout journey, because of Goa's many rivers and estuaries. For two hours we jolted slowly between still, palm-guarded paddy-fields, or over steep hills entangled in dense green jungle, or past tidy hamlets of red-brown thatched cottages, or over wide, slow rivers serenely reflecting a deep blue sky. I couldn't help longing to be on foot, with a pack-animal to carry my kit; but another year or so must pass before I can revert to that way of life.

In four and a half centuries the Portuguese naturally made a much deeper impression on Goa (area 3,800 square kilometres: population 837,180 in 1971) than the British could make on their unwieldy empire in less than half that time. Margao is emphatically not an Indian town – not even to the extent that the British-built hill-stations now are – but neither is it Portuguese, despite a few imposing buildings with Moorish touches. Like the rest of Goa, it has its own unique, unmistakable character.

One immediately senses the effect on local attitudes of the hippy influx. The Goans are by nature welcoming and warm-hearted, and not unduly disposed to take financial advantage of the tourist, but many do now feel it necessary to be politely on guard with outsiders. Much hippy behaviour grossly offends Indians of every sort, though this country's high standards of tolerance and hospitality usually preserve the offenders from being made to feel uncomfortable or unwelcome. In Goa, however, with its strong Christian minority, I had thought people might be less temperate in their reactions to such hobbies as nudity and drug-taking; but apparently this is not so.

When we got down from our bus it was two o'clock, and hot and still in the streets of Margao. Most of the shops were shut – I was looking for a liquor store – so we sat drinking tea under a tattered awning, watching a couple of American hippies rolling a joint. When someone beckoned from the tea-house door the

young man jumped up with more alacrity than hippies are
wont to display and hurried round to the side of the building.
His companion then looked at us, smiled hazily and asked,
'You want some grass?'
'No thank you,' I said, 'my vices are of another generation.
I'm looking for a liquor store. But it seems they're all closed.'
The girl stood up. 'I'm Felicity,' she said, shaking pastry-
crumbs out of the folds of her voluminous ankle-length robe.
'Come, I'll show you – there's always one open down here.' And
she took the trouble to guide us for half a mile through dusty,
sun-stricken streets. At the door of the shop she nodded and
turned away, having given a perfect example of the sort of
disinterested kindness practised by many hippies but for which
the tribe gets too little credit.

Colva is a scattered settlement, rather than a town or village,
and my heart sank when the bus stopped on the edge of the
beach beside a shack in which Coke and other such fizzy
potions are sold. The place seemed to be infested with foreigners.
Not less than ten were visible at a glance, including a flaxen-
haired youth who was strolling under the near-by palms, stark
naked, his eyes fixed raptly on the horizon as though it were
vouchsafing him some vision not normally granted to man – as,
indeed, it doubtless was. Rachel considered him closely for a
moment and made an unprintable judgement before turning her
attention to the camping possibilities of the terrain.

As we walked on to the beach it became apparent that Colva
is not, after all, too seriously infested; pale, smooth sands stretch
for many miles with no trace of development and away from
the bus stop there are few people to be seen. Close to the sea,
palms flourish on low, scrubby sand-dunes where I reckoned it
should be possible to camp comfortably; but first we would
bathe, and then return to the settlement to eat before looking
for a sleeping-spot. Floating in clear green water, listening to
pure white surf singing on golden sands beneath an azure sky,
I felt as unreal as a figure in a travel brochure for millionaires.

The local fisherfolk – whose boats and nets are strewn all over
the beach – seem very shy, though willing to be friendly with
Rachel. They are almost black-skinned, quite tall and beautifully proportioned. (Good advertisements for a fish and coconut
diet.) The women wear gay blouses and swirling skirts, the men

only a cod-piece attached to a string around their waist, or sometimes to a belt of silver links. As we bathed they were constantly passing to and fro, the women and girls carrying on their heads enormous circular wicker baskets, or earthenware or brass jars. Twice we saw crews loading elaborate nets into heavy boats, which were then pushed on rollers into the sea. It delighted me to watch these men – all grace, strength and skill – performing a ritual unchanged for millennia. As they worked they chanted a slow, haunting song and seemed to be thoroughly enjoying themselves. These aboriginal inhabitants of Goa have never interbred with invaders.

Back at the settlement we met a pathetic American youth named Bob who had the unmistakable appearance of one suffering from chronic dysentery. When I explained that we were going to sleep out he jumped like a shot rabbit and told us that a hippy sleeping on the dunes had had his throat slit three nights ago. The naked body was found only this morning and has not yet been identified, nor have the police any idea who the killer might be, so we are now installed in a typical Goan fisherman's hut at Rs.5 a night. It is half-full of nets and other equipment, with a roof and walls of palm-fronds, interwoven with palm-trunks, and a floor of loose, fine sand. The beds are strips of coir laid on the sand and since there is no door the place has its limitations as a protection against throat-slitters. However, our landlord's cottage is scarcely thirty yards away and his pi-dogs are large, fierce and vociferous.

From our non-door we have a splendid view of the sea; I threw a stone to see if the waves were within a stone's throw and if I were a better stone-thrower they would be. Rachel rejoices in the innumerable small black pigs and minute piglets, and in the brown-and-cream goats and mangy pi-dogs (too much fish produces mange) who roam around near by. The whole beach is permeated by a strong but pleasant fishy smell: noisy flocks of gulls and crows see to it that no fish rots. Slightly less pleasant-smelling is my present form of illumination – a wick floating in a small tin of shark's oil.

20 November.   Colva Beach.

This has been an extremely idle day: I can think of none other quite like it in my entire life. Yet now my muscles are reminding

me that 'idle' is not the *mot juste*; since morning I must
have swum seven or eight miles, up and down, parallel to the
beach.

I am writing this sitting in the doorway of our hut, with a
glass of Feni (the local spirit, distilled from cashew-nuts)
beside me, and through a fringe of palms, stirring in the evening breeze, I can see a fleet of ancient fishing-boats sailing away
into the gold and crimson sunset. But this is a place and a time
for purple prose, so I must exercise restraint.

A coconut-picker has just been distracting me: I delight in
watching them as they swarm up these immensely tall trees,
with no aid but a few shallow footholds cut in the bark, and
send huge nuts thudding on to the sand. Nuts are now 75 paise
each – a few years ago a rupee bought half a dozen – but one
nut provides a full meal for two.

A ripple of morbid excitement went through the settlement
today as the police from Margao man-hunted. They have
apparently established that the murdered man was a German –
good detective work since he wore nothing, carried no documents
and had communicated with nobody during his fortnight or so
amongst these dunes. Such a degree of withdrawal is common
at a certain stage of drug-addiction, when the victim himself
hardly knows who he is, but the Goan police do not realise
this and clearly suspect Colva's foreign colony of an unhelpful
conspiracy of silence.

21 November.   Colva Beach.

The hazards of tropical life are upon us. This morning Rachel
trod on a malevolent dead fish with a frill of four-inch spikes
around its neck. One spike penetrated far into her right foot,
which bled profusely, but prolonged immersion in sea-water
seems to have cured it.

When I looked up just now I saw a line of five young women
walking by the edge of the waves, balancing enormous wicker
fish-baskets on their heads. They moved with marvellous grace
and against a turquoise sea their full-skirted gowns – orange,
blue, pink, yellow, red, green, mauve – billowed and glowed
brilliantly. Life on Colva beach is full of such pictures, making
the ugliness and suffering of Bombay seem not part of the same
human existence. But the snag about even a rudimentary tourist

industry is that it inexorably raises barriers between travellers and residents. Here the Us and Them atmosphere is already so strong that one can only admire the locals from a distance.

This is being another slightly unreal day; it is just too idyllic to waken on golden sand in a palm-leaf hut, and to look through a non-door at a milky blue early sky, and to hear the gentle hiss of the surf behind the shrieking of parrots and the immemorial chanting of fishermen beaching their boats.

Later. The first disaster of the trip: despite all my security precautions someone stole between 500 and 600 rupees while we were having our sunset swim. As usual I had put my purse – containing watch, cash and traveller's cheques – in the pocket of my shorts, which were left close to the water with my boots on top to make an easily watched pile. I could have sworn I never took my eyes off that pile for more than thirty seconds and it was a nightmarish moment when I put my hand into my empty pocket. To be without one paise some 6,000 miles from home is not funny. Immediately I found myself thinking, 'Thank God it's a hippy colony!' for in such situations the less way-out type of hippy may be seen at his concerned best.

On the way back to our hut I paused to ask a young Australian couple – camping under the palms in a tiny tent – if they had noticed anything suspicious. They had not, but instantly offered to lend me Rs.10 and to baby-sit Rachel while I went to the police in Margao. (Here there is neither policeman nor telephone.) No one believed the police would even pretend to attempt to recover the money – responsible Indians themselves admit the rule of law has virtually collapsed since the British left – yet the average European's first reaction to any crime is to report it to the police. Though one may know this exercise to be pointless it still has a therapeutic effect, probably because it is our way of sublimating a primitive longing for revenge.

Leaving Rachel with the Australians, I hurried between the palms to our hut – and saw my purse lying on the floor the moment I stepped through the doorway. My first thought was that it must have slipped out of my pocket before we went for our bathe, but all the cash had been taken, including the coins, though all the cheques and my watch have been returned. So I feel certain the thief was not an Indian, who could use traveller's cheques as currency notes and to whom a Swiss watch would seem a treasure beyond price – even one bought for 30 shillings in Kathmandu eight years ago. It is, however, easy to imagine a destitute hippy lurking among the palms, or behind a beached boat, and being irresistibly tempted to solve his pressing financial problems at my expense. The hippy conscience is a curious, unpredictable thing and it does not surprise me that such a thief would go to some trouble to return unwanted loot. Very likely if the same young man – or woman – suddenly inherited a fortune they would give most of it away.

This is Colva's third major robbery from a foreigner in ten days. Last week an unfortunate English girl, on the way home from a working holiday in Tokyo, was robbed of £400, a gold watch and her passport. (British passports are currently fetching £300 each in India.) Such a calamity makes our loss look pretty insignificant and when I heard about it my lust for vengeance ebbed and I decided not to bother trekking to and from Margao police station.

22 November. Karwar.

Last night four sympathetic fellow-foreigners arrived at our hut to cheer me with a mixture of Feni and Arlem beer and their mission was entirely successful. We sat happily on the sand, beneath a black sky that was lively with the golden blazing of tropical stars, and soon I had decided that money-losses were of no consequence and that all was right with my world. But I woke this morning feeling dreadfully otherwise. Clearly the aforementioned mixture is injudicious and the thought of our stolen money seemed the last straw.

Then our landlord's toothless wife called, as usual, with a little present for my breakfast – a thick, cold, moist slab of slightly sweetened rice-bread flavoured with coconut. Despite its promising ingredients, this bread is repulsive beyond anything I have ever eaten: but, because its cook always sat smiling in the doorway to observe my enjoyment of her gift, I had hitherto forced myself to masticate gallantly while looking as though taking an intelligent interest in her rapid Konkani monologue. This morning, however, being past such well-mannered heroism, I implied that I was hoarding the choice morsel for consumption on the bus. Whereupon our friend hastened away to return half an hour later, beaming, with two more slabs.

After our early swim I left Rachel digging a canal with a Swedish hippy and sought a large pot of tea in the recently built tourist restaurant – a small, inoffensive building. For obvious reasons I retired to the least bright corner but was soon pursued by the only other breakfaster, a bustling Bombay whizz-kid who even at the best of times would have done my equilibrium no good. He informed me that he was 'associated with the Taj Group of hotels' and had come to Colva to plan another excrescence to match that now being built near Calangute beach on the once-magnificent ramparts of an old Portuguese fortress. He was full of contempt for the shiftless Goans who, he claimed, were simply not interested in the profitable development of their territory. However, he assured me that things are about to improve. Apart from his own present endeavours, a hotel complex (which sounds like what I've got, but must mean something quite different) is being built near Colva by a Goan company; and Goan millionaire mine-owners are planning a five-star hotel at Siridao; and a Bombay travel agency is planning another five-star hotel at Bogmalo beach. And so 'the death of the goose' is being as ruthlessly and obtusely organised in Goa as in Ireland.

At our present pace it will not take humanity many more years to obliterate every trace of natural beauty on this planet; then people will look back on the Landscape Age as we look back on the Ice Age, believing it once existed yet unable to imagine it.

From Margao to Karwar is only forty-five miles but the journey took three and a half hours; Indian buses are probably the world's least frustrating motor vehicles. They always arrive (unless they crash, instantly killing everyone on board), yet they move so slowly, and stop so often for so long, that one can observe quite an amount of local life from a well-chosen seat.

This afternoon we passed first between newly harvested,

golden-brown fields where pillars of blue-grey smoke marked
bonfires of burning maize stalks. Then for miles our road
twisted through lonely mountains covered in dense, shadowy
jungle, or plantations of teak or eucalyptus – the last popular
as quick-growing firewood. A few brown rhesus monkeys sat or
sauntered by the roadside but Rachel missed them. In buses I
refrain from pointing out things of interest, feeling she must be
left to observe and absorb at her own pace. There is so much –
details I take for granted – to delight and amaze her: full-grown
bulls gently wandering between the benches in a bus stand
waiting-room; cows with brilliantly painted horns wearing
silver necklaces or garlands of flowers; flocks of bright green
parakeets flying parallel with the road, racing the bus and, not
surprisingly, overtaking it; petite women-coolies carrying great
loads of earth or bricks or timber beams on their heads and
babies on their hips; elaborately carved wayside temples;
gigantic banyan-trees like bits of Gothic architecture gone
wrong; cascades of bougainvillaea and poinsettia; demented-
seeming, nearly naked *sadhus* moaning *mantras* as they hold their
begging-bowls under one's nose.

A group of slim, ebony-skinned tribal people boarded the bus
for a short time in the mountains but kept aloof from the other
passengers. The men wore only the most meagre of loin-cloths
and the bare-breasted young women were laden with necklaces
of tiny black beads – each necklace must have weighed at least
two pounds – and with large golden ornaments in their noses
and ears. They also wore countless tinkling glass bangles on
their slender arms and many silver rings on their toes.

At the State border two armed military policemen came
aboard to check all the luggage. Then they beckoned to three
men who left the bus and followed them behind a small palm-
frond shelter. A few moments later the men returned, openly
replacing their rolls of rupees in their shirt pockets. Goa has
long been a notorious smugglers' colony and since the Government of India banned the import of luxury articles the Goans
have been supplying foreign status-symbol goods to both the
newly rich, who want to flaunt their new riches, and the
traditionally rich, who want to maintain their normal standard
of living. Nor do the State police on either side of the border
overlook the opportunities thus provided. Also, alcohol is sold

throughout Goa for about half the price demanded in heavily taxed Mysore State. So it was tactful of the police to ignore my rucksack.

Over the border, we were still in unpeopled, heavily forested country, but the well-kept Goan road was replaced by a rough dusty track. Then we came to a village – to a town – to more villages – and were back in the 'teeming millions' belt. As the sun set I could see tiny lamps burning before crude shrines in domestic courtyards on the edge of the darkening forest.

At last the bus stopped, its front wheels only feet away from the lapping waters of the Kalinadi river estuary. Boarding the antique, overcrowded ferry-boat, I took Rachel on my knee and admired the ribbons of pink and gold cloud reflected in the wide waters. Then, turning to look towards the open sea, I saw a picture of unforgettable loveliness. The dark expanse of the estuary was catching the last russet-and-green sunset tints on its ripples, and to the north palms were etched black against a royal blue sky, and to the west, silhouetted superbly against the final fiery band above the horizon, a solitary, slim boatman stood astride his loaded craft, leaning on a long pole, straining to push off.

In India one rarely sees an ugly face but beside us on the bus today sat one of the ill-favoured minority who also suffered, poor lad, from severe acne. He passed the time by picking obsessively at his pimples and talking pidgin English to me, despite the evident impossibility of my being able to hear him above the rattling and roaring of our vehicle. On arrival at the ferry he solicitously helped us on to the boat, and off again at the other side, and then he insisted on taking us to the dak-bungalow in an auto-rickshaw. While I was thanking him, he predictably murmured 'It is my duty' and faded away into the night. Unfortunately the dak-bungalow was full; so, because of our spotty friend's conviction that a dak-bungalow is the only suitable accommodation for foreigners, we found ourselves stranded two miles from the town's hotels. While we were discussing what to do next an engineer from Bangalore intro-duced himself and as he knew Karwar well we gladly joined him in the search for rooms. A short, stout, middle-aged man, he spoke excellent English. I wondered if he would prove sufficiently Anglicised to offer to carry my water-bottle or foodbag but, though himself carrying only a fat brief-case, he made no attempt to share the white woman's burden.

For Rachel's sake, this was the sort of situation I had hoped to avoid, since I believe a small child can be expected to rough it only if allowed enough sleep at regular hours. However, she was thoroughly enjoying being out under the stars as we pushed our way through the noisy, crowded bazaar from one full hotel, or doss-house, to another. Children usually revel in unalarming crises which prove that grown-ups are not always able to organise things exactly as they want them.

Eventually we gave up and went to a vegetarian restaurant where we sat by open windows in the purdah compartment and much astonishment was expressed at the speed with which I – having eaten nothing all day – dispatched a moderately hot curry and a foot-high mound of rice. In South India food is served either on a large circular metal tray – usually, nowadays, of stainless steel – or, more sensibly, on a large square of banana-leaf. No cutlery is used and every restaurant is provided with hand-basins for the rinsing of hands and mouths before and after meals; if running water is not available a barrel or water-jar and several dippers will be placed beside the basins. The majority of South Indian restaurants are owned and run by Brahmans, since food cooked by the highest caste may be eaten by most Hindus. Usually in such establishments the floors are not very well swept, the tables are a trifle grubby, the walls are badly in need of paint, the hand-basins are fairly revolting and the latrines are quite unspeakable – but in the kitchens all will be well. Probably, in fact, a lot better than in most European hotel kitchens.

When we stood up to leave, our friend abruptly announced that he had decided to take us to the Government Polytechnic College, where the warden – a friend of his – would certainly allow us to doss down. So off we went in another rickshaw, weaving and honking and bouncing through the packed streets, back to the dak-bungalow suburb where the handsome, British-built college also stands, overlooking the sea.

The warden is away for the night, but his deputy received us most warmly – we might have been expected guests – and at once decided the luckless foreigners must have the warden's room. Within seconds of Rachel's lying on the narrow cot under the mosquito-net she was asleep and I then returned to the huge, high-ceilinged, almost unfurnished room where our host had been having his supper off a steel tray when we intruded. He ordered tea for me and we were joined by several of his staff, including three Tamils and a Madrasi Christian. All were dressed in *lunghis* and loose shirts and each man carried with him his own light chair, though they might well have felt more relaxed sitting on the floor. Our host wears thick horn-rimmed spectacles, which suit his long, lean, very dark face, and he is obviously a man of outstanding ability. For hours we sat happily drinking tea and discussing South Indian languages, Bangladesh, Northern Ireland, the caste system, cow-worship, Watergate and Indian attitudes to birth control. I found these teachers excellent company. It is always the half-educated Indians who get one down. The educated and the uneducated each have their own style of charm and graciousness.

When the conversation turned to birth control I mentioned something that has been haunting me for the past few days – a colossal advertisement in Bombay's railway station proclaiming 'Sterilisation "The Best Method". Many Lucky Prizes Awards/ Certificates to Promoters and Patients who Under Go Vasectomy from 20 Jan. '73 to 7 March '73.'

The deputy-warden and most of his staff agreed that, despite the inevitability of such a campaign, there is something disquieting – even sinister – about attempts to solve a population problem by depriving men and women, for ever, of their procreative powers. I asked their opinion of the sixty or so recanalisation centres, to which men who wish to replace dead children may apply; but it seems these operations carry no guarantee of success and the centres are little more than a propaganda device to reassure parents who fear sterilisation because of India's high infant mortality rates.

I have always been anti-sterilisation, perceiving behind the idea an insult and a threat to human dignity. Yet looking around any Indian railway station, or walking through any Indian bazaar, one realises there is now merely a choice of threats. And perhaps sterilisation is preferable to slaughtering or being slaughtered by one's neighbour.

The statistics are well known. An Indian is born every $1\frac{1}{2}$ seconds, which means that more than 55,000 are born a day, which means that at present a country with 2·4 per cent of the world's land and 1½ per cent of the world's income is supporting 14 per cent of the world's population. These are menacing figures, particularly when one has personally tasted the flavour of Indian urban life. Our struggle to get on a bus at Juhu beach was only slightly annoying; but for those who have no escape from the consequences of over-population, which in Indian cities constantly offend almost every sense, such experiences can be infuriating. During the hot weather, especially, they often provoke to uncontrollable violence people whose nerves are already frayed by hunger and money-worries.

A decade ago, when the world first heard of the Indian government's sterilisation campaign, many people were deeply shocked; now one is half-inclined to wish it luck. And it is being moderately effective; the deputy warden told me that well over 2 million men were sterilised during 1971–72. In 1965 India's Birth Control Programme was given 'top priority' and launched on a 'war footing' and in the fourth Five-Year Plan some Rs.3,000 million were to be set aside for its promotion: so no one can say the Indians have not been trying. Yet the population went up from 361 million in 1951 to 548 million in 1971. By now it must be nearly 600 million and if one dares to look ahead one can see the spectre of compulsory sterilisation on the horizon. My teacher friends emphasised that this would be repugnant to most Indians, but then we gloomily agreed that many ethical scruples may have had to be disregarded, all over the world, before the end of the twentieth century.

Now I am back in the warden's room, where I have had to close the window, because of weirdly zooming insects, and switch on the fan. Considering the status of its usual occupant, this apartment is very simple. The only furnishings are the cot, a long narrow table laden with books and papers, two camp-chairs and a steel filing-cabinet. Over a small shelf in one corner hangs a picture of a blue-bodied Shiva – representative of life-energy in all its manifestations – with a third eye in the middle of his forehead and wearing a necklace of serpents. On the shelf are the remains of a *puja* offering, a safety razor and a small tin of Nescafé.

Some moments ago a kind student looked in to tell me our bus for Mundgod leaves at eight-thirty in the morning. When I first asked about this, nobody here had ever heard of Mundgod – a small town four miles from the Tibetan Refugee Settlement where we are going to spend the next few days. This settlement is run by an outstanding Tibetan refugee leader, T. C. Tethong, and his Canadian wife Judy, an old friend of mine. To get there it seems we must take one bus down the coast to Kumta, another to climb into the *ghats* and a third from Sirsi to Mundgod. My map tells me a more direct route would be through Kadra and Yellapur, but I suppose the local man knows best.

3

Tibetans in Mundgod

23 November. Mundgod Tibetan Settlement.

Four and a half months ago I stood in hot sunshine on a steep mountainside overlooking a deep green valley. Far above, long lines of freshly printed prayer-flags were suspended between pine-trees and all round me hundreds of Tibetans were chattering, laughing and praying. The women looked gay in ankle-length *chubas* and striped aprons; some of the older men had retained their pigtails, tied across the crown of the head, and a few wore turquoise and gold pendants on the left ear to mark their positions as lay state officials. Grey-haired peasants with calm, strong, wrinkled faces twirled prayer-wheels, wafts of incense came from the tall temple half-way down the slope and a four-man band was playing rousing Tibetan dance music. Occasionally lamas in orange and maroon robes passed through the crowd and were greeted reverently. Everyone looked happy and excited for we had gathered together to celebrate the thirty-eighth birthday of His Holiness the fourteenth Dalai Lama.

That was in Switzerland, well off the tourist track and three miles from the nearest village. Many of the more prosperous young Tibetans had come to the monastery by car from the nearby towns where they worked as watchmakers, carpenters or factory hands. They moved awkwardly in their long robes, now worn only on special occasions, and their wives fed babies from shining, sterilised bottles. The older children were drinking Coca-Cola through straws and exchanging remarks in Swiss German. Almost everyone was lavishly decked out in silver, jade and turquoise jewellery, but these ornaments were brand new. The old pieces had been sold in India for a few rupees when the refugees were starving.

Ten years ago I lived on another mountainside, also steep and pine-clad and criss-crossed with prayer-flags. That was at

Dharamsala in the Himalayan foothills, where in those days most Tibetans wore lousy rags and the air reeked of makeshift latrines and so many orphaned children died every week – of dysentery, bronchitis, measles, scurvy and malnutrition – that one dared not allow oneself to feel for them.

Why, then, was I overcome by sadness as I looked around at the healthy, well-dressed, contented Tibetan community in Switzerland? United in loving families, secure in their well-paid jobs, accepted and admired by the Swiss, it seemed that for these 700 or 800 migrants, at least, the refugee story had had a happy ending. Yet to be among them oppressed me almost intolerably.

At eleven o'clock we moved into the temple and a long, long queue formed to lay ceremonial white muslin scarves before His Holiness's portrait. The altar was laden with butter lamps (an expensive expression of devotion in Switzerland), and with little mounds of rice and sacrificial cakes; and, watching the Tibetans ritualistically presenting their scarves, I wondered what – if anything – all this meant to youngsters who had lived most of their lives in Switzerland and would never live anywhere else. There was a striking contrast between the expressions and general demeanour of the young Tibetans, reared in Switzerland, and their elders, reared in Tibet. It sounds glib to say that the faces of the older Tibetans were marked by a serenity that passeth European understanding; yet this is the simple truth.

The scarf-bearing queue was still long when suddenly I knew I could take no more. The emotion I had been trying to suppress all morning had the strength and quality of one's feelings at the death-bed of a beloved friend. As we left the temple, Rachel asked, with the animal perception of a 4½-year-old, 'Why are you so sad today? This is a birthday party.' But of course I could not explain.

Remembering all that today, as we walked from Mundgod town, I half dreaded arriving at this settlement. I am absurdly vulnerable about Tibetans. A sentimental fool, perhaps, but in good company; many distinguished scholars deplore the erosion of Tibet's traditional culture no less than I do.

We saw no motor traffic and few people on our narrow road.
All around stretched miles of golden stubble, green pulses and
dark ploughland, encircled in the distance by powder-blue
mountains. The silence was broken only by the calls of jewelled
birds, the occasional creaking of straw-laden ox-carts or the
tinkling of cow-bells. The light had an exhilarating clarity, a
cool breeze blew – we were at about 2,000 feet – and small
cotton-wool clouds sailed high.

Suddenly I stopped and pointed into one of the wild mango-
trees that grow by the roadside. Rachel looked and went scarlet
with excitement.

'Monkeys!' she whispered ecstatically. 'Millions and millions
of monkeys!'

'About a dozen,' I corrected prosaically.

Half a mile farther on we turned a corner and far away in a
stubble-field I saw what was unmistakably a group of Tibetans.
Their physique and very way of moving is so utterly different
from the Indians that they were at once identifiable and, as we
drew nearer, I heard their familiar and beautiful harvest song:
a most poignant sound. From the edge of the field we could see
three elderly men and two young women threshing grain; they
were dressed in rags and darkly sunburnt but their faces revealed
what the Tibetans in Switzerland have lost. When they
noticed us I waved and called '*Tashi Dele!*' and they waved
back and laughed and bowed and stuck out their tongues. (The
origin of this custom had to be hastily explained to an appalled
Rachel.) As we walked on my heart was full of hope; it seemed
everything might be all right at Mundgod.

I found Judy astonishingly unchanged by marriage and the
thirties. Tall and slender in her *chuba*, she still looks like an
18-year-old and it is hard to believe she first came to India ten
years ago, to work as a C.U.S.O. volunteer under the gruelling
conditions I have described in another book.

Soon we were sitting drinking tea on the wide veranda of an
attractive guest-bungalow vividly decorated in Tibetan style;
this building is somewhat misleadingly known as 'The Palace'
because it was built primarily for the Dalai Lama's use during
his visits to South India. Judy and her husband, who is known
as T.C., live in a tiny three-roomed bungalow, less than half the
size of 'The Palace', on the same rise of land overlooking the

administrative heart of the settlement – the office of His Holiness's representative (T.C.), the office of the Co-operative Society (of which T.C. is chairman) and a branch of the local bank. Near by are the workshop, school, hospital, shop and old people's home for those who have no surviving relatives. And all around, replacing the dense forest that grew here only seven years ago, are the level, neat fields now owned by the refugees, not all of whose nine villages could be seen from our veranda.

As the sun was setting in glory we watched eighteen tractors being driven back to the workshop compound, while Tibetan songs and laughter rang faintly across ploughland and stubble; and I began to be aware that this settlement is successful beyond anything I had imagined possible. Then I felt more than ever curious to meet T.C., who is one of the few Tibetan aristocrats to have been influenced, as a refugee among refugees, by *noblesse oblige*. Since the first stampede into India fourteen years ago, after the tragic Lhasa uprising of March 1959, he has devoted his life to his compatriots – apart from three years spent in Germany, at the request of the Dalai Lama, acquiring a political science degree.

When we met at dinner I quickly came to understand why His Holiness regards Tsewang Choegral Tethong as one of his more dependable lieutenants. There is nothing facile about the leader of Mundgod – even his muscular, compact figure, which makes him look shorter than he is, has an uncompromising quality about it – yet he exercises that special brand of charm which is based on sincerity. Though never effusive, he is consistently kind; and after a few hours one has realised that he is also just, patient, obstinate when necessary and devout with that little-spoken-of yet deeply felt religious faith characteristic of educated lay Tibetans.

Now I long to explore Mundgod and examine in detail the Tethongs' achievement. T.C. confirmed my suspicion that we should have come today via Yellapur, but I am glad we did not miss that drive to Kumta through the high green spurs of the Western Ghats, where they slope steeply to meet mile after mile of lonely golden beaches, washed by a sapphire sea.

24 November.   Mundgod Tibetan Settlement.
In 1965, when the Indian Ministry of External Affairs offered the Tibetans 5,000 acres of virgin forest near Mundgod, T.C. came south with a small team to survey the possibilities; but for various reasons – mainly bureaucratic – reclamation work did not begin until December 1966. Four bulldozers were lent by Swiss Aid, the United Nations High Commission for Refugees and Oxfam, and for these the Government of India provided fuel, operators and mechanics. Of the 300 Tibetans who came from the Himalayan road-camps in November 1966 some 75 per cent were farmers and 100 per cent were eager beavers. A Government-sponsored transit-camp of tents was set up and the workers were paid Rs.1.25 a day plus their rations. Three years of bulldozing, clearing and building followed, and by the end of 1969 the reclamation had been completed and the fields were ready to be sown. (Though reclamation, one feels, is not quite the right word for subduing virgin forest.)

Meanwhile, at the end of 1967 sixteen British-made tractors had been presented by the World Council of Churches and 300 farmers had come from the Kulu valley; and a few months later another 300 or so arrived from the Kailasa region of West Tibet, via a detention camp in U.P. (The Indian fear of Chinese spies entering the country as Tibetan refugees has perhaps been allowed to become a phobia; yet such things have occasionally happened, and could happen again, and the Tibetans themselves are in favour of careful checking lest His Holiness might be assassinated when giving a mass-audience to newly arrived refugees.) In April 1968 another 700 men, women and children came from the road-camps around Simla, and in November 1968 over 500 Ledakhi nomads arrived, including a few lazy trouble-makers who sound not unlike the difficult Dolpo nomads I was once up against in Nepal. Early in 1969 a second group of newly escaped West Tibetans arrived via the detention camps, and throughout that year other small groups came from Bhutan, Rajput and Delhi. By the end of 1970 the population of the settlement had been officially completed, with over 3,000 Tibetans living in nine villages; but a trickle of individual refugees still continues to flow southward and no one in real need is turned away.

The villages vary considerably in size but there are a total of 397 double houses for almost 800 families, and each family has 120 feet by 60 feet of kitchen-garden where banana and papaya-trees flourish – and vegetables and flowers, if the owners are energetic enough and the water-supply is adequate. Each village has its own water-storage tank, providing clean water from deep wells, but there is no sanitation – just the fields – and Judy is trying to introduce the sensible system of human manure conservation traditionally used in Tibet. (Though obviously it would have to be modified to suit a hot climate.)

At the time of land-distribution four acres were allocated to each five adults, plus half an acre for each child, so already economic inequality is apparent as the households with expanding families become poorer. For many years the more sophisticated Tibetans have been deliberately limiting their families and in Tibet some spontaneous form of birth control, possibly connected with the effect of high altitudes on hormones, seemed to keep the peasant birth rate down. Now, however, the ordinary refugee is very chary indeed of operations, pills, loops, caps or even the condom, which throughout India may be bought almost anywhere for the nominal sum of 5 paise and has recently become quite popular amongst Indian men. Unfortunately Tibetan peasants seem to think birth control in some way shameful or 'inauspicious' and, as they are particularly vigorous gossips, fear of what the neighbours might say is enough to keep them away from family-planning clinics. There is nothing in their religion to support this bias, so it is possible that they are now under the influence of some deep instinct of self-preservation. No one wants them to get caught up in the Indian vicious circle of malnutrition and stunted intelligence, but at this stage in their history is it, in fact, desirable to restrict the replacement of those uncounted tens of thousands 'eliminated' during the past fifteen years?

Before land distribution took place the acres already cleared were farmed collectively but – Tibetans not being natural collectivists – the output was low. However, by May 1971 each family had its own plot and production promptly soared. Ever since, the settlers' output per acre has been far above the local average, despite the poorish quality of the soil and a chronic shortage of fertilisers. In November 1967 the Co-operative

Society was formed to handle crop selling, and seed and fertiliser buying. It flourishes, and very few members try to avoid paying their debts.

T.C. also runs a workshop where all the settlement's mechanical repairs are carried out, the necessary spare parts being made from scrap-iron. Despite their non-technological cultural background, most Tibetan youths have a marked flair for this sort of thing. The workshop serves, too, as a training centre for boys from both the Mundgod and Bylekuppa settlements, and T.C. would like to be able to employ all the surplus Mundgod school-leavers by making small spare parts on a contract basis. One hopes he will succeed. Unless their leaders take some such action – and training programme funds are readily available from Refugee Year donations – many of the younger refugees will soon have no alternative but to beg. True, they are free to set up as traders or craftsmen in Mundgod bazaar, or to seek labouring jobs outside the settlement: but such jobs for hundreds of school-leavers will not be easy to find, though the local people – to their credit – are very well disposed towards Tibetans. These Indians surely have legitimate grounds, if such can be said to exist, for envy and jealousy. Nobody has ever given them free land, the free means to reclaim and till it, free seeds, free fertilisers, free food and free housing. But, of course, it may be argued that neither has anybody ever deprived them of all they once possessed – the flaw in this argument being that so many Indians have never possessed anything.

After breakfast, we walked across to the gigantic, noisy workshop where several groups of alert young Tibetans in greasy overalls were manipulating complicated tools. They looked happy and absorbed, these members of the first generation of refugees to grow up with few, if any, memories of their homeland. Yet watching them I felt a pang, when I thought back to the simple way of life their own fathers still knew, scarcely twenty years ago, beyond the Himalayas. Even if political developments were to make a return to Tibet possible, neither the refugees nor their country can ever regain the Age of Freedom when most journeys meant riding contentedly for many days over the silent steppes. ('Freedom from what?' my more irritated progressive readers may inquire impatiently at this stage. And the short answer is,

'Freedom from the abominable effects of industrialisation, the consumer society and the internal combustion engine.')

Leaving T.C. in the workshop, the rest of us went on to the hospital, which is administered by Judy. These refugees have adjusted well to a climate which, though not hot by South Indian standards, is extremely hot by Tibetan standards; but tuberculosis remains a major problem. The most important members of the hospital staff are, of necessity, Indian, though the Tibetans would like to be able to supply their own doctors and nurses. Unfortunately, however, not all the young refugees trained abroad at vast expense are keen on returning to the relative hardships of life in India. The gadgets and glitter of the West have an almost hypnotic fascination for people in whose own country many peasants still use flint and steel to make fire; even His Holiness is not immune to this fascination, so it is absurd to expect adolescent refugees to withstand it.

I strolled through a few of the villages today and visited several homes. Although these 397 houses started out as identical bungalows, with red-tiled roofs, whitewashed walls and concrete floors, hardly any two are alike by now. Most families have added one or more rooms, using their own cash and labour and sometimes improvising rather impermanent walls of bamboo-matting plastered with cowdung. On the whole such building efforts add little to the beauty of a village, but they certainly preserve it from the drabness of uniformity. Each family has built its own mud stove but as usual there are no chimneys so every room is impregnated with wood smoke. Western-type furniture is rare, Tibetan couches and carpets being used instead. Every living-room has an altar in one corner, more or less elaborate but always with a decorated picture of His Holiness and a row of silver butter-lamps.

The two monasteries here are the pathetic remains of Drepung and Ganden, to which are attached small groups of Nyingmapa and Sakyapa lamas. In all, 600 monks came to Mundgod from their notoriously unhealthy camp at Buxa and many of them are still plagued by lung diseases contracted there. The monks live in little houses like everyone else's but the temples are fine buildings, in the traditional Tibetan style, and there is also a Drepung debating hall. The villagers give just as

many sons to the monasteries as they did in Tibet, so one sees
dozens of little monks around the place; from The Palace we
can hear their treble chanting carried on the breeze at prayer-
times. Each monastery has 300 adult monks who have been
granted plots at the rate of two acres to three monks – a meagre
ration indeed, when one thinks of the old days. The monks still
farm collectively, but with them the system works well because
of monastic discipline. Their relations with the lay-people are
essentially as they were in Tibet and they perform the same
ceremonies, in addition to cultivating their land. However,
though time could be found for both ritual and agricultural
activities it was soon realised the student monks could not also
be expected to do the amount of intensive studying needed to
keep their religious tradition alive. So His Holiness has just
started a scheme whereby the twenty brightest students will
be supported by their communities, by the settlement and by
the Tibetan Government-in-Exile while completing their
studies. Then they will take to the fields with the rest, leaving
their juniors to concentrate on the awesome courses of philosophy and metaphysics which, after many years slogging, entitles
a Tibetan monk to be called a 'lama', or teacher. This seems an
excellent scheme and some people feel it may even herald a
religious renaissance amongst the refugees. But this is perhaps
being too optimistic.

25 November. Mundgod Tibetan Settlement.

Yesterday Rachel several times begged to be taken to the
near-by jungle to monkey-watch, so early this morning we set
off, armed with 'rustling sticks' against the local cobras, kraits
and vipers, all of which are said to be numerous. A brisk fifty-
minute walk across pale gold stubble-fields, and up slopes
entangled in green scrub and coarse reddish grass, took us to the
settlement boundary. We crossed a narrow stream of cool,
quick water, and then were in a green meadow that sloped
slightly up to the edge of the trees. Against a clear sky the
parakeets were emerald streaks, harshly warning the forest of
our approach, and in the distance I could see the branches of a
conspicuously tall banyan-tree moving agitatedly as a troop of
langurs heeded that warning.

Our monkey-watching was not nearly as successful on that

isolated hillside as it had been on the road from Mundgod, where the monkeys are accustomed to human traffic. But during our wanderings through the thin forest, interspersed with grassy glades, I felt no less thrilled than Rachel to be surrounded by such a variety of exotic birds, butterflies, beetles, trees, vines, shrubs and flowering plants. According to T.C., the most troublesome local animal is the wild pig, which can wreck a whole maize crop in one night, and we saw much evidence of porcine rootings in the glades. (We have just had wild roast pork for supper – delicious.)

At last I suggested that if we wanted more than a glimpse of the langurs we had better sit very quietly behind a screen of shrubs and wait for them to reappear. Sitting quietly is altogether against Rachel's principles, but today the motive was strong enough and after not many minutes we saw a fine male langur loping across the grass, his silver coat gleaming where the sunlight fell through the trees. He was followed by two females, and then chatterings and screams made us both look up to see a whole gang of adolescents at play in that giant banyan. Forgetting herself, Rachel squealed with excitement and at once the tall male reappeared and raced across the grass not ten yards from us, swearing angrily, his white whiskers bristling against his black face. As he swept up the banyan the youngsters leaped on to another tree, and then another, and gradually the scoldings and rustlings died away. I looked at Rachel and quoted:

"His hide was very mangy and his face was very red,
And ever and anon he scratched with energy his head.
His manners were not always nice, but how my spirit cried
To be an artless *Bandar* loose upon the mountainside!"

My literal-minded daughter frowned. 'Their hides weren't mangy,' she said. 'And their faces were black.'

On the way home I told her the story of Rama and his wife Sita, and Ravana and Hanuman, the monkey-king who was also a langur and probably the first detective in world literature. Then I told her that many Indians used to – and perhaps some still do – believe the English to be the descendants of Hanuman and a female servant of Ravana, the demon-king who held Sita a prisoner. This servant treated Sita so well that Rama promised her she should be the mother of a race who would one day rule India. And then Hanuman married her.

'But human beings and monkeys don't mate!' protested Rachel. 'Anyway, I think some of the *Indians* look more like monkeys. The English look like us.'

'Ssh!' I said. 'You'll have the Race Relations Board after you.'

'*What* is the Race Relations Board?' – and that kept us going until we got back to a late breakfast.

Mundgod's atmosphere is an excellent antidote to the affluent society; one sees many poor people, yet never a discontented face. I enjoy standing at the main settlement crossroads, just looking and listening. Usually a few figures are moving along the tracks: maybe an old man with braids across his head, twirling his prayer-wheel, on his way to gain merit by walking around the new *stupa* near the hospital; or a young woman with baby on back going to the Tibetan-run store to buy material for a new *chuba* and also twirling her prayer-wheel; or a group of children, clutching dog-eared copybooks, chasing each other home from school. Then a tractor will come busily bumping along to plough another field, or a Tibetan-owned truck, loaded with surplus rice for the market, will drive towards the public road, or one of the richer farmers may be seen manoeuvring his bullock-team with the assistance of a Harijan servant. The local Indians consider the Tibetans very good employers. And, judging by appearances, the local cattle find the Tibetans very good owners; all the settlement cattle are in markedly better condition than their Indian-owned brethren.

I do not find it easy to convey the elation I feel this evening. During previous visits to India I have known the Tibetans only as penniless, landless, homeless wanderers, often separated from their children through death or misfortune. Therefore to see them tilling their own fields, repairing their own machinery, sweeping their own floors, selling their own produce and – above all – playing with and loving their own children is an eminently heart-warming experience. It seems to me that here, miraculously, the authentic spirit of Tibet has been revived.

All the qualities that made the Tibetans so admirable and lovable and enviable when first one knew them flourish throughout this settlement. The fact that most of the villagers have never been exposed to any but the most superficial non-Tibetan influence is no doubt partly responsible, and Mundgod's isolation must also help. The whole settlement is Tibetan-run – which of course means that it is, in a refugee context, artificial, and what I have called 'the authentic spirit of Tibet' may soon be quenched here as elsewhere. I remember Professor Tucci making the interesting point, in one of his tomes, that whereas Hinayana Buddhism can co-exist with the most advanced social theories, Mahayana Buddhism, of which Tibetan Lamaism is an eccentric offshoot, is virtually incapable of surviving in the modern world. He concluded that when its formalism broke up it would be hard to find a substitute, and I suppose one feels Mundgod to be such a special place because here this formalism has been successfully, if only temporarily, re-established.

26 November. Mundgod Tibetan Settlement.

Today, while Rachel played with her Tibetan contemporaries, I spent hours in the villages listening to the grim recent histories of families and individuals; and yet again I marvelled at the fortitude of the ordinary Tibetan. In this oasis of calm and contentment Tibetan Buddhism emerges as a most powerful spiritual force, however much outsiders may scoff at its crude animist traits, exuberant demonology, comic superstitions and money-spinning lamas.

I feel the Tethongs do not realise how much they have achieved here. The factors that went to make Mundgod may be divided into four groups; one: practical help from the Government of India and the refugee charities; two: guidance and support from the Dalai Lama; three: the industry and discipline of the settlers themselves; and four – uniting all the rest – the dedication, energy, endurance and imagination of Judy and T.C.

Tibetan refugees, being exiles from a hierarchical, feudal society, need immensely strong leadership during a resettlement phase, and advice of one sort or another every hour of the day, and encouragement, understanding and unsentimental love.

All this they got from the Tethongs in a way and to an extent that has enabled them to become what they now are – independent, happy, free and still unspoiled.

Being all the time on the spot (holidays are not part of the Tethong life-style), Judy and T.C. are perhaps more aware of the daily frustrations and the innumerable minor flaws of the settlement than of its remarkable atmosphere. Throughout a middle-aged lifetime I have felt for few people the wholehearted admiration and respect I feel for this couple. To administer funds wisely, to organise practical affairs efficiently, to treat people kindly – all that is accomplished often (though not often enough) in the refugee world. But to have resettled a group of people as culturally fragile as the Tibetans, without destroying their spiritual integrity, is a rare and very wonderful achievement.

From here we go to the Bylekuppa settlement, a few hundred miles farther south, not far from Mysore City, and it will be interesting to see how that earlier and bigger settlement compares with Mundgod.

4

Discovering Coorg

27 November. Udipi.

This evening I feel lonely not only for the Tibetans but for
the various livestock in our Palace suite: the two busy little
lizards; the swarms of minute, industrious ants who were always
dragging around the colossal (relatively) corpse of some beetle,
moth or cockroach; and the pretty light-brown frog who lived
in the loo and leaped out whenever the lid was lifted (how
alliterative can I get!) to take refuge on the wall until the plug
had been pulled and his home made habitable again. Sometimes
he had a long wait since the water-supply was almost as erratic
as the electricity, which went off at least three times a night for
periods of anything from ten minutes to three hours.

During the four-hour journey down the Malabar coast from
Kumta to Udipi we crossed three rivers as they were about to
enter the sea, and the fertile, vividly green, palmy landscape
that Rachel calls 'fatly populated'. Near Udipi our road ran
for a few miles close to the beach, where fine sand shone with a
strange rosy patina while the setting sun laid a trembling,
molten path across the water. Then we crossed the wide Kolluri
estuary, and overlooking it stood a steep, solitary peak of the
Western Ghats, those high, royal blue mountains that run from
Gujerat to Cape Comorin, isolating the fertile coast from the
harsher plains and hills and plateaux of South–Central India.

I thought our Malabar travelling-companions exceptionally
likeable, yet everywhere in India one is aware of being kept at
arm's length – sometimes literally. This is partly a consequence
of the caste laws, which still strongly influence many who
have given up formally obeying them, and partly a result of my
being a woman and therefore, according to traditional Hindu
beliefs, an essentially inferior person.

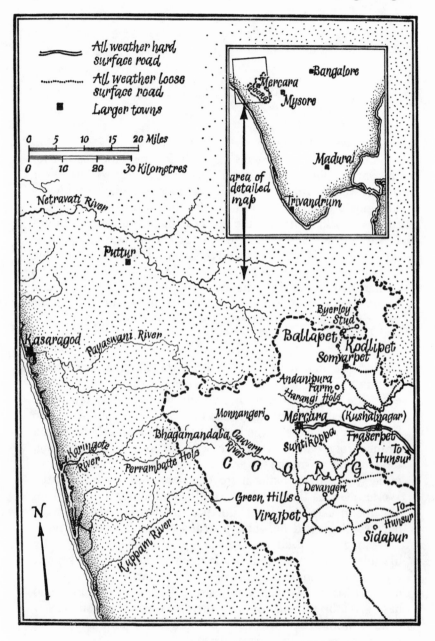

Perhaps some outsiders are drawn to this opaque world of one of man's oldest societies – where foreigners are never fully accepted, and can never fully understand – simply because they intuitively recognise how good it is for the soul to be cut down to size. Jolting slowly along those lovely roads today, I briefly *felt* unimportant and insignificant, in a way one couldn't possibly do at home. It was an odd but not unpleasing sensation: and there was a perceptible element of escapism in it. In Europe one knows one is unimportant and insignificant, but having been brought up in an ego-nurturing tradition one rarely or never feels it – and if somebody or something did make one feel it, that person, event or circumstance would almost certainly be resented.

This evening I think I can identify one of the things that went wrong during my first stay in India. After a slow journey through the Middle East, and through places as gloriously un-Westernised as Gilgit and the Hindu Kush, I found the degree of apparent Westernisation anti-climactic. Now, however, having flown direct from London – and perhaps having in the intervening decade become a little less obtuse – India's Westernisation seems to me very superficial: though that is another too sweeping generalisation, since even Hinduism has been modified by industrialisation. Yet only slightly, so far. On the whole, the British influence, like that of many earlier conquerors, is being inexorably assimilated into India's *dharma*, which eventually will be a little changed by this contribution as by all the others – though the changes will not necessarily be those the British would have wished to effect.

At Bhatkal, a biggish port town half-way between Kumta and Udipi, Rachel was a little scared to see several groups of Moplak women in silken *burkhas* on the streets and at the bus stand. One can understand how these completely shrouded figures, moving about so swiftly and silently in their dusty slippers – though apparently unable to see – could make a child feel faintly uneasy. Yet cheerful colours are fashionable in Bhatkal this winter. In one group I counted eight different shades: sky-blue, pale pink, turquoise, orange, mauve, green, pale yellow – and black. Very likely the lady in black was an elderly chaperone.

For over 2,000 years Arabs have been trading with the Malabar Coast and the present-day Moplahs (Muslim merchants) claim to be descended from ninth-century settlers. From what I have seen of the men, they must never have intermarried with Indians to any great extent for they remain perceptibly Semitic. Most of the native Muslims and many of the native Christians are the descendents of low-caste Hindus or outcastes who went over to Islam, or Christianity, hoping thereby to improve their social position – a move which was rarely successful. If the bonds of the caste system could be so easily broken Indian society would have evolved along very different lines.

It was after dark when we arrived here and having tried four full hotels I turned reluctantly towards the posh-looking tourist hotel, expecting to have to pay Lakshmi-knows-what; but as Udipi never has any tourists the charge for a single room, with a fan, is only Rs.5. Already the interior of this new building looks very shoddy and the latrines stink so frightfully that my fastidious daughter had to be taken out to the gutter.

Tomorrow I must buy some candles, before the feeble bulbs in these hotel rooms have ruined my eyes for ever.

28 November. *Mercara.*

We left Udipi at ten-thirty this morning, after a fascinating three-hour 'explore' (Rachel's term). I am no lover of crowds, but Indian towns – when not poverty-dominated – vibrate with a contagious vitality and I thoroughly enjoyed Udipi's bazaar. The people seemed happy, healthy, relaxed, friendly; and during the busy early morning hours the streets were flooded with colour – brilliant saris, shimmering silk *burkhas*, the vivid sweeping skirts of tribal women, the men's equally vivid ankle-length *lunghis* (which a few swift tucking movements transform into knee-length kilts) and, contrasting with all the rest, the white robes of orthodox Brahmans or the white saris of Hindu widows.

The usual wide range of goods was being carried through the market on a wonderful diversity of heads from 6-year-old girls with bundles of freshly cut grass to 80-year-old men with rolls of bamboo matting twice the length of themselves. There were improbable loads of tin kitchen utensils tied up in old fishing-nets and balanced with circus-artiste skill; trays of coconuts, cauliflowers, cucumbers, tomatoes, radishes, aubergines, fresh

sardines, salted sardines, oranges, limes, supportas, jack-fruit
and plantains; bales of firewood and sisal and sugar-cane and
bamboo rods; tremendous towers of wicker baskets, perilously
balanced stacks of new-fired ochre pitchers, tins of kerosene,
crates of hens, baskets of bricks, very long planks, bulging
sacks, locked tin trunks and a new-born, orphaned calf in a
round wicker basket on the head of a worried-looking young
woman.

Throughout the bazaar cattle were being deferred to by all
and Rachel is still an incredulous observer of the amiability of
Indian bulls. Inevitably she finds the Hindu attitude to cows
difficult to understand, though I notice she has not simply
dismissed it as 'a silly custom'.

I cannot agree with Dr Johnson that, 'Pity is not natural to
man. Children are always cruel. Savages are always cruel. Pity
is acquired and improved by the cultivation of reason'. Like
many small children, Rachel has had, for some time now, strong
tendencies towards vegetarianism. By nature she is most
sympathetic towards this aspect of Hinduism, though she
relishes her meat course and realises that it is kinder painlessly
to kill an animal, and eat it, than to allow it to die agonisingly
of hunger and thirst.

We went to the bus stand at ten o'clock to secure a good seat
on the ten-thirty Mangalore bus. The usual chaos prevailed,
yet despite this chaos most Indian buses do depart and arrive on
time. The Indian road transport system is, unexpectedly, a
miracle of organisation and a credit to all concerned.

At its terminus a bus stands ready to leave for at least forty
minutes before departure time, yet only when the engine has
been switched on do the majority of passengers appear, sprint-
ing from nowhere to hurl themselves aboard with shouts of
alarm and indignation. Indians relish drama and obviously
enjoy *almost* missing the bus.

As we moved out of Udipi we were at last feeling the heat,
though while the bus was moving – the windows were unglazed
– we felt not too uncomfortable. As soon as it stopped, however –
which it did six times during the forty-mile run – we both began
to sweat spectacularly.

We were on the back seat among the Harijans and looking
down that bus was like being at a flower show, so many young

women had decorated their glossy black coiffures with exotic
scented blossoms, fresh from the jungle. Those are the little
touches that make India – for all its obtrusive squalor – seem so
much more graceful than present-day Europe.

We arrived at Mangalore just as a crowded bus was about to
leave for Mercara and leaped on board to find two front seats
inexplicably empty; I can only suppose the watches of the
passengers concerned were inaccurate beyond the Indian
average. When I handed over our fares I was, for the first time,
given tickets previously used. This meant the conductor was
pocketing our fare, having got back the used tickets from
accommodating passengers to whom he had no doubt paid a
consideration. I hesitated. Should I demand a valid ticket,
thereby upholding Western standards of morality? Or should I
respect local customs, remembering that for Rs.2 the conductor
– who probably has a wife and ten children at home – could
buy himself a good square meal? I decided on the latter course
and put my change and the dud tickets in my purse. Then I
felt someone lightly touching my shoulder and looked around to
see an elderly Brahman wearing a pained expression. 'You must
ask for a good ticket,' he said reprovingly. 'Bus conductors are
not poor. They have to pay a lot to get such a job. He should not
be allowed to cheat. Please ask for a good ticket.'

'Very well,' I said, shamefacedly, at once seeing the
Brahman's point of view. By contributing one's mite of acceptance to this sort of thing, one is simply perpetuating a tradition
that India could well do without. And, of course, the conductor
cheerfully gave me a valid ticket on request, with the air of a
man who has played a good game and knows how to take a
beating.

The eighty-five-mile drive into the province of Coorg took us
back over the Western Ghats and as we climbed almost 4,000
feet from the coast the splendour of the landscape exceeded
anything we had yet seen. Dense jungle, in which many of the
trees were ablaze with blossom, covered the lower slopes. Next
came a vast rubber plantation, where the tappers were at work,
and then we were amongst a massive array of tumbled blue
ridges and peaks. The air felt deliciously cool and on every side
mountains rose steeply from deep, narrow, wild ravines, while
occasionally one glimpsed, far below in a paddy-valley, the

vivid green of a new crop or the gold of stubble. Over its final fifteen miles this road climbs 2,900 feet and at a certain point, where the gradient is one-in-twelve, our Brahman friend again tapped me on the shoulder. 'You must know,' he said, 'that the building of this road was begun in 1837 by a very brave young countryman of yours. You have heard of Lieutenant Fast?'

I shook my head, explaining, 'We come from Ireland, so I'm afraid Mr Fast was not our countryman.'

'Oh?' said the puzzled Brahman. 'Well maybe Lieutenant Fast also came from Ireland. He was British, you see, and he died of jungle fever here, on the job. He was the engineer. We still call it Fast's Ghat. Not the younger people, of course. They call it Sampaje Ghat. But we old people don't mind remembering that the British built all our roads. There were not even cart-tracks when they came to Coorg. The Rajas never wanted roads built. They were afraid easy roads might mean easy invasions.'

'And weren't they right?' I said, drily.

The old Brahman looked at me with sudden quick suspicion. 'Are you anti-British? Anti-Imperialist? Do you have a war in Ireland? A civil war with Britain? Or am I becoming confused from the papers?'

'Not at all,' I said, 'that is an excellent description of what we have. But I'm not in the least anti-British – only anti-Imperialist.'

The Brahman gestured with his slim, wrinkled hands. 'Imperialism there has to be. It is part of the evolution of mankind. It is a necessary evil.'

It was my turn to look surprised, for such an historical approach is rather un-Indian. 'Are you a teacher?' I enquired.

The Brahman smiled. 'I was a Professor at Madras, but many years since I have retired. According to the *Laws of Manu* I should now be a *Sannyasin*, a holy beggar. But my wife might not like that. She might even join the Women's Lib!' He chuckled at my expression on hearing this allusion from Brahmanical lips. He was a charming old man and I was sorry to say good-bye at Mercara bus stand.

We soon found another Rs.5 hotel which is much more primitive than last night's, with no running water or anything fancy like that. However, we step out from our two-bedded cell on to a long balcony, level with the near-by mountain-tops and

overlooking most of the red-tiled roofs of the town – a view
which more than compensates for the state of the latrines. On
the far side of the wide, shallow bowl containing Mercara's
bazaar one can see the glint of two identical imposing gilded
domes, which must be investigated tomorrow, and the steep
green slopes that form the sides of this bowl are dotted with neat
white bungalows. As for the glory of the surrounding mountains
– when I look at them I guiltily wish that I were free to go
trekking at my own pace. Why has nobody ever heard of
Coorg? Or have I been alone in my ignorance of this most
enchanting region? We shall certainly spend a few days here,
though I had intended merely stopping overnight in Mercara
and continuing to Bylekuppa tomorrow.

29 November.   Mercara.

After a seven o'clock breakfast of tea and potato-cakes we
walked some way down Fast's Ghat to explore what we merely
glimpsed yesterday, from the bus.

Mercara's average temperature is 66 °F. and as we trotted
downhill the sun was warm, the breeze fresh and the sky
intensely blue – an almost incredible colour, to northern eyes.
At intervals, in the cool depths of the forest, we saw sudden
glorious flourishes of colour – tall trees laden with pink or cream
or red flowers; and blue-jays, hoopoes, mynahs, weaver-birds
and subaltern's pheasants were all busily breakfasting, and we
chased gaudy butterflies as big as sparrows, and once Rachel
came within inches of treading on a small snake. Probably it
was harmless, but at the time my maternal blood ran cold. One
is a much less light-hearted traveller with foal at foot.

We took short cuts at the hair-pin bends and whenever we
wandered by mistake into a compound everyone was extraordinarily friendly. Even the wives or daughters of not very
well-off farmers spoke intelligible English and were without that
withdrawn, wary shyness which marks most Hindu women.
Obviously the people of Coorg are no less exceptional than the
landscape; both men and women make one feel welcome to a
degree that is most uncommon in India. Also there is a splendid
feeling of being isolated here, in a cosy sort of way – a quality
in the atmosphere difficult to define but very attractive.

·   ·   ·   ·   ·

Across the street from our hotel, dominating Mercara and the southern and western approaches to it, stands a strongly fortified hill-top – the work of Mudduraja, a seventeenth-century Lingayat ruler. In the middle of the fort is that ruler's undistinguished palace, long since converted into the Commissioner's office, and on the way up from the road one passes the hall-door of Coorg's old-fashioned, no-nonsense gaol, where gaunt prisoners peer from tiny, heavily barred windows far above the ground, and armed guards look as though they would shoot first and ask questions afterwards should a helicopter chance to land in the courtyard.

Also inside the fort is a Mahatma Gandhi Memorial Library with a delightful notice in the entrance hall: 'Serene Silence, please! Have respect for thought!' – a typically Hindu sentiment. Several earnest-looking young men were sitting around large tables studying fat tomes, or consulting yellowed newspaper files, and in the large English language section (General) Patricia Lynch and Bertrand Russell stood shoulder to shoulder. But the selection of books in English on India was most impressive, though there were only two volumes on Coorg. A nice young librarian lent me the Coorg district volume of the Mysore State Gazetteer of India for 1965, very properly insisting on a Rs.15 deposit, and when he escorted us to the door I asked him the significance of the two realistic-looking grey stone elephants which stand at one end of the fortress compound and are marked 'Historic Monument. Do not touch.'

The young man smiled. 'British people always liked those monuments – so my father told me. They reminded the Coorgs how lucky they were to have British rulers. They were put up by the last Raja, who was very cruel and mad and enjoyed hurting people. Every morning he liked to be wakened by two special elephants trumpeting under his bedroom window over there' – he pointed across the compound. 'Then one night he sent a message to the mahouts that he didn't want to be wakened next morning, but they never got it. So in a temper when he was wakened too early he ordered the elephants and mahouts to be killed on the spot. But then he got his temper back and felt very sorry because they were such clever elephants. So he had those statues put up to honour them.'

'And what about the mahouts?' I asked.

The young man gestured vaguely. 'They were just riders,' he explained. 'Very clever and well-trained elephants are most valuable.'

From the fort we walked to the other side of Mercara to investigate those conspicuous gilded domes which mark the mausoleums of two Lingayat rulers of Coorg: Doddavirarajendra (died 1809) and his brother Lingarajendra (died 1820). On a high, grassy ridge, directly overlooking Mercara and that apparently infinite turmoil of blue mountains which is Coorg, some six or seven acres were levelled to build the twin tombs. Both are massive, square buildings in Islamic style, with minaret-like corner towers surmounted by statues of Nandi, the sacred Hindu bull, and on each dome is a gilded ball and weathercock. The windows have solid brass bars and the syenite blocks of the window frames are handsomely carved, as are the pillars (representing various manifestations of Shiva) which flank the stone steps leading up to locked doors. Obviously these memorials were devised by a somewhat eccentric family and what they may lack in formal beauty they make up for in individuality and sheer impressiveness. They are, in fact, admirably suited to rulers who were power-hungry, cunning, erratic, considerably talented and religiously eclectic – or perhaps 'omnivorous' would be a better word.

On the steep path up to the ridge we were overtaken by about twenty fascinated school-children who soon swept Rachel off to play on the smooth green turf around the tombs. This gave me a chance to sit in the sun studying the *Coorg Gazetteer*, which is quite informative about Doddavirarajendra and Lingarajendra. The former had no son and wanted his daughter Devammaji to succeed him, but she was only ten when her father died – having in his last years gone very mad and ordered the executions of many near relatives, principal officers of State and palace guards. Uncle Lingarajendra then usurped the throne and for nine years ruled energetically and efficiently, if unethically. He was succeeded by his dotty 20-year-old son, Chickavirarajendra, who felt so unsure of his position that he soon became even dottier and organised the killing of an inordinate number of his own relations. His subjects then complained about him to the British overlords of neighbouring Mysore, who presumably were not displeased to be regarded by the Coorgs as protectors.

Naturally, Vira Raja (as Chickkavirarajendra is usually called) was particularly anxious to kill his cousin Devammaji – the rightful heiress to the throne – and her husband Chennabasappa: so the young couple took refuge with the British Resident in Mysore, who refused to hand them back to an enraged Vira Raja. Vira Raja next wrote a series of rude letters to the Resident and, when these were ignored, begged several neighbouring rulers for military help against the foreign foe. If the British were looking for an excuse to annex Coorg this was it. Early in 1834 they accused Vira Raja of maladministration and made threatening noises. The Raja was then advised to surrender by his four Coorg dewans, who had long since come to despise the Lingayat dynasty and were openly pro-British – especially their leader, one Bopanna Apparanda.

I won't go into the earlier history of Coorg, which is bedevilled by gentlemen bearing such names as Satyavakya Kongunivarmmadharmma-maharajadhiraja and seems in any case rather obscure. But originally the Lingayat rulers were 'outsiders', so his subjects felt no obligation to remain loyal once Vira Raja had proved unworthy of respect. Moreover, the Coorgs had already, in the campaigns against Tippu Sultan, established a tradition of co-operation with the British and at the close of the eighteenth century a British Resident had been appointed to the Raja's Court. So it is not surprising that satisfaction was expressed when Lieutenant-Colonel J. S. Fraser, representing the Governor General of India, met the assembled leaders of Coorg at Kushalnagar in April 1834 and informed them that their ruler had been deposed.

Colonel Fraser then asked the leaders 'to express their wishes without apprehension or reserve, in regard to the form of government which they desired to be established for the future government of the country.' Without hesitation the Coorgs requested that their country be ruled by those laws and regulations already in force throughout the East India Company's dominions. Whereupon Colonel Fraser proclaimed Coorg annexed, because the people wished to be ruled by Britain, and on 6 April 1834 the Union Jack went up over Mercara Fort.

Thus did the British Lion acquire a valuable property without having to unsheathe his claws even once, the Coorgs being
the only martial race on the subcontinent never to have taken
up arms against the Raj. The Indian author of the *Mysore
Gazetteer* for 1965 gratefully points out that 'Coorg was under
British rule from 1834 to 1947, over a century and a decade.
The benefits conferred by the British rule were many and
varied. The English built this state from a small loose-knit
feudal principality into a prosperous and well-administered
unit.' So here we have one imperialist story with a happy
ending, and I suppose most people have never heard of Coorg
simply because 'good news is no news'. While all sorts of grue-
somely thrilling things were happening on The Frontier or in
the Punjab, or in Lucknow or Calcutta or Sind or Maharashtra,
the British and the Coorgs were being awfully nice to each other
in Coorg.

There was, however, one person for whom this story did not
have a happy ending – the 'Baddy', Vira Raja. On surrendering
Coorg he expressed a wish to be retained as Raja, though he
appreciated he could never again be more than a figurehead,
and he was extremely annoyed when hustled off to Benares on a
pension. Having brooded over this grievance for years he went
to London in 1852, with two of his wives and his favourite
daughter, to complain personally to the British government.
Nobody was interested, but Queen Victoria took pity on the
first Indian prince to visit England and did a lot to help this
forlorn little group of exiles. (Presumably she either did not
know, or with regal tact pretended not to know, the status of
the second lady in His Highness's entourage.) Eventually
Gowramma, the favourite daughter, became a Christian and
married an Englishman. Her father died in London in September 1859 and not long after she and her only son also died –
both of consumption. And thus ended the Lingayat dynasty
which had ruled Coorg for 230 years.

Looking up from my Gazetteer, I noticed that Rachel had her
playmates – all of whom were 8 or 10 years old – completely
under control. Everybody was doing exactly as she wanted them
to do, and this is not the first time during the past fortnight that

I have observed such a development. It worries me slightly that without one word of any common language a white child, who is being brought up in a totally unimperialistic environment of liberty, equality and fraternity, should unconsciously and effortlessly take up where the Raj left off.

On the way back to our hotel I suddenly remembered, as we passed the Rotary Club, that when last heard of an English friend of mine was running a stud-farm in Mysore State. So few British residents remain in South India that it seemed likely somebody at the Club would have heard of the Fosters, and I soon discovered that their place is only forty miles north of Mercara, on the Coorg–Hassan border. Moreover, a helpful Rotarian said we could probably get a lift to Byerley Stud tomorrow with a local racehorse owner. A. C. Thimmiah – a cousin of the famous General – was then contacted by telephone and gladly agreed to meet us on the club veranda at 9.30 a.m.

30 November. Byerley Stud, near Ballupet.

We woke to an Irish morning; thin, drifting cloud was draped over Mercara's mountains and the air felt cool and moist. 'A fine soft day, thank God!'

Punctually at nine-thirty Mr Thimmiah appeared, accompanied by his vivacious 25-year-old daughter, Sita. A. C. Thimmiah – who prefers to be known as Tim – lives on an estate fifteen miles south of Mercara. He has a kindly, gentle glance and an interesting smile – half-sardonic, half-shy – and for all his patrician ways there is about him an immediately endearing air of simplicity, goodness and modesty. He is one of those rare people who inspire affection the moment one meets them, before a relationship can be said to exist at all; and his hobby is expatiating on Coorg, so he must have rejoiced to find himself in the back of the car with such a willing listener.

From Mercara our road descended gradually to Kushalnagar, winding through mile after dark green mile of coffee-estates, with Coorg's ever-present jumble of blue mountains lying beyond a series of deep, heavily forested valleys. Tim explained that the whole character of this region changed after coffee-planting was introduced – probably by Moplah traders from the coast – about the middle of the last century. Captain Le Hardy, the first British Superintendent of Coorg, encouraged the

pioneer planters and Europeans soon made it the area's main
cash crop. Finding the people and climate extraordinarily
agreeable, many Europeans settled here, as owners or managers
of plantations, and employed thousands of former slaves –
freed when the British annexed Coorg – and further thousands
of landless peasants from Mysore, Cochin, Hassan and South
Kanara. Coffee-taxes provided the government with much
revenue and soon cardamom jungles were being leased to the
highest bidder, which meant even more revenue. New towns
were built, old towns flourished and trade increased as imported
articles became popular. Yet Coorgs remained the principal
landowners, despite the influx of foreigners, and the whole
Coorg community benefited enormously from the coffee-trade.
However, there has to be a snag. By 1870 much of the forest
had been converted to estates and now the annual rainfall is
decreasing; even in the remaining forests the once-famous
Coorg bamboo-thickets have declined. From time immemorial
this region has regularly produced an abundance of rice for
export to Malabar, but if the rainfall continues to decrease the
paddy-crop must eventually suffer.

Kushalnagar is a straggling, dusty little town some 2,000 feet
lower than Mercara and only a few miles from the old Mysore–
Coorg border. During British days it was called Fraserpet, in
honour of that Colonel Fraser already mentioned, and Tim still
uses this name. As we drove slowly through the crowded bazaar
he told me that one of his great-grandfathers was Bopanna
Apparanda – usually known as Dewan Bopu – who, as Vira
Raja's Chief Minister, was mainly responsible for persuading
the last ruler of Coorg to surrender to the British. At
Kushalnagar Dewan Bopu officially welcomed Colonel Fraser
to Coorg, and soon afterwards became Captain Le Hardy's
right-hand man. During the Kanara rebellion of 1836–37 he
led his own private army to fight at Sulya and Puttur, and then
led a separate thousand-man expedition to put down 'im-
postors' in another direction. Afterwards, the British offered
generous rewards to their allies. But Dewan Bopu, like every
other Coorg leader, declined with thanks, pointing out that 'We
Kodavas do not require pay because to fight is our duty which
we owe to our country to secure our tranquillity'. Later, during
the Mutiny, Coorg volunteers stood guard at the Mysore,

Malabar and Mangalore boundary posts and were rewarded
for this spontaneous display of loyalty by being exempted from
the 1861 Indian Arms act, which made it an offence for all other
'natives' to carry arms.

As we drove into north Coorg, Tim explained that amidst the
darkly tangled jungle on the steep mountains grew millions of
rupees worth of teak, ebony, eucalyptus, rosewood, sandalwood
and *ood* – a sweet-smelling wood of which I had never heard
before. One rosewood tree, which will have taken sixty or
seventy years to mature, is at present worth about £10,000.
Pepper-vines, cardamom and various spices also grow wild in
these forests, and a few timid aboriginal tribes survive in the
remotest corners, only rarely emerging; but their numbers,
sadly, are dwindling.

Beyond the small town of Kodlipet the landscape changed to
sweeping uplands of golden grass and low green scrub. Then,
near the Coorg border, we exchanged the narrow main road for
a bumpy dirt track and soon – for no particular reason, as it
seemed – we had bounced off the track to drive for a few miles
over open scrubland, leading apparently nowhere. When
suddenly we were amidst trim paddocks, full of glossy mares and
lively foals, I had the impression of a conjuring trick

This eighty-acre stud-farm employs twenty-eight locals –
mostly syces – for whom solidly built little houses are provided
near by. According to Tim, the place was a wilderness when the
Fosters took over; now it is a thriving example of what can be
done in India with not much money but a great deal of thought
and hard work. Apart from their bloodstock interests, Fred and
Shelagh are keen to improve the local cattle and their approach
to this problem is immeasurably more sensible than that of most
international aid organisations. Like many Indian problems,
this one seems insoluble at village level. Planters, landowners
and state-run experimental farms can all afford to improve
their stock, but what does this profit the half-starved villager
and his family? Of what use is a fine sturdy heifer from an
Ayrshire or Charollais bull if she cannot get the feed she needs
to keep her big frame fit? Before you improve village cattle you
must improve the available fodder and Fred is now experimenting to find out which of the various new strains of grass is best
suited to this area.

There is a nice sense of historical continuity about the
Fosters' present way of life. Their ancestors were pioneers in
New Zealand and India and they are still carrying on the tradition in this remote corner of Mysore, much of which was
originally opened up by Fred's father. Their little bungalow is
emphatically a Pioneers' home, rather than an Exploiters', and
to our great delight the 'guest room' is an ancient and honourable horse-box called Genghis Khan, which has several times
done the India–Britain–India round trip behind an even more
ancient and honourable Land-Rover.

Also staying here for the week-end are the Fosters' only remaining European neighbours, David and Jane Hughes, who
manage a company plantation eighty miles away, at the far end
of Coorg. For the few Europeans who have not yet uprooted
from rural India loneliness is obviously something of a problem,
though they may have adjusted gracefully to an independent
India and acquired many Indian friends. However, it is hard
to imagine such people, whose families have usually been
India-based for generations, at ease against any other background. They still need India: and I strongly suspect that
India, though she would never admit it, still needs them.

After lunch we strolled around the farm, which on all sides
overlooks silent miles of untouched country, stretching away in
green-brown-gold undulations to the lavender shadows of
distant mountains. In every sense, the atmosphere here is totally
unpolluted. Indian atmospheres tend to be very strong, whatever their quality. On that evening last week when we entered
Mysore State from Goa, our bus passed through a village on the
edge of the forest where I was quite overcome by an awareness
of evil – a feeling altogether unexpected and inexplicable, but
none the less definite for that. (I omitted it from my diary that
night because I was still trying to shake off the unpleasant
after-effects.) Similarly, amidst this tranquil isolation one is very
aware of Good being in the ascendancy: perhaps Varuna dwells
here.

1 December. Byerley Stud.

We breakfasted on the veranda (bacon and eggs, naturally)
while files of almost black-skinned men and women servants
passed to and fro, their bare feet noiseless on the dewy grass,

their ornaments tinkling and flashing, their eyes respectfully averted from the sahibs and mem-sahibs, who were putting away more good food in fifteen minutes than the average Indian can lay hands on in a month.

One of the stable girls is particularly striking: tall, lithe and elegant in an emerald-green sari, with ebony hair tied in a glossy, waist-length tress. Her regular, fine-boned features wear a permanent expression of faintly amused disdain and she is unmistakably a personality. However, as a guest I would be wasting my time trying to establish contact; in India, any attempt to run with the hare and the hounds inevitably leaves all concerned feeling thoroughly embarrassed. But I can't help wondering what she and her contemporaries make of European employers: certain subtle changes of attitude must surely have taken place during the past quarter-century. A whole genera-tion has grown up that was born free – if 'free' is an allowable adjective for India's poverty-bound millions – and even in a backwater like this the no-longer-ruling sahibs and mem-sahibs must be suffering from some loss of status. And yet – while writing these words I have remembered Rachel's bossing of her Indian playmates, who seem never to resent the domin-eering white child. Plainly the British control of their Indian Empire was based on something more than Might, though I honestly do not know whether I believe that 'something' to have been a defect in the Indian character, or a virtue in the British, or a combination of virtues and vices on both sides that just happened to make possible the domination of millions by thousands.

Throughout today I have felt as though I had slipped back fifty or a hundred years in time, not because there is anything imperialistic about the way of life at Byerley Stud but because much of our conversation could have been lifted straight from an Edmund Candler novel, with occasional lapses into Flora Annie Steel. And of course having servants of any kind about the place does strike the visitor fresh from Europe as too quaint for words. Their presence gives an entirely different flavour to life, which is nice for a change, though personally I should not care for it permanently. However, the villagers working here undoubtedly appreciate being well paid, housed, fed and clothed; they would never be able to comprehend my democratic distaste for the sort of relationship that is traditional in India between masters and servants and that appears to them as a right and proper extension of the caste system.

Before the Thimmiahs left yesterday it was arranged that we should go to stay with them on 9 December, for *Huthri*. This is the most important of all Coorg's religious festivals and the occasion when every family member returns to the ancestral home. Meanwhile, we should have time to visit (at last!) Bylekuppa Tibetan Camp, and to spend a day or two in Mysore City looking up Kay Webb – a medical missionary with whom I worked in Nepal. I feel tonight that Fate has taken over the organising of this journey and is making a pretty good job of it.

5

Musings in Mysore

Having said our good-byes to the Fosters, Rachel and I strolled for a couple of hours along a narrow, pot-holed, tree-lined road. The only traffic was an occasional herd of cattle being driven by ragged, grim-faced men, none of whom returned our greetings. We passed a few huts with shaggy straw thatches and glimpsed a few toddlers who fled from our strange white faces, howling with terror. Perhaps their mothers use Europeans as bogy-men.

At noon the remains of a bus picked us up. Its seats were torn, its glazed windows broken, its floorboards sagging in the middle and its brakes so imperfect that at every stop wooden blocks had to be thrust under the back wheels by a small boy specially employed for the purpose. As long as the road remained level we crawled along at ten or twelve m.p.h., the engine sounding like a concrete-mixer, but at the foot of the first slope we stopped dead where we would have seriously impeded any other traffic had it existed. I soon realised that this was no crisis, but common form. All the standing passengers scrambled out without comment and proceeded to walk up the hill, followed by the bus containing its legal load (according to the notice over the engine) of thirty-eight seated passengers. In due course I counted forty-three illegal passengers re-entering through the back door and several others squeezed into the cab. We then went careering down a steep mountain at hair-whitening speed and I began to understand India's bus-disaster statistics; had we gone over that parapet none of us could possibly have survived. In reports of bus crashes one usually reads that the driver and conductor, if amongst the survivors, have 'absconded'. (A favourite word of Indian journalists.) But those drivers and conductors who escape both death and imprisonment must be rich men, since for them the fares of the illegal passengers are clear profit.

On buses one often observes sex discrimination in action. At Kodlipet, where we changed into a marginally less decrepit bus, a poorly dressed young couple came aboard when there was only one seat vacant – in the 'Ladies'' section. The obviously pregnant wife was holding a baby boy, but it was the husband who sat down and took the baby on his knee. His woman was to be left strap-hanging for two hours and she had to refuse my seat because I was in the 'Men's' section. I then offered it to her husband, so that she could have his; but though he had no right to be in the Ladies' section he simply gave me a stony stare, knowing that in any dispute public sympathy would be on his side.

It was five-thirty when we arrived here so for Rachel's sake I decided to stay in a hotel – Rs.3 for a twin-bedded room! – though we are only seven or eight miles from Bylekuppa.

3 December. Bylekuppa Tibetan Settlement.

Last night my sleep was disturbed every few minutes by fleas, mosquitoes, pi-dogs fighting under our ground-floor window, jackals howling in the compound and strident Indian jazz being played over a public amplifier from 4.10 a.m. onwards.

As we walked out of Kushalnagar at seven-thirty we saw many prosperous-looking Tibetans coming into the town on their own bicycles or scooters or bullock-carts, or in settlement jeeps or trucks. At the Bylekuppa police-checkpost I had to produce a letter of introduction from T.C. and the security precautions here underline the essential difference between this settlement and Mundgod. Bylekuppa was started in 1963, amidst considerable controversy and publicity, and it has always been under Indian supervision and influence. Also, being on the main Mangalore–Mysore road it is over-exposed to Western curiosity and interference. But one must not expect perfection everywhere and, as T.C. readily admits, Mundgod has benefited through avoiding the mistakes made here during the first experimental resettling of large numbers of Tibetans in South India.

Despite these mistakes, most of Bylekuppa's 8,000 Tibetans

are now prospering. Some have built, independently, little houses for married children on their own fields, and the majority are probably better off, materially, than they could ever have been in Tibet. Whether they are as well off in other respects is a matter of opinion.

As I write – in the settlement guest-bungalow, drinking the settlement beer – I find myself rapidly becoming incompetent to comment further. This beer is a Sikkimese variation on the *chang* theme and is made here from *ragi*, a highly nutritious grain known as 'the national millet of Mysore'. It is served in a huge glass jar placed in a shallow dish and filled to the brim with fermenting *ragi*, from which protrudes a bamboo 'straw'. To mix one's drink one slowly pours hot water from a half-gallon kettle on to the grain. After a few minutes the brew is ready to be imbibed through the 'straw' and one thinks how pleasant and innocent it is. One adds some more water, and imbibes again, and after repeating this ritual a few times one begins to spill a little of the water as one adds it . . .

4 December. Mysore City.

On the Mysore plateau many solitary, spreading trees grow in the wide, red-brown fields, giving the landscape a slightly English look – accentuated today by a scatter of bulky white clouds drifting across the deep blue sky. It could have been a perfect June day at home, and as Mysore is almost 2,500 feet above sea-level it was not too hot even when we arrived in the city centre at one o'clock.

A helpful receptionist at the Holdsworth Memorial Hospital told us that Kay will be back from her village leper-clinics tomorrow afternoon and we then rambled off in search of suitable accommodation. In this 'Palas Hotel' our Rs.3 room has no window, scarcely enough space for me to turn around when wearing a rucksack and so much wild-life on the floor (already I have counted six species of insect) that I shall have to sleep beside Rachel on the narrow plank bed. Judging by the goings-on in the corridors, the place is an ill-disguised brothel; but since I am above the age of provoking sexual assault, and Rachel below it, this detail is of no practical consequence. More disquieting is the fact that the restaurant washing-up is done on the floor of the filthy latrine just outside our bedroom door – something I did not observe until after we had enjoyed an excellent lunch.

Mysore City is said to have deteriorated since the British left but I find it most attractive. It is small enough to be tackled on foot and there are few motor vehicles on the wide, straight, tree-lined streets, most of which run between solid, well-kept, cream-washed buildings with terraced roofs and spacious gardens. The traffic consists mainly of horse-gharries, pedal-cycles, bullock-carts and multitudes of wandering cattle, many of whom lie complacently in the middle of main roads chewing the cud as though the internal combustion engine had never been invented. One has to like a city in which the cow still takes precedence over the car.

The people, too, are congenial – except in the State-run tourist bureau, where I found the staff most unhelpful. In a desperate effort to arouse their sense of duty I murmured something about collecting material for a travel-book, but this merely prompted them to exchange smiles. Plainly they found it impossible to believe that anyone so poorly clad and generally unimpressive could sign her name, never mind write a book. Indians tend to rely heavily on outward appearances when judging foreigners, which is natural enough. Occasionally, however, the use of this criterion, unaided by any other, leads to regrettable *contretemps* with sartorially eccentric visitors who are really quite respectable.

5 December.   Mysore City.

I notice, with some unease, that the older I get the more sentimental I feel about kings and queens, emperors and emirs, the Nizam and the Wali and suchlike personages. But perhaps this is less a symptom of senile decay than an emotional retreat from a world which daily becomes more anarchic, ugly and false. In Europe the lot of the average man has in some ways been greatly improved over the past half-century, but in India technology seems only strong enough to erode valuable traditions, without providing even the limited amount of good we have derived from it. Hence modern India encourages one to look back, even more wistfully than usual, to an age when life was slower, more rhythmic and more dignified – and yet in many ways gayer, freer, more colourful and more spontaneous.

So wandered my thoughts early this morning, as we strolled along neat gravel paths between neat lawns in the vast compound of Mysore City's famous fort. All around us stretched handsome red-brown fortifications, ahead rose soaring twin temples – the 'private chapels' of the ex-rulers – and dominating all else was the Maharaja's Palace, built in 1897 and extravagantly though not displeasingly ornate. Indeed, from the romantic tourist's point of view it is eminently satisfactory, being just the sort of edifice in which an Eastern Potentate might be expected to reside.

The feudal past looks good in Mysore. By the end of the eighteenth century the British had defeated the Muslim interloper, Tippu Sultan, and restored to the throne an old and much-loved Hindu dynasty. This restoration was not, however, immediately successful on the practical level, and British administrators were appointed in 1831. A succession of dedicated Englishmen ran the State efficiently for the next half-century, until the Wadeyars again took over, this time proving not merely competent but brilliant rulers. During the 1930s Gandhi described Mysore as 'a model state'. More than any of their princely rivals, the Wadeyar Maharajas fulfilled the immemorial Hindu ideal of Kingship – which was fitting, since the history of Mysore is inextricably interwoven with the legends of the Ramayana and Mahabharata.

In the business of government the Maharajas were assisted not only by British political agents but by a number of distinguished dewans, many of whom were Muslims – though none the less loved and trusted by their Hindu masters on that account. Yet the man now generally regarded as 'the maker of modern Mysore' started off as a poor Hindu village lad. His name was Dr M. Visvesvaraya and he is known as 'the Engineer-Statesman' because he organised the building of an astonishing number of dams, canals, factories, hospitals, schools and colleges – including India's first polytechnic. Already I have several times been told the story of his two fountain-pens. So determined was he to give a good example that he used separate pens for personal and official work and bought the personal one, and the ink to fill it, out of his own pocket. To such obsessional behaviour does India reduce honest men.

During its final princely period, Mysore attracted many scientists, artists and musicians. The Maharajas – fine scholars themselves – were generous and perceptive patrons of every form of creative endeavour and Jayachamaraja Wadeyar, the last Maharaja, is a composer of distinction. But now he can no longer afford to subsidise young musicians and I find this very sad.

However, one must not wax too sentimental/romantic/monarchist. Of the 562 'native princes' left theoretically in control of two-fifths of India in the autumn of 1858, hundreds were ineffectual and dozens were downright nasty. When Queen Victoria made further annexations of territory impossible, by announcing that the Raj was to replace John Company, most old Company hands were outraged and Lord Elphinstone – a nephew of the incomparable Mountstuart Elphinstone – foretold that the princely states could be useful only as 'sinks to receive all the corrupt matter that abounds in India'. The following century justified his cynicism, in many cases, though it is wildly misleading to generalise thus about 'princely states' when some consisted of only a few acres and others of more than 80,000 square miles.

Had the mutiny been delayed for a decade, John Company might well have secured that remaining two-fifths of the subcontinent – or most of it – and thus the government of a new Indian democratic Republic would have been spared the embarrassment of coping with old Indian undemocratic princes. For their own reasons, the princes had consistently opposed the idea of an independent India, in which they would no longer enjoy British protection. However, thanks to the combined efforts of S. V. Patel, Lord Mountbatten and Pandit Nehru, they proved less intractable than had been expected. Most were concerned with the trappings rather than the realities of power and so were easily enough brought to heel when Mr Nehru – temporarily, and not for the last time, neglecting his pacific image – brusquely declared that any princely state which chose to stay out of the new India would be treated as 'hostile'. Two years later the states had all been absorbed into the Republic and their rulers soothed with promises that they and their heirs forever would receive annual pensions ('Privy Purses'), and be allowed to retain their private property, honorary titles, personal flags and the various other princely perks to which so many of them attached such importance.

Unfortunately, however, that is not – could not be, in modern India – the end of the story. Anti-Congress politicians saw the concessions granted to the princes as useful ammunition since public opinion, throughout what had been British India, was in an understandably anti-prince mood. Typical of the criticisms made by secularised agitators was the accusation that the princes had insensitively flaunted loads of precious stones in public while their people starved around them. This taunt ignored the fact that the wearing of as many jewels as could possibly be fitted on to one man's person was often part of a Hindu ruler's duty. In Mysore, most of the Maharaja's subjects believed jewels to have magic properties capable of spreading beauty, abundance and security throughout the land if – but only if – the jewels were worn by him whose body symbolised the people of the state.

After years of wrangling the government gave way to the agitators in 1971 and withdrew the princes' pensions and privileges – though the saving was negligible in an all-India context. At least where Mysore was concerned, this seems to have been a blatant example of 'democracy' enforcing the will of an articulate minority at the expense of an inarticulate majority, who even today remain deeply attached to their ex-ruler.

In 1956, when many of India's state boundaries were redrawn – generally on a linguistic basis – Mysore was doubled in area and almost doubled in population by the inclusion of much of the old states of Bombay and Hyderabad, and what had been the separate province of Coorg. This new geographical entity – last month renamed Karnataka – has an area of 74,000 square miles and a population of 30 millions, out of whom some 17 millions speak Kannada, Karnataka's official language. Other languages spoken by significant numbers are Telugu, Urdu, Marathi, Tamil, Tulu, Konkani, Malayalam, Banjari, Hindi and – in Coorg – Kodagu. Kodagu and Tulu – the language of South Kanara – both use the Kannada script but each of the other languages has its own script though Old Kannada and Tamil are so alike they were once thought to be dialects of the same language.

The ancient Karnataka–Vijayanagar kingdom, of which the

state of Mysore was the residue, lost its identity in the mid-
seventeenth century during the Muslim conquest of the
Karnatic. Previously, it had stretched from the sacred River
Godavari to the even more sacred River Cauvery and for three
centuries its rulers had dedicated themselves to preserving their
ancient Hindu society from destruction by Islam. Frequently
their armies were beaten but the fact that one now finds South
India so different from North India is a measure of their
success on other and ultimately more important battlefields.

Although Karnataka has been designed to approximate in
area and ethnic content to the old Vijayanagar kingdom, the
majority of modern Kannadigas naturally cannot feel towards
their new state as they did towards Mysore under the Wadeyars.
For almost 3,000 years, while empires waxed and waned, the
small Hindu kingdom remained a constant feature of Indian
life, especially in the south, and from the peasants' point of
view a secular democratic state is a poor substitute. Despite
long periods spent under the suzerainty of various imperial
powers the rulers of South Indian kingdoms usually retained
considerable local control and their mere presence gave
emotional stability to the social structure, however inept or
corrupt individual rulers might be. In theory, Indians should
feel much more secure these days, when they can choose at
the polls the sort of rulers they want, but for the people of a
caste-dominated society a feudal overlordship of some kind is
more psychologically comfortable than parliamentary democracy. Several years ago Dr Radhakrishnan wrote, '. . . caste . . .
today has become a political evil; it has become an administrative evil. We are utilising caste loyalties for the purpose of
winning our elections or getting people into jobs, exercising
some form of favouritism or nepotism.' The recent abrupt
political Westernisation of India has probably been the most
traumatic single event in the whole history of the subcontinent
and a growing number of Indians believe the process should
somehow have been accomplished more gradually.

I felt acutely aware of the past as we entered the sumptuous
though now desolate-feeling Sajje Hall, where the Maharaja
used to give audience to his people every September, during
the Navaratri festival. Rachel was greatly taken by the throne,
which is made of fig-wood overlaid with ivory, plated with gold

and silver and carved with innumerable figures from Hindu mythology.

On our way out of the fort, when I turned aside for a moment to try to get a photograph of the zenana wing, a poorly dressed elderly man emerged from a distant doorway and came running towards us, angrily shouting and gesticulating. At first I, too, felt angry, for we had been much plagued, in and around the palace, by aggressive pseudo-guides demanding rupees. But then I noticed something different about this shabby little man who was pointing to the ornate zenana windows while vigorously shaking his head and trying to talk English. He did not want rupees: he simply wanted us to go away.

At last I got the message – 'Maharana still here! No allowed visitors to this side! Away with quickness!' He paused, and suddenly the right word came. '*Private* here!' he exclaimed triumphantly. 'Away! Private! No looking! This *only* for Maharana!'

I apologised profusely, and asked why there was no warning notice. But the guardian of the zenana merely repeated, 'Away with quickness! Private! Here lives our Maharana!'

We went away then, 'with quickness', and I was sadly aware of having seen, in the eyes of this scruffy retainer, the last glowing embers of a reverence and loyalty such as 'the elected representatives of the people' rarely inspire in any country.

Outside the gateway by which we left the fort several men were saying their morning prayers in a small public temple. Rachel wanted to ring the temple bell but I explained that not even Hindu women – never mind *mleccha* girls – are allowed to do this. However, consolation was at hand. On the little temple veranda sat two tame rhesus monkeys, tied to the wall by long chains and still wrapped in their night attire – a communal piece of cotton. They hailed Rachel's appearance with jibber-jabbers of joy and she spent half an hour playing with her cousins, after I had prudently removed her spectacles and hair-band. Every few moments they reduced her to paroxysms of laughter, and she and they combined had the same effect on many of the passers-by while I sat enjoying the morning sun, and admiring the massive lines of the fortifications, and appreciating the friendliness of the atmosphere.

.   .   .   .   .

As we approached Mysore yesterday my eye was drawn across the level plateau to a conspicuous, isolated mountain not far from the city's outskirts. This is Chamundi Hill (3,489 feet), on which stands a much-visited temple dedicated to Chamundi – the family goddess of the Wadeyars – who once upon a time killed two demons, named Chanda and Mundi, on the site of the temple. In fact Chamundi is just another of the goddess Kali's many names; my only complaint against Hinduism is that, not content with having tens of thousands of gods and goddesses, many of these deities confront the bewildered *mleccha* with a memory-defeating multiplicity of names. But the important thing is not to be misled by all this into regarding Hinduism as an essentially polytheistic religion. The late K. M. Sen explained the situation with his customary succinctness: 'Depending on the social traditions of particular sections of the people, Hindus show a particular attachment to a particular figure in Hindu mythology and worship God in that form. The Nameless and the Formless is called by different names, and the different forms are attributed to Him, but it is not forgotten that He is One.' Incidentally, travellers in India should keep K. M. Sen's *Hinduism* permanently within reach. A Pelican book – published in 1961 – it weighs only a few ounces, and to the outsider who is trying to look sympathetically in, but is not a trained philosopher, it is more valuable than a dozen weightier tomes I could mention.

Kali is of course Siva's wife and she is also known as Sati, Gauri, Annapurna, Parvati, Durga, Bhawani and Devi. As Kali she requires to be frequently mollified by sacrifices of a bloody nature and recently, in some remote Maharashtrian village, a 6-year-old boy was killed to placate her. Nowadays human sacrifices are made only by those generally regarded as insane, but it is not surprising that most foreigners despair of ever understanding a religion which can directly inspire one sort of devotee to murder a child and another to refrain from killing a gnat. E. M. Forster perfectly describes the *mleccha's* difficulty in *A Passage to India*: 'The fissures in the Indian soil are infinite: Hinduism, so solid from a distance, is riven into sects and clans, which radiate and join and change their names according to the aspect from which they are approached'.

Buses frequently leave Mysore's bus stand for the top of

Chamundi Hill, but because of the temple's popularity as a place of pilgrimage it is extremely difficult to board one. Twice this morning we were left behind, having been at the head of the queue, and for this I blame my own absurd European reaction to people in a hurry. Instinctively one moves aside to let them pass and today I had to make a real effort of will to overcome this automatic reaction. I also had to make an effort of muscle to push, pull or slap people out of the way as we boarded the third bus. Rachel was nearly trampled underfoot and became momentarily panic-stricken, yet this was a bus with separate entrances for men and women, so I only had to deal with the weaker sex. The strength of some of those wiry little peasant women, who could curl up in my rucksack, is quite extraordinary.

Here I again noticed a bus conductor treating women and low-caste men as though they were draught-animals, shouting at them abusively and occasionally even striking them. For a people who are widely believed to profess a philosophy of *ahimsa*, or non-violence, the Indians seem inordinately aggressive in their daily lives. It was Gandhi who created, almost single-handed, the false impression that they are gentle and peaceful. All the still influential kings and heroes of Sanskrit literature were expected to be ferocious slayers of men and, apart from the Mahatma's not entirely successful *ahimsa* campaign, there is nothing whatever in the past 2,000 years of Indian history to support the view that Hindus are basically pacifist. Their violence, indeed, is part of the mystery of India, for it always seems to have causes and cures unknown to us.

This morning's pandemonium, for instance, seemed almost a mini-civil war. First men, women and children fought tooth (literally: I was bitten on the forearm) and nail to board that bus, and then the seething mob of women was set upon by the conductor and clouted and shouted at to get it so arranged that another dozen could be fitted in. Yet ten minutes later the conductor and his women victims were laughing and joking together, like old friends, and men who had recently been doing each other grievous bodily harm were cordially exchanging newspapers. At which point I remembered N. C. Chaudhuri's remark that 'Somehow an alkali is always present with the acid of Hindu life: it is a marvellous and boundless tolerance of bad language and blows, which is some sort of a conditioned reflex

of forgiveness. The Hindu possesses a faculty of callous charity.'
He needs it, too.

Chamundi Hill is so precipitous that Mysore quickly shrinks
to toytown proportions and on clear days the surrounding
country can be overlooked in every direction for at least 100
miles. Two-thirds of the way up we stopped for everyone to
unwedge themselves and pay homage to a sixteen-foot statue of
Nandi, hewn out of solid rock in 1659. Despite the early hour he
was wearing fresh garlands on his forehead and the bell of his
gigantic necklace was draped with marigolds. Our fellow-
passengers produced further garlands and Rachel asked in a
penetrating whisper, 'Do they believe bulls are gods? Is that a
statue of a *real* bull? Why is he so big? Is he prehistoric?'

'No,' I said, 'he's not prehistoric and he's not real and
Hindus don't think bulls are gods. But some of them worship
Nandi as a symbol of the god Shiva, and he is generally regarded as a sort of chamberlain, or guardian, of all Shiva's
temples. And he represents, and protects, all four-footed
animals.'

'I see,' said Rachel, untruthfully.

As Chamundi temple is now being turned into a tourist
attraction its environs are becoming unattractive. When we
arrived a canopied figure of Chamundi, which normally
resides in the innermost sanctum, was being carried round a
courtyard on a palanquin and perfunctorily whisked with yak-
tails. In attendance were four grossly fat priests covered in
sandalwood ash and red powder – the first fat Indians I have
seen since leaving Bombay. The contrast was most striking
between those pot-bellied parasites, with greed ever shining in
their eyes, and the throngs of simple, prayerful, underfed
worshippers devoutly doing their *pujas* and repeatedly handing
coins to the priests or their attendants. As soon as we appeared,
two of these minions were deputed to harass us, which they did
with considerable verve but no success.

Although Hindu priests are not supposed to minister to a
temple for more than three years few have ever been willing to
retire from working this particular gold mine and by now there
are separate priestly sub-castes whose ill-educated members do
not intermarry with other Brahmans. These men are mildly
derided by most people, yet nobody can worship in the temples

without their expensive professional aid. It is never easy to trace Indian beliefs, customs or laws back to source, but one cannot help suspecting a link between the intricate refinements of Hindu ritualism and priestly greed. Although the person who brings the offering must perform his own *puja* he cannot do so – even if himself a Brahman – without professional help, and only by paying for this can he retain the merit of his *puja*. The ritual fee has thus become an indispensable part of the rite, just as in Ireland no Catholic would go empty-handed to his parish priest to request the celebration of a mass for his 'special intention'. Indeed, the French writer Madeleine Biardeau – perhaps the most perceptive contemporary student of India – remarks that 'it is tempting to compare what has remained of ancient Vedic ritual, which prescribes this or that *puja* to obtain this or that result – and quite often an entirely profane result – with what one knows of the Roman Catholic religion'. However that may be, the fact remains that many visitors leave India convinced that Brahmans are a bad lot, though in fact the temple-priests form only a tiny part of the Brahman population. Many Brahmans are true ascetics; many others – like our friend on the bus to Mercara – are charming and cultivated gentlemen; and a high-powered minority are scholars who regard it as their duty to hand on the torch of Hindu culture – free of charge – to the next generation.

Quite close to Chamundi temple is a garishly painted little bungalow with a large notice over the entrance proclaiming it to be 'The Godly Museum'. It belongs to a new sect called the Prajapita Brahma Kumaris which has its headquarters at the Godly University on Mount Abu, a place better known as the site of the Dilwara temples. From a half-demented-looking young woman at the desk inside the door I bought for 10 paise a booklet which informed me that 'in 1937, Incorporeal God Almighty whom we know as "Shiva" (World Benefactor) descended in the corporeal body of a jewel merchant, and blessing him with numerous meaningful divine visions revealed to him that a world war would soon be coming, in which nuclear weapons would be used and the present vicious Iron-aged world would meet its tragic end by means of that war, natural calamities and civil wars. On the other hand, he saw the visions of the forthcoming Golden-aged Deity World . . . He got the most blissful vision of God also and His Divine voice called him up to become instrumental for the re-establishment of the ensuing Golden-aged viceless and peaceful Deity World ... He became a medium to God Shiva whom some people also call "Jehovah" ... This Institution is now teaching God's knowledge and Easy Raj Yoga through 250 Godly Service Centres in various towns and villages of India ... Scientists only recently landed on the moon but this Institution knew beforehand that there was no life on the moon. Divine Insight also reveals to you regions beyond the sun, the moon and the stars without any expense or difficulty ... Several persons have given up easily such sticky habits as drinking, smoking, etc., because as a result of having acquired Godly Knowledge, they no longer feel any necessity for them ... They are now delighted to have purity, mental health and happiness as a routine, through the Easy Raj Yoga taught by this Godly University.'

Godly Museums try to explain the Easy Raj Yoga principles and methods through pictures and wall-charts which – to judge by the Mysore examples – are the work of a mentally retarded religious maniac. Various motifs from European popular religious 'art' are incorporated, including the Sacred Heart and the Blessed Virgin (looking slightly dazed, as well she might in these surroundings). Abraham and Mohammad also feature in a bizarre representation of the Kalpa Tree, and Rachel particularly liked the chart inscribed 'Skeliton of Bones and Flesh', which taught that we have a 'Mind to Think' and an 'Intelect to Decide'. Another chart taught that 'World History and Geography Repeat Dramatically Every 5,000 years' – at which point I felt I had had enough. As we withdrew, the receptionist presented me with another booklet and said she hoped I would soon attain Self-realisation, Bliss, Liberation, Fruition and Purity.

In India people will eagerly experiment with any spiritual novelty that comes their way; nor have we any right to assume that those experiments must always be unsuccessful just because they seem totally haywire to us. At least experimenting Hindus are spared the conflicts and punishments that once were endured by experimenting Christians. Despite the rigidity of many of its taboos, Hinduism has no central authority to forbid or discourage unorthodoxy. Indeed, to the Indian

mind there is no such thing as 'Hinduism'; the term was coined
by foreigners to describe that complex of distinctively Indian
yet often dissimilar faiths which they encountered on the
subcontinent. The Indians themselves, when referring to what
we call Hinduism, use the ancient and very satisfying word
dharma. Dharma means a whole way of life and thought and
feeling, and therefore not only covers religious beliefs and
practices but includes the processes by which these have formed
the Indian peoples' characters, and influenced the development
of their society, over the past three or four thousand years.

The Indian *dharma* is so peculiarly flexible that it can take even
the Prajapita Brahma Kumaris in its stride. At first I was a little
startled to read that this network of oddly Godly Museums has
been commended by the President of India, State Governors,
cabinet ministers, judges of the Supreme Court and so forth;
but then I saw how natural it was, in India, that the highest in
the land should approve of any sincere spiritual movement,
however apparently crazy.

By two o'clock we had collected our kit from the hotel and
were on the way to meet Kay. Then suddenly Rachel said,
'Stop! I hear a band!' (She has become passionately addicted
to every form of Indian music.) Obeying, I too could hear gay,
martial airs and then, in the near distance, we saw half a dozen
drummers and pipers crossing the road at an intersection. They
were following a palanquin clumsily decorated with plantain
leaves, coconuts, papayas, bunches of bananas and branches of
bougainvillaea, and behind them trailed a procession of a
hundred or so shabbily dressed men and women. The palanquin was preceded by a boy of about twelve, carrying a smoul-
dering length of sandalwood, so I knew that despite the gay
music a corpse was on its way to the burning ghats. When I had
explained the situation Rachel exclaimed, 'Let's follow and see
what happens!' Which we did – this being a traveller's attitude
of which I thoroughly approve – though the procession led us
away from the hospital.

Rachel seemed a little disappointed by her first corpse. 'He
doesn't *look* very dead,' she observed. Nor did he, poor chap, as
he sat cross-legged amidst the bougainvillaea, wearing a grey
woollen turban, red *lunghi* and brown sports jacket. His
brow was streaked with ash and saffron and a support had been

tied beneath his chin. He may not have been very dearly
beloved, since even the chief mourners looked bored rather than
distressed. Everyone seemed to welcome our attendance, as a
form of light relief, but the burning ghats were miles away and
we had to turn back at three o'clock, lest we might miss Kay.

On the hospital veranda we were joined by the first white
person we had seen in Mysore City – an elderly Englishwoman,
kindly looking and frail, with 'missionary' stamped all over her.
When we had chatted amiably for some moments, about nothing in particular, she suddenly turned to Rachel and asked 'Do
you love Jesus?'

I held my breath, foreseeing some artless regurgitation of
K. M. Sen.

'Yes,' said Rachel, 'and I love Ganesh and Hanuman.
Especially Ganesh. He has such a nice fat tummy. He's Shiva's
son,' she added helpfully.

The missionary's reaction was even worse than I had
expected. She looked so hurt – as though personally insulted –
that I truly felt sorry for her. Avoiding my gaze, she asked in a
taut sort of voice – 'Does the child not know there is only one
God?'

'Of course I know!' said Rachel quickly and rather huffily,
resenting the slight on her theology. 'But he has lots of different
names.'

There seemed no point in my adding anything to that stark
statement, which brought a flush of outrage to the unfortunate
missionary's cheeks. As I made some inane remark about the
Mysore climate our companion stood up, stiffly said good-bye
and walked away. Watching her go, I wondered how many
years she has devoted to her Christianising campaign. Probably
forty or fifty – a lifetime – only to see, at the end of it, not
Hindus coming increasingly to appreciate Christianity but
Christians coming increasingly to appreciate Hinduism.

Yet it is perhaps foolish to waste sympathy on the remnants
of a class well described by J. R. Ackerley, to whom a typical
1930s mem-sahib said, 'You'll never understand the dark and
tortuous minds of the natives . . . and if you do I shan't like you
– you won't be healthy.' Granted, few *mlecchas* can understand
the Hindu mind, however hard they try, but it now seems
exceedingly strange that so many Europeans spent most of their

lives in India without even wanting to know what makes the 'natives' tick. Probably this intellectual aloofness was partly based on a fear of Hinduism's pervasive eroticism. We find India's alleged obscenities innocent indeed, beside our own home-grown pornography, but in many books by what were then known as Anglo-Indians one perceives revulsion overlaying fascination whenever Hindu sexuality is hinted at. This is a very unpleasant aspect of the British–Indian relationship and it persisted until the Empire expired.

In retrospect, one can see that British arrogance in India was not always as simple as it looked. But whether it sprang from a genuine, uncomplicated racial superiority-complex, or was a cover for fundamental uncertainties, it alienated countless thoughtful Indians who might otherwise have taken a friendly interest in Western spirituality. Many British missionaries gave the impression that for them Christianity was the one true faith less because Christ had founded it than because Englishmen practised it – and look how civilised, clever, well-organised and advanced *they* were!

Of course there was the occasional realist, like Thomas Edwardes, who in 1880 observed that 'Neither Buddhism, Hinduism nor Mohammedanism ... can be expected to fall asunder and evaporate at the touch of the Ithuriel spear of Christianity. These religions are part of the race characteristics of the peoples who possess them, and are worked into the very tissue of their lives ... and, until events arise that shall materially alter the conditions of their existence, these historic faiths will retain their supremacy ... in the lives of their adherents.'

Educated Hindus have always distinguished between conversion in response to outside pressure and conversion as a result of some personal inner change. The first, which in their experience has usually had political overtones, they see as a threat to social and national order: the second they can and do sympathise with. However, despite Hinduism's traditional tolerance there has been a strong post-Independence move to make 'conversions' illegal and, though unlikely to succeed, this is a significant symptom of India's new nationalism. The extremist Hindus, such as the Rashtriya Swayamasevak Sangh – one of whose members assassinated Gandhi – interpret missionary efforts as 'an integral part of the domination of white races over Asia'. And basically they are right, though few of the men who ruled India were themselves pro-missionary.

More important than the extremists' attitude is the resentment felt by politicians and industrialists because some aboriginal tribes are being encouraged by their Roman Catholic and Lutheran friends to fight for various forms of national autonomy. This could cause endless trouble, as much of India's unexploited mineral wealth is in aboriginal territory. Already missionary and industrial activities have undermined the tribal way of life and it is certain that these primitive hunting peoples, who have survived for so long amidst India's jungly mountains, are now doomed.

Yet one cannot ignore the immense amount of good that has been done all over India by medical missionaries. Kay is a typical example, as selflessly dedicated to 'the cause' as anyone could be. By worldly standards there is nothing in it for her – no money, fame, glamour, adventure – nothing but hard work and discomfort and worry and frustration and the consoling conviction that she is doing God's will. At four-thirty she returned from three days of camping out near her jungle leper-clinics and swept us off to spend the night on her bedroom floor. Since our Nepalese days she seems to have became a shade more paternalistic (sorry: maternalistic) in her approach to 'heathens', but otherwise she is splendidly unchanged. And, despite certain radical differences in our outlooks, it has done me good to see her again.

6

Andanipura Farm

6 December. Andanipura Farm, near Kudige.

Last week, on the way to Byerley Stud, Tim pointed out an estate near the village of Kudige which belongs to his wife's brother, K. C. Appayya, who is one of Coorg's few experimental farmers. I expressed an interest in Mr Appayya's agricultural theories – and at once, with characteristic impulsive kindness, Tim announced that he would arrange for us to spend a couple of nights at Andanipura before we moved down to South Coorg for *Huthri*. At the time I felt ungratefully lukewarm about this plan, since a tour of the stately homes of Coorg was not really the object of our journey, but the Appayyas are such a warm-hearted and fascinating couple that I am now blessing Tim for having introduced us.

This morning we got a bus from Mysore to Kushalnagar, and from there to Kudige we shared a ramshackle five-seater car with fourteen other passengers – which meant paying only 50 paise for the four-mile journey. Rachel went free, though she must have added considerably to the already acute discomfort of the pyramid of men on whom she sat.

Our taxi put us down where the Andanipura track meets the motor road and we walked for half a mile between acres of wild heliotrope until suddenly this house came into view – a new, crescent-shaped bungalow, surrounded by banks of white and scarlet flowers. As we aproached the vine-draped veranda 'Casey' – his Cambridge nickname – came hopping down the steps to meet us. A rotund, bright-eyed little man, with the air of one who cannot help enjoying life, he irresistibly reminded me of a cock-robin – an impression reinforced by his quick, darting movements while he poured drinks, and said how happy he was to meet us, all the while making rapid, pecking movements of the head as though each word had to be captured before being articulated.

Then his wife appeared, in a turquoise Coorg sari spangled with tiny golden stars and tied on the left shoulder with a golden brooch. As we stood up to greet her I was reminded of a Botticelli Madonna. In India womanly beauty often has an ethereal quality and even Rachel was overcome by Shanti's loveliness. When we went to our room she said – 'I think our hostess would look like a queen if she wore a crown'.

Within moments the Appayyas had made us feel like dear friends instead of total strangers, and before sitting down to a superbly cooked lunch I had my first bath for a week and massacred the numerous fleas which had been my constant companions since that night we spent in Kushalnagar's Hilton. So this afternoon all is right with my world.

The siesta-habit is a great boon to writers; while everyone else snoozes I can get on with my diary. I am now sitting on the veranda, facing a semicircle of mountains and overlooking the Appayyas' farmlands. There are gay expanses of sunflowers in full bloom, and guava orchards, and glowing acres of paddy, and across wide fields from which a tobacco crop has just been harvested pairs of small black oxen are drawing simple wooden ploughs. Casey uses tractors sparingly; with the oil-crisis gathering momentum oxen make more sense. Of course most South Indian farmers will scarcely notice this crisis, since they are still using 'agricultural machinery' first invented 5,000 years ago.

Casey hopes to be able to improve production in the less fertile parts of Coorg and here he has demonstrably made a good start. However, he is worried by recent rumours about State government plans to confiscate big estates and divide them among the villagers, paying the owners Rs.60 (£3) per acre as compensation. Even to my politically naïve ears, this sounds more like a vote-catching device than a genuine programme. But what disturbs Casey is that such threats could so easily be carried out, without anyone paying the slightest attention to the landowners' pleas. Power has very definitely shifted, in modern India, to the hands of the career politicians.

I know too little about the intricacies of this problem to have strong views on it, though I cannot but sympathise with men like Tim and Casey, who clearly do not abuse their privileges. According to the *Gazetteer*, Coorg, fifteen years ago, had some

60,000 agricultural holdings, of which 42,000 were under five acres, 6,700 between five and ten acres, 10,040 between ten and fifteen acres, 880 between fifteen and thirty acres and 806 above thirty acres. The 'Gazetteer' gave no indication of the average size of the 'above thirty acres' estates, but I am told that Tim – admittedly one of Coorg's chief landowners – holds some 500 acres of coffee, apart from his paddy, grazing and forest. So on the one hand it does seem an excellent idea to give the peasants more land, though the estates of the rich 806 might not go very far amongst the poor 42,000. On the other hand, any drastic land redistribution would inevitably lead to a perilous drop in food production at a time when India desperately needs more and more food for those 55,000 additional citizens born every day. But if the *status quo* is maintained, how are the peasants to gain the funds and experience needed to cultivate larger holdings efficiently?

I always seem to end my digressions on Indian problems with a question mark.

7 December. Andanipura Farm.

The hospitality here is so generous that by bedtime last night I was in no fit state to do my usual late writing stint. We had a memorable evening, during which – while still able to focus – I got out my map and with Casey's aid established the boundaries of Coorg. It is a small district, by Indian standards – only about 1,585 square miles. Its greatest length is just over sixty miles, its greatest width scarcely forty. To the east it merges into the high Mysore plateau, to the west its mountainous frontier is twenty to thirty miles from the Malabar coast. Most of its rivers flow east and are too shallow to be navigable.

The Appayyas, like Tim, enjoy nothing better than explaining and speculating about their own distinctive culture. The speculation centres on the origin of the Coorg race, a puzzle which greatly intrigues those Coorgs who have read the informed guesses made by foreign experts about their forbears. Yesterday, for example, on the Mysore bus, a charming old gentleman from Mercara enthusiastically presented me with his own personal theories, but unfortunately I could only catch one word in ten above the roar of the engine. When the bus stopped at Hunsur, and we got out to drink tea together, I gathered that 'a singular tendency towards brachycephalism distinguishes Coorgs from other South Indian races'. This might have enlightened me had I known what the 'ism' in question means. But I do not, and as I was about to request a translation we saw the driver rinsing out his mouth and had to hurry back to our seats.

From the start of their association with this region, the British were impressed by the Coorgs' comparative indifference to the taboos of the caste-system and by their marked independence of Brahmanism. These traits set them decisively apart from other South Indians, as do their traditional costumes and fair skins. Yet the Coorg language is purely Dravidian and more closely allied to Tamil and Malayalam than to Kannada. This is the sort of contradiction that makes the 'Coorg origins' problem seem insoluble.

The *Puranas* prove Coorg to have been long recognised as a region with a separate identity (The *Puranas* – 'Ancient Stories' – are a vast collection of myth and folklore accumulated during the first millennium A.D.) According to the Cauvery *Purana*, the Coorgs are descended from a *Kshatria* (Aryan warrior) father and *sudra* (non-Aryan slave) mother and so are called *Ugras*, a word meaning fierce, formidable and powerful, and also used to describe a tribe of mixed caste origins. This ties in very nicely with the Coorgs' attitude to caste taboos; and they have had the best of both worlds, being traditionally regarded as equal to the *Kshatrias*, except in the possession of the four Vedas and six Angas.

Casey quoted Fr Henry Heras of the St Xavier's Historical Society, who believed the Coorgs to have been mentioned in Mohenjodaro inscriptions; but this left me unimpressed, since the Indus Valley script has not yet been 'cracked'. He also quoted Professor Ghurye of Bombay, who believes they belong to the Indo-Scythian race. Another pleasing and not impossible theory is that they have some Roman blood. This could be a result of intermarriage either with the numerous Roman traders who appear to have settled in South India during the reigns of Augustus and Tiberius, or with the Roman mercenaries employed by early Pandyan rulers, if these fled to the safety of mountainous Coorg when the Pandyan Kingdom collapsed in the eighth century.

Everyone in Coorg must have their own favourite answer to this ethnological riddle, so I decided last evening to sponsor the delightful though highly improbable theory that the Coorgs are descended from yet another group of Alexander's ubiquitous soldiers.

The Appayyas have two children, and though Shanti is 36 years old and her daughter Kalpana 16 years old they look like sisters – as do many Indian mothers and daughters of the privileged classes. Obviously being a Repressed Indian wife and mother is a much less ageing occupation than being a Liberated Western wife and mother.

The 12-year-old son of the house, just home from school for the short winter holidays, promises to be as handsome as his parents. I cannot even attempt to spell him since the use of traditional Hindu names has very properly been resumed, after a period during which it was fashionable in Coorg to call one's children Bobby, Tommy, Mickey, Kitty, Pam, Betty and so on. Many Coorg children are sent away to school at the age of 4; but judging by the affectionate Appayya family atmosphere, this does nothing to alienate them from their parents.

Kalpana expects to begin her university career in six months' time, at either Bangalore or Madras, but the present student unrest in India is so extreme that her parents naturally feel uneasy about the prospect of their ewe lamb falling among rioters. Yet they are as determined as she that she shall get a degree. This surprised me at first, since Karnataka's sixteen engineering colleges, nine medical colleges and four universities annually produce many thousands of graduates who cannot hope for appropriate jobs unless they know how to manipulate the relevant set of strings. However, when Kalpana graduates she will be looking for a husband rather than a job and I soon realised that in her circle 'attending college' is regarded much as 'finishing abroad' once was in Britain. Neither Shanti nor Casey seemed to see my point when I hinted last night – after their daughter had gone to bed – that for a girl of her personality, intelligence and beauty a university degree was surely superfluous, unless she proposed to use it. Since formal education first came within their reach, in the 1830s, the Coorgs – both men and women, of all classes – have been avid for it, and they remain reluctant to admit that nowadays the intelligent

daughter of intelligent parents can complete her education more
effectively at home than at a grossly overcrowded and under-
staffed college.

At the moment utter chaos prevails in Bangalore University,
and conditions seem not much better in Madras. I have been
following a curious drama in the newspapers, to do with a recent
speech made by Mr Basavalingappa, one of the Karnataka
State Ministers, who innocently deplored the numbers of trashy
novelettes now being written in Kannada. South Indians have
become so touchy about language issues that the poor man was
immediately accused of being anti-Kannada – the worst
imaginable crime in Karnataka. After days of serious student
rioting all but two of Karnataka's eleven Cabinet Ministers
resigned yesterday in protest against their colleague's remark
and the Chief Minister begged everyone – but particularly the
students – to 'put an end to this pointless controversy'. Of
course there must be more involved than appears in the papers:
Mr Basavalingappa has recently been at the centre of other
rows. Moreover, he is a Harijan, and so cannot afford to be too
controversial lest he might provoke inter-caste friction. The
powerful conservative element in rural India strongly resents the
fact that Harijans can now become high government officials.

I am beginning to feel vaguely guilty about having fallen so
deeply in love with Coorg. I set out, after all, to tour South
India, and my lingering here seems suspiciously like escapism.
Undeniably, Coorg is a place apart – clean, quiet, uncrowded,
unmodernised, not impoverished at any level of society, never
too hot or too cold at any time of the day or night and populated
by exceptionally congenial people. Add a truly magnificent
landscape to all this and you have Paradise. No wonder the
Coorgs are so proud of their country, with something more than
the normal regional pride of Indians.

Atmosphere is such a mysterious thing. Why or how could I
feel so sure, on our first evening in Mercara, that for me Coorg
was somewhere special? I then knew nothing whatever about
the place, so no part of my initial reaction can be attributed to
preconceived ideas; yet my antennae were functioning with
flawless precision – as most people's do, if their owners are
willing to rely on them.

.   .   .   .   .

Later. This afternoon, when I mentioned that I would like to live for a couple of months in Coorg, Casey said it would be impossible to rent accommodation since letting rooms or houses is not part of the local way of life. But then he added, reassuringly, that Tim would solve my problem; and I fancy there are few Coorg problems beyond the ingenuity of that descendant of dewans.

Until Casey explained, I had not realised that there are no Coorg villages, as we understand the term. Instead, the Coorgs live either in large, isolated houses on their estates, or in groups of several smaller houses occupied by members of a joint family and surrounded by the family lands. A scattering of such homesteads is known as a *grama* and corresponds to what we in Ireland call a 'townland'. A group of *gramas* forms a *nad* and in Coorg today there are six *taluks*, divided into twenty-four *nads*. Such real villages as exist are occupied by Moplah traders or non-Coorg Hindu merchants and craftsmen.

After tea we all strolled down to the farm buildings, accompanied by two sloppy Labradors. Casey employs about ninety farm workers – men and women – and his openly feudal relationship with them seems to suit everybody. He told me that the 80,000 true Coorgs now form only about one-sixth of the population of Coorg, but are so dominant a minority that their culture has powerfully influenced most of their neighbours. Coorg customs have been adopted by thousands whose forefathers were freed slaves, or plantation workers imported from near-by states a century ago, or tribesmen forced by the reduction of the forests to become part of the farming community. As a pleasing result of this, the graceful traditional Coorg women's costume may even now be seen all over the countryside, worn by the peasantry, though the majority of the younger 'genuine' Coorg women have foolishly abandoned it.

Shanti and I went back to the house together, leaving the rest pottering about the farmyard, and as we walked through gay acres of sunflowers the conversation turned to recent pro-women changes in the laws of India.

According to Coorg Civil Law, which in this respect follows the general Hindu law, a daughter only has the right of maintenance from her father's family property until marriage, and after marriage no right either of share or inheritance. In

theory, however, all ancient tribal, regional or religious laws
have been superseded since Independence by new laws giving
women full equality with men, so that they may now own
property and insist on full and equal shares in any family
inheritance. But most villagers, of both sexes, disapprove of this
violent tampering with the fundamentals of Hindu society.
They do not want their country reduced to the level of that
pernicious, permissive Western world of which, through their
transistors, they from time to time hear faint and disquieting
rumours; and they cannot conceive of a moral world in which
men and women are treated as equals. It is one of history's
minor ironies that these particular changes should have been
enforced immediately an Indian government came to power,
when for so long the Raj had scrupulously avoided offending
Hindu susceptibilities.

Yet the influence of the Raj did appreciably improve the
position of many urban women and this new legislation must
eventually bring about a change in rural India. Listening to
Shanti, I got the impression she would prefer not to see an
abrupt change, even if such a thing were possible; and on such a
basic point as arranged marriages few mature Indians – outside
of a tiny cosmopolitan 'sub-caste' which is no longer truly
Indian – are prepared to advocate any change, ever. Even a
couple as liberal as the Appayyas would feel deeply distressed
should their daughter set out on a personal husband-hunt
instead of depending on her parents' judgement.

I asked Shanti what the average parents' priorities are as they
cast about for suitable mates for their young, and she replied
without hesitation that all Coorgs consider 'blood' the most
important qualification – by which I assume she meant caste
and sub-caste. Next comes 'honour' (that is, moral character),
and then property, health, looks and accomplishments. On the
question of honour a boy's parents pay special attention to the
character of a girl's mother and Shanti quoted a Coorg pro-
verb – 'If the mother has a white tail the daughter will at least
have a white spot'. So if a girl can produce a mother with an
unblemished reputation it does not much matter what unsavoury
predilections she may have inherited from her father.

Shanti also remarked on a change I have recently heard
mentioned by several other Indians – the tendency amongst

today's youngsters to abandon that love-match ideal which twenty or twenty-five years ago was the dream of every progressive young Indian. Some of those youngsters are themselves the victims of love-matches gone wrong, and many others know that a high percentage of such marriages failed. This failure rate is hardly surprising since there is little in the Indian's cultural background to help them to create the sort of relationship that should develop out of a love-match.

According to Casey, the Coorg Civil Law is still widely respected and Coorgs have only recently been permitted to own private property. Until the joint-family system was weakened by migration, no individual could acquire or inherit property that was separate from the family possessions. Now, however, men are allowed to leave to their children – without having first to seek permission from the *Koravakara* (Head of the House) – all property acquired through their personal effort. But the Coorg who has prospered in some far-away city is still criticised if he does not annually donate a generous portion of his wealth to the family pool. And nothing is allowed to interfere with the cultivation of the joint-family lands by the joint-family for the benefit of the joint-family.

It seemed to me, listening to Casey's explanations, that the *Koravakara* is not to be envied. As the eldest son, he has all the worry and responsibility, when he succeeds his father, of managing the entire estate, yet he is not entitled to an even fractionally larger share of anything than his brothers – or his widowed sisters-in-law, on behalf of their sons, should his brothers predecease him.

The adoption laws are interesting. A childless Coorg widow may adopt a son to inherit her husband's share of property, and so may a Coorg male who is himself disqualified from inheriting through disease or blindness, or an unmarried Coorg female who has no brothers. (Spinsters are very rare in India but they can happen, usually because of some physiological defect.) An illegitimate son or daughter may not, however, be adopted, nor can a boy be purchased. Most people prefer to adopt a spare son of a daughter of their own household, if such is available. Adoptions are not recorded in writing, but a little ceremony takes place in the presence of relatives and friends; and, if adoptive parents subsequently produce a son of their own, he and the adopted boy have equal rights and the latter, being the elder, will eventually become the *Koravakara*. Many childless Hindu men adopt because they fear *Putt*, a place of torment reserved by some unspecified but obviously unreasonable god for those who have no son to perform the last rites over their corpse. But Coorgs are made of sterner stuff. They don't believe in *Putt* and their motives for adoption are always strictly practical.

7

The *Huthri* Festival

8 December.   Green Hills, near Virajpet.

This address – sounding so like a stockbroker's fine detached residence in darkest Surrey – is a typical period aberration on the part of a wealthy Coorg landowner and Cambridge graduate of the early twentieth century.

For some odd reason, now quite forgotten, a Swiss architect designed Green Hills in about 1910, when Tim's father moved out of the ancestral home. By my humble standards – or, indeed, by normal Coorg standards – it is an imposing mini-palace, full of ebony and teak and rosewood, and silver and ivory and brass, and ancient armour, and swords that were wielded in famous battles, and of course the inevitable, magnificent shikar trophies which Rachel and I find so very off-putting. However, though Tim was one of the most celebrated hunters of his generation, and prided himself on always going into the forests on foot, even he has at last been bitten by the conservation bug. But it may already be too late to save the Coorg tiger.

This morning the Appayyas insisted on providing us with an ancient retainer as escort, which I felt was taking concern for one's guests a bit far. Obviously none of them could imagine a foreign woman, who spoke only English, being able to find her way unaided from Andanipura to Green Hills – a distance of some thirty miles.

When we changed buses at Mercara I bought today's *Deccan Herald* and read: 'Three Killed in Bus Capsize: A bus proceeding from Coimbatore to Velanthavalam village had more than one hundred passengers at the time of the accident ... The driver was reported to have absconded, while the conductor surrendered at the Madukkarai police station.' Folding up the newspaper I looked around and estimated there were no more than sixty-five people in our forty-four-seater bus, so we seemed likely enough to survive.

The road from Mercara to Green Hills'– which is five miles north of the market town of Virajpet – winds through South Coorg, where the landscape is less rugged than in the north but even more beautiful. This whole area – Yedenal Kanad Taluk – is extraordinarily fertile and generally considered the centre of Coorg life. Many leading families live here and Virajpet, though a smaller town than Mercara, is the province's most important commercial centre.

I find myself automatically using the word 'province' when writing of Coorg, though the term is no longer technically correct. Under the British, Coorg was a province – the smallest in India, administered by a commissioner – but now it is merely one of Karnataka's many districts. However, I may perhaps be allowed this inaccuracy, in view of Coorg's 'natural' – as distinct from political – independence.

The bus put us down at the freshly painted white wooden gates of the Green Hills estate and as we walked up a long drive I could for a moment have believed myself in some quiet corner of England. On either side, green parkland was dotted with handsome trees; near by grazed a few fine horses and a herd of even finer cows, and in the distance, beyond the big house amidst its brilliant abundance of flowers and shrubs, lay the long, uneven line of the Ghats. Their gentle blue contrasted with the vivid, sharp, almost incredible blue of this Coorg sky – a sky such as one would never, it must be admitted, see in England. Nor would one pass there a nursery of orange-tree saplings and baby coffee-bushes, each infant protected by a wicker shield; and the bull would not be a glossy red Sindhi with a splendid hump, nor would the house be surrounded by graceful groves of immensely tall areca-nut and coconut-palms.

We arrived just as lunch was being served on the veranda and Sita introduced us to her mother, her two brothers, various visiting relatives and five dogs including a Great Dane the size of a pony. More relatives will arrive this evening for the *Huthri* Festival tomorrow.

One has to admire the Coorgs' devotion to their own customs. Observing the Thimmiah family today, I noticed that

when junior members meet their elders they bow respectfully
to touch the older person's knees with the fingertips, which are
then pressed to their own forehead and, finally, to their superior's feet. This form of obeisance takes longer to describe
than to carry out: the whole series of gestures is somehow
swiftly accomplished in one graceful movement. And it pleases
me to see such a tradition maintained, even in the most sophisticated circles.

Huthri literally means 'new rice crop' and the festivities go on
for about a week. These celebrations are simple – mainly
dancing, singing, eating and drinking – but *Huthri* is greatly
looked forward to as the one occasion when nothing short of
serious illness prevents every family member from returning to
the ancestral home. The central event is the solemn cutting of
the first sheaf of paddy by the head of the family. This must be
done on the night of a full moon, in either November or
December, at a precise moment which has been declared
auspicious by the *Kanias* (astrologers). No one yet knows when
the 1973 auspicious moment will be, but tomorrow's newspapers are expected to publish it. I felt slightly cheated on being
told this; an announcement about a ceremony that may well
antedate the written word – never mind the printed word –
by thousands of years should surely be publicised in some more
romantic way than through the newspapers.

A thorough spring-cleaning of every house, outbuilding,
yard and garden precedes *Huthri*, and today all doorways and
windows were decorated with festoons of mango and peepul
branches and garlands of flowers. The pathways and gateways
from the fields to the house must also be decorated with
elaborate floral arches, and this afternoon Rachel and I went
for a long walk so that none of the busy household would feel it
necessary to entertain us.

On our way we explored one of Tim's big plantations where
the coffee-berries were swelling and ripening beneath towering,
ancient shade-trees. As coffee-bushes need shade the forests
never had to be completely cleared to make way for the
plantations and walking through coffee is always a delight;
enough trees remain for the insect and bird life to flourish and

this afternoon we saw three sensationally large butterflies and several jewel-like birds.

As we were leaving the plantation I happened to notice, in an uncleared patch of forest near the road, one of those primitive non-shrines which seem much more relevant to the religious life of Indian peasants than the ornate, Brahman-dominated temples. A long, flat stone (not a *lingam*) lay on the ground amidst the tangled roots of a gigantic tree that seemed as old as the earth itself. No attempt had been made to erect even the crudest shelter over this altar-like boulder but many small objects were piled near by and, when my eyes had got used to the perpetual twilight beneath that dense canopy of leaves, I saw the simple pottery votive offerings of people whose ancestors were worshipping thus before ever Brahmanistic Hinduism was heard of. These clumsily made little figures represented elephants, cattle, goats, dogs or pigs and some looked fresh from the fire. We circled the colossal tree under which the stone lay, following a path trodden by countless generations, and I noticed that piles of broken pottery almost covered the complex roots. I wondered then if human sacrifices had ever been made in this appropriate setting. But if once upon a time such rites did take place the victims must have been as happy to die as Christian martyrs, for there is now no stain of terror or brutality on the atmosphere. (In letting my mind run on these morbid lines, I was not being unduly fanciful. Up to the middle of the last century, at Kirindadu and Konincheri villages in near-by Katiednad, a human sacrifice was offered to Bhadra Kali in the June and December of every third year. Then gradually, as the British influence spread, human victims were replaced by animals.)

When I asked Tim about the stone slab in the sacred grove he said – rather surprisingly – that he had never heard of it, but that it could be one of those altars dedicated to the local god Bete-Ayyappa – Lord-father of hunting expeditions – which are found all over Coorg in forests and fields. He added that in honour of this god the Coorgs have reserved a certain tract of forest in each *nad* which is considered sacred and where no trees may be cut. Despite Coorg's abundant forest wealth, the indiscriminate felling of trees has always been discouraged and very ancient customs – which have the force of laws – specify which trees should be used for fuel, which for building, which for furniture and so on. It is laid down that only the branches should be cut; nobody has the right to fell a tree unless he has already planted two.

9 December.

By dinner-time last night all the family had assembled for today's *Huthri* ceremonies and a more congenial gathering it would be hard to imagine. I am still searching for words to convey exactly what it is that makes the Coorgs seem so endearing. Perhaps I came across a clue to it this morning, when reading an early book on Coorg borrowed from Tim's library. Some 120 years ago a Swiss missionary – Dr Moegling – wrote of the Coorgs that 'strangers are received among them and naturalised without difficulty.' And for the ordinary traveller it is not only heart-warming but flattering to be made to feel immediately at home by people who, though Westernised in many superficial ways, have so far remained emphatically a race apart.

This evening's ceremonies began at seven-thirty when we were sitting on the veranda sipping our gins or whiskies. Suddenly Sita said, 'Listen!' – and we heard the distant beating of drums and clashing of cymbals and the occasional long, solemn note of a horn. As the music drew nearer I moved to sit on the broad wooden parapet at the edge of the veranda, overlooking a level stretch of freshly swept beaten earth – some fifty yards by twenty – on which the *Holeyas* would dance. These are the labourers who work in the paddy-valleys and many of whose ancestors have been the *Holeyas* of Tim's ancestors for centuries.

There was nothing outwardly remarkable about the forty or so men and boys who soon appeared, dressed in everyday clothes and led by a five-man band. At first they seemed rather self-conscious but then something took hold of them – the music? the home-distilled Arak they had been drinking? or simply the *Huthri* spirit? – and for two hours they danced and chanted like beings possessed by some happy demon. This was a glorious scene, lit by the full moon – slim, agile figures leaping and crouching, and twisting and wriggling, and bounding and swaying in their improvised dances. It was every man for himself, from a turbaned greybeard who must have been well over 70 years old to a chubby, vigorously pirouetting 4-year-old. And overhead the leaves of the tall palms stirred and glinted against a blue velvet sky, while fireworks of every conceivable sort were being let off at frequent intervals by the small boys of the family.

Meanwhile, the menfolk had been taking a purifying bath and dressing in their traditional costume, which is so dignified, attractive and practical that I cannot imagine why they ever abandoned it in favour of Western clothes. The coat – called a *kupya*, and usually made of thick black cloth – reaches a little below the knees and has a vee-neck, elbow-length sleeves and a scarlet and gold silken tasselled sash. Under it is worn a white shirt and into the sash is tucked a *peechekathi* or an *odikathi*, or both. The former is a short, sharp dagger with an ivory handle and a silver and gold ornamental scabbard; the latter is a heavy, curved knife very like the Gurkha kukri. On ceremonial occasions the male Coorg costume must include a *peechekathi*, attached to the silken sash by a long silver chain decorated with exquisite silver miniatures of all the traditional Coorg weapons. The unique, flat-topped Coorg turban completes this striking outfit and the legs and feet should be left bare; but nowadays almost everybody is hookworm-conscious and wears light sandals. A strong streak of egalitarianism runs through Coorg society and at ceremonial gatherings it is impossible to tell the difference, by their attire, between the poorest farmer and the richest coffee planter.

For *Huthri* each member of the local community makes his contribution, the potter bringing a new pot, the mat-weaver a new mat, the basket-maker a new basket, the carpenter a new wooden bowl; and at nine-thirty, when we went to the *Nellakki Nadubade* or inner hall of the house – which amongst the ancestor-revering Coorgs serves as a family chapel – I saw the uses to which these things are put. At one end of the room the sacred brass wall-lamp, now lit, hung from the ceiling at face-level and directly below it the new mat was spread on the floor, touching the wall. On it stood the new basket, containing auspicious bitter-gourd, mango and peepul leaves, and also an old basket containing some of last year's paddy to welcome this year's crop. The new earthen pot held flour made from fried boiled rice, and beside it stood small bowls full of milk, honey, sesame and ground coconut. On a three-legged stool was laid the billhook with which Tim would cut the first sheaf, beside a dish-lamp complete with rice, betel leaves and areca nuts.

As we all stood before the wall-lamp Tim invoked the blessing of the god Igguthappa and the *Karona* (family ancestor), and then each member of the family saluted him in the traditional way and received his blessings. At this point the *Koravakara's* wife becomes the most important person in the ceremony and Mrs Thimmiah, bearing the dish-lamp, led us in procession from the house to the fields.

We were preceded by several torch-bearers holding aloft blazing plantain stumps to light our way down the steep slope immediately below the house, and at intervals other stumps wrapped in oil-soaked rags flared beside the pathways, making the blossoms on the flower-bedecked archways glow with a strange, subtle radiance. All the time the tempo of the music was quickening and it reached a crescendo when we stepped from the shadows of the tall coffee-bushes and the paddy came suddenly into view, looking like a wide lake of silver beneath the brilliance of the tropical moon.

The swathes to be ceremonially cut had already been prepared and we approached them by walking in single file along the narrow tops of the dykes. Then Tim looked at his watch, poured milk and honey on the roots of a paddy clump, accepted the billhook from the youth who had been carrying it in a special bamboo container and, to a frenzy of music and exhilarated chanting, cut the first stalks of this year's harvest. At once a henchman rushed to the edge of the group and fired a single shot into the air to summon Igguthappa – and everyone began an immemorial chant to invoke the god's blessings on the crop. As I write this is still going on somewhere out in the vast, shadowy courtyard. The words mean 'Increase, O God!' and sound like 'Poli, Poli, *Deva*! Poli, Poli, *Deva*!' '*Poli*' is said very quickly, while '*Deva*' is almost drawled.

Next, the *Poludu Kuthu* (a special wooden vessel) was filled with sheaves and placed on the head of the young man – Tim's son – who had been chosen for the great honour of carrying it back to the house. Other sheaves were handed to everyone present and I found it deeply moving to walk with the rest towards the threshing-yard holding those cool, dew-wet stalks, which collectively mean so much to some 500 million Indians. It is impossible, against the Coorg background, to think of this ceremony as merely 'a quaint local custom' or 'interesting old superstition'. Perhaps it is no more than that: perhaps all religious ritual everywhere is no more than that – who knows? But, if there is a God, then I think we came close to him tonight as we stood chanting in the moonlight.

Marking the centre of each Coorg threshing-floor is a plain stone pillar about four feet high, around which, for *Huthri*, an elaborate pattern is drawn on the ground with white chalk. I took off my shoes at this stage, to join in the prayerful procession, and we circled the pillar three times before laying our paddy at its base while Mrs Thimmiah performed another *puja*. Then we picked the sheaves up again and climbed the steep path through the coffee back to the house, to lay them finally beneath the sacred wall-lamp. Before entering the house the *Kuthi*-bearer paused on the threshold to have his feet washed by Sita – the unmarried daughter – and to receive from her a drink of milk. He then laid the *Kuthi* on the mat below the lamp and, after a few moments, several young servants took some of the new paddy to weave it into garlands which were placed on every door-handle and window-latch in the house.

Having saluted his elders and received their blessings the *Kuthi*-bearer went into the kitchen to mix a dough known as *Elakki Puttu*. This consists of rice-flour, fried gingelly seeds, bitter-gourd peel, grated coconut, mashed plantain, milk, honey and some tiny pebbles and coins, added for much the same reason as we add foreign objects to our barm bracks or Christmas puddings. I had followed the *Kuthi*-bearer and I watched as he placed a little dough on six peepul leaves (one for each resident member of the family) and threw the leaves at the ceiling, calling the name of an ancestor at each throw. All the little balls stuck, which means the ancestors are well pleased with their descendants. And so they should be, in this family.

Meanwhile, two wooden trestle tables had been laid with shiny squares of plantain leaf in the *Nellakki Nadubade*, and Sita was peeling a few grains from the new crop. She added these to a sweet porridge of which she placed a portion on a leaf – with a morsel from each of the seven ceremonial dishes we were about to eat – as an offering to the ancestors, and when we had all taken our seats Tim asked ritualistically, 'Shall we partake of the new crop?' We then did so, by eating a little porridge; and I came on a pebble and a coin which means I am to live long *and* become rich.

I certainly feel rich tonight, though my new wealth has nothing to do with coins. Occasionally the traveller chances on an experience that seems enormously important, even if its significance cannot easily be expressed or explained, and though nothing could be simpler than these *Huthri* ceremonies I know I shall never forget them. Altogether apart from the feeling engendered – which was so genuinely religious, in its joyous, primitive way – the sheer visual beauty of that paddy-cutting ritual was overwhelming. The Coorgs are a handsome race and all those fine faces, seen in profile against the darkness by the light of flaring torches, made a picture that would have inspired Rembrandt. Nor was there any intrusive twentieth-century detail to spoil the vision of Sita, superb in a Coorg sari of crimson silk, following her mother – a slim figure in silver – as Mrs Thimmiah bore that flickering dish-lamp along the narrow path while the workers' happy, rhythmic, full-throated chanting went echoing across the valley.

Probably, however, it is a mistake to consider the religious feeling and the visual scene as separate phenomena. Very likely they are interdependent, people responding to the one all the more readily because of the other. The builders of the great cathedrals seem to have known a thing or two about this matter, though my impression is that modern architects understand it only imperfectly. But perhaps thirteenth-century conservatives thought Chartres disgustingly eccentric and irreverent.

10 December

I woke at dawn this morning, despite having been so late to bed, and went for a solitary walk through the early freshness of coffee-plantation, paddy-valley and bird-busy forest. And I wondered, as I walked, what the *Huthri* festival now means to Westernised Coorgs. More, I suspect, than Christmas now means to many Christians – though one might not think so to see the Thimmiahs lounging about in their jeans and T-shirts while sipping their cocktails, reading their *New Yorkers*, listening to their stereo Johann Strauss and conversing in their Cambridge English (the first language of the Coorg élite). It interests me that so many Coorgs seem emotionally and intellectually capable of moving from East to West and back again without showing any sign of inner conflict or loss of integrity. This is a facility more usually found in practice amongst Muslims than amongst Hindus, though in theory the Hindu philosophy should be the more conducive to it.

As we sat on the veranda last evening, watching the dancers, I was very conscious of the chasm between Indian landowners and labourers; but later, when we were all in the fields, at the heart of the *Huthri* ceremonies, I realised that at a certain level there is less of a chasm here than in Europe. Landowners and labourers recognise each other as being equally important, in different ways, and – at least where this family is concerned – are truly united in mutual loyalty and respect.

A Socialist would of course be appalled by the Coorg scene, which is as shamelessly feudal as anything I have ever come across. Tim talks cheerfully about 'allowing my people to smoke' or 'forbidding my people to gamble' as though democracy died with the City States. On the other hand, in addition to a just wage he gives 'his people' generous paddy rations for two meals a day, subsidises their weddings and funerals, pays their medical expenses when they fall ill and has so organised their lives that few of them are ever in debt though throughout India millions of agricultural labourers spend most of their lives in the grip of money-lenders. According to himself, Tim is an 'average' Coorg landowner and I would like to be able to believe this. He once stood for parliament, causing the local Congress candidate to lose his deposit, but the wheeling and dealing of politics so disgusted him that he soon left the democratic arena to concentrate on doing his own feudal thing.

Contrary to my usual custom – but not surprisingly – I slept after lunch and woke to hear music in the distance. The bandsmen and singers had returned for a ritual praising of the family, from the founder-ancestor, called the *Karona*, down to the youngest living grandson, aged three. As I write this (at

10 p.m.) the musicians are still sitting on long benches against
the wall in the prayer-room, chanting their strangely moving
refrain, while the sacred lamp burns steadily before them. At
intervals throughout the evening members of the assembled
family went into the prayer-room and sat for a time, listening –
and then returned to the veranda to get on with their game of
scrabble. Tim has told me that tomorrow the ceremonial
Huthri Dance of Seven *Nads* is to be held near by. He added,
sadly, that since the cinema came to Virajpet the locals have
been losing interest in their festivals and the quality of both
music and dancing has deteriorated. In an effort to encourage
the boys to learn from the men, he himself sometimes tours the
nads; but even in Coorg mass-entertainment is winning.

Rachel is 5 years old today and despite the inevitable shortage of cards and presents it was a most successful birthday,
complete with home-made chocolate cake for tea.

11 December.

This really is superb walking country, with climate to match.
I spent most of today on the move: before breakfast with Sita,
Rachel and the dogs, after breakfast with Rachel, and after
lunch on my own. In all directions little tracks run to and fro
and up and down, across the paddy and through the coffee and
over the steep slopes. And every turn of every path presents a
new combination of the region's beauties; blue mountains
fortifying the horizon, protecting the peace of Coorg: long
paddy-valleys lying between the dark green of the forested
ridges like magic lakes of gold: wild heliotrope covering the open
scrubland like a pale purple mist: neat acres of coffee fringed
with lines of slim silver oaks and shaded by trees of an awesome
height: and occasional handsome dwellings marked by warm
red-brown tiles, gleaming white walls, groves of palms and
plantains and cascades of bougainvillaea and poinsettia.

This afternoon, as I walked alone, I thanked Fate for having
guided me to Coorg. With a 5-year-old fellow-traveller I cannot
seek out those remote areas which most appeal to me and it is
rare indeed to find a 'developed' region free of brash advertisements, domineering pylons, strident petrol-stations, abundant
litter, synthetic building materials and hideously artificial
colours. But here, in this 'finest of the kingdoms of Jambudwipa'

a civilised harmony still exists between landscape and people. So perfectly do the artistry of nature and of man complement each other that one feels miraculously restored to the Garden of Eden, to the world as it was before Eve ate the apple of technology.

At about half past four I overtook several groups of friendly, curious, gracefully robed women who were also on their way to watch the *Huthri* dancing, due to begin soon on a level expanse of grassy common land. Beneath the solitary, giant sampige tree in the centre of the common, Rachel was awaiting me with a swarm of young friends she had somehow acquired since lunch-time, and she announced that the local Harijans were about to perform an overture to the formal *Huthri* dances.

Then, on the far side of the common, a quartet of weirdly comic figures came bounding on to the grass. The leader was almost black-skinned, smeared all over with white chalk and naked from the waist up – apart from a battered trilby, an elaborate garland of orange flowers and a blatantly false beard of goat-hair. Around his waist he wore a ragged cotton mini-skirt, held in place by a rope from which hung a dozen clanging pewter bells, and he had been kept well topped-up with a Arak during the past several days. He was followed by another man whose huge engaging grin revealed a magnificent mouthful of even white teeth and whose great bush of tangled hair may not have been as verminous as it looked. This character was clad in someone's cast-off army shorts and had a moth-eaten tiger-skin draped across his ebony torso. Like his friends, he was brandishing a long wooden staff and exuding Arak fumes. The other two performers were tall youths disguised as women and even without knowing the language one soon gathered that this entertainment would not have amused a certain Empress of India.

The adult Coorgs standing under the sampige rather pointedly ignored the Harijans as they gambolled, danced, yelled, sang, leaped high in the air and shook their long staffs. During a mock fight they rolled on the ground feigning mortal injuries (and feigning other things when the young 'women' fell beside them), while two small boys played a monotonous yet pleasing melody on long, curved horns. This boisterous, undisciplined clowning went on until the Coorg dancers appeared, forming a dramatic contrast to the Harijans as they crossed the common in a stately double line, their costumes immaculate, their bearing kingly, their movements, when the dancing began, stylised and gracious.

Forty-two men from seven villages were taking part and all carried short bamboo canes with which they duelled ritualistically while dancing in a circle to music provided by the drummers and horn-players. The leading pair wore white, the rest black, and as those handsome men circled rhythmically against a background of mighty trees I reflected that seldom, in the 1970s, is folk dancing performed for fun – not self-consciously, to preserve customs, or cunningly, to please tourists. But my pleasure can never be unalloyed when I chance upon such fragile and doomed links with the past. One knows that before Rachel is grown even Coorg will have opted for that pseudo-culture which 'kills time' (grimly significant phrase) but leaves the spirit starving.

Why do some people remain so passionately attached to traditional customs, while others can happily jettison them? The traditionalists, I suppose, are just silly romantic fools – or maybe cowards. It certainly frightens me to think that within my own lifetime customs which had survived for incalculable periods have been discarded in country after country, by race after race. Why should we assume that those links which previously bound the living to the dead are now worthless? It was only a few hours ago, under the sampige tree, that I glimpsed a possible answer to this question.

The dancers were still indefatigably dancing, though the clear evening sky had changed from pale blue to faint apricot, and then to a strange and lovely shade of violet. And suddenly it seemed to me that because our world has been so radically altered within the past half-century many of those things we were bred to value are, quite simply, no longer valuable; in modern society they have no place, they fulfil no function. So they must go, as the leaves in the autumn, leaving us, unprotected, to face the consequences of our own terrifying ingenuity.

Tomorrow we leave for a few weeks in the extreme south and Tim has guaranteed to have some suitably primitive accommodation organised for us on our return to Coorg.

8

A Glance at Kerala:
Cochin's Kathakali Dance

12 December.   Tellicherry.

This morning's journey from Virajpet to the Kerala state border was a continuous descent through dense forests where cardamom groves flourish in the undergrowth and not a trace of humanity is to be seen. On such roads I find it very hard to reconcile myself to bus travel.

The border consists of a shallow, clear green river running over elephantine boulders at the bottom of a deep ravine. In a one-street village on the Kerala side the Karnataka State-run buses turn around to go home, leaving their passengers to board the Kerala buses, which also turn around here. Kerala's rich green hills rise straight up from the village street and to the east looms the high blue bulk of the Ghats. This is the sort of hidden-away little place, with a 'lost' feeling, which I particularly enjoy.

In the ramshackle mini-bazaar an astonishing amount of salted fish was on sale, and many baskets of fresh fish are brought every day by bus from the coast. At noon we went into a tiny eating-house and ate off plantain leaves provided by a little boy who carried them down the street on his head in a neat, freshly cut roll, tied with grass, and received 10 paise for his labour. Before the food was served each customer carefully washed his own 'plate' with a tumbler of water – letting the water run on to the earth floor – and after the meal he tossed his leaf over the balcony towards the river far below. If it landed in the bushes on the cliff-side it was immediately set upon by the local cats and crows, watched enviously by the local pi-dogs, who could not cope with the precipice.

After lunch we set off to walk through lush magnificence until a bus overtook us. For a mile or so we had the river on our left and on our right were hibiscus and bamboo-clumps, marking the edge of the forest. Despite a total lack of cultivable land, quite a few little thatched dwellings, of mud-brick and/or coconut matting, had been erected along the edge of the precipice above the river. Their occupants were black-skinned, thick-lipped, curly haired, bright-eyed and well-built. Most of them greeted us cheerfully, when they had recovered from their incredulity on seeing a more or less white woman and child strolling down the road, but the toddlers were terrified and fled shrieking to the shelter of mother's skirts.

In countries as developed as India one expects 'the media' to have by now given everybody an approximate idea of what everybody else looks like. But of course this is nonsense in the case of – for instance – Kerala's Ezhavas. Formerly these people were not merely 'untouchable' but 'unapproachable' and they are still a 'Depressed Class', to use the quaint official euphemism for impoverished groups who suffer from persisting (though now illegal) caste discrimination. The annual *per capita* income in Kerala is £26.30, so obviously the poorest class cannot afford to take their children to the coast, where they might glimpse foreign tourists or at least see pages from magazines, pasted on tea-house walls, which would give them some visual idea of white people.

We had been walking for about an hour when the countryside opened up. On every side stretched plantations of cashew and eucalyptus, groves of coconut-palms and plantains, low green scrub, stands of bamboo, patches of tapioca and the remnants of primeval forest where the black pepper vine thrives. One is overwhelmed here by the sheer abundance – the boundless exuberance – of Kerala's fertility. It is as though the Lord of Creation had given way, at this point, to the promptings of a wild and joyous extravagance.

We stopped at a cross-roads to drink scalding sweet tea in the shade of a lean-to decorated with crudely printed Communist posters and a large picture of St Francis Xavier looking uncharacteristically soulful. The Hammer and Sickle marked the crossroads, fluttering merrily atop a high bamboo flagstaff, and opposite the lean-to some twenty barefooted boys and girls were sitting on the ground outside a thatched schoolhouse, busily doing their English lesson. No teacher was in sight but they looked up from their studies only to help each other. I began then to believe all I had heard about the Malayalis' devotion to scholarship. And when the bus picked us up half an hour later we had just passed a large, tree-surrounded convent school from which hundreds of girls were pouring like lava down the sides of some intellectual volcano. Observing them, I wondered what effect that molten stream was destined soon to have on the Communistic, under-employed Malayalis. But – looking ahead – volcanic soil is very fertile.

From our seats at the back of the bus we had a good view, when the road began to descend to coast level, of the most densely populated region I have ever seen. Villages and towns merged one into another, people moved in throngs or stood talking in groups as big as a successful public meeting, the Red Flag fluttered gaily, gaudy wayside shrines contained smirking statues of the Virgin Mary, the Hammer and Sickle was neatly painted in white on ochre gable walls, Christian churches were frequently conspicuous and the hot, heavy air was laden with what a disdainful Coorg friend accurately described as 'the classic Malabar stench of shit, piss and rotting fish'.

Judging by the literature with which they were laden, most of our fellow-passengers were students. The lovely, flower-wreathed girl beside me cherished on her lap a gigantic tome of American provenance entitled *Industrial Psychology and Capitalism.* She gladly allowed me to look at it but the jargon was so way-out it might as well have been in Malayalam; and I did wonder how much of it was comprehensible to its present borrower from the college library. When we passed a gleaming new church – its grounds criss-crossed with bunting made of fresh blossoms – I asked our student friend if there was some special festival on and she explained the church was to be dedicated this evening. Then she sighed and confessed that she was worried. It was her new parish church and she longed to go to the dedication service, but her father was addressing a Communist rally in a near-by town at the same time and she had promised weeks ago to help with the refreshments for the visiting speakers. So what was she to do? When I suggested that she should go early to the rally venue, do her bit on the refreshments and hurry back to the church she immediately brightened. 'Of course! Why didn't I think of that?'

When we arrived in Tellicherry at five-thirty we walked the length and breadth of the town, looking for accommodation, and in seven hotels were told 'No room'. 'This is because India has too much population,' Rachel observed cheerfully. But I fear it is a bit more complicated than that. In three hotels an amiable youth at the desk had booked us in and was about to hand us the key when his paunchy Brahman boss appeared, gave us a hostile stare and said 'All rooms are full!' However, remembering the racial discrimination once practised in India by Europeans I feel I must not complain. Although two Wongs don't make a white, as the Bishop of Hong Kong said to the couple with the blonde baby.

By seven-thirty the railway station – where I am writing this – seemed our only hope and we could have had a good free night's rest but for an unfortunate remark by the kindly station master to the effect that the nine-fifty night train to Ernakulam would solve all our problems. Apart from the daftness of travelling when the country is invisible, I can think of few things more hellish than an eight-hour nocturnal journey without a berth in a third-class Indian railway compartment. However, Rachel seized on the idea as a monkey on a banana and resolutely closed her ears to maternal words of wisdom; so I soon gave in, feeling she had earned this concession by being, on the whole, such a reasonable travelling companion.

In the ticket hall the male queue stretched for over fifty yards – its end was out of sight – but there were only two other women in the female queue. Inevitably I was asked to get a ticket for a man, which I gladly did. He was a very young father carrying a sleeping toddler of fourteen months and whimpering, new-born twins. Their mother, he explained pathetically, was still in hospital 'with a terrible complication – I sadly worry she will die'.

13 December. Cochin.

Between Tellicherry and here all my nightmares came true; and since Rachel enjoyed every ghastly moment of the journey it did not even serve the purpose of teaching her that Mother Knows Best. There was standing room only so she perched happily on my rucksack in the corridor when not sitting on the knees of strange men up and down the train, telling them her life-story. Apart from an hour's doze around midnight she never closed an eye, yet remained in high spirits. It is becoming noticeable that the rougher the going the better she copes, but the same cannot be said for her ageing mamma. I stood all night by an open door in the corridor swigging Koday's Rum and enjoying the waning moon behind the palms, while thinking how foolish it is to travel by train. Indian buses are as cheap as third-class on the railways and much more convenient from every point of view except speed (and, of course, safety).

We arrived here at 5.30 a.m. and went wandering around in a semi-coma of exhaustion looking for a hotel with a conscious *chowkidar*. Coming out of one narrow side-street, just as the darkness was turning grey, I walked straight into something white and hard and long and curved. Yes, an elephant's tusk. And beyond it, looming colossal in the dawn-light, was the owner, carrying a bundle of palm-fronds the size of a haystack in his trunk and an amused mahout on his neck. A collision with an elephant was just what we had needed to cheer us up and Rachel insisted on our following him. There was something almost eerie about the speed and silence with which that huge bulk moved through the greyness along the empty streets. Indeed, the speed was so considerable that even Rachel was willing to give up when we saw the door of a tea-house opening.

We emerged, refreshed, into full daylight and soon found this enormous new tourist hotel close to the sea. By our standards it is Hiltonian: Rs.10 for a single room with private Western loo and shower attached, and a fan and large table and comfortable chair. The bed has a foam-rubber mattress and everything is newly painted and scrupulously clean. By seven o'clock Rachel was asleep, but I can never sleep in the daytime when I have reached this point of exhaustion. So I shall now lie down and do some Kerala homework.

Later. According to legend, Kerala was raised from the sea by Parasurama, a Brahman incarnation of Vishnu who undertook to perform this labour with his battle-axe as a penance for having vengefully and destructively waged war against the *Kshatrias*. Yet the credit for Kerala's Golden Age is given not to Parasurama but to a demon, King Mahabali, whose reign ended when he was banished by the dwarf Vamana, another incarnation of Vishnu. Mahabali's reign represents the pre-Aryan era when the indigenous, caste-free peoples of Kerala were in control of their own destiny; and Vamana represents the fair-skinned invaders who imposed their own rigid social system on the dark-skinned and henceforth despised natives. Every August the Malayalis celebrate the imaginary return of Mahabali, during whose reign social equality, health and prosperity were enjoyed by all the people of Kerala. And surely it is no coincidence that in this State, which has dreamed for centuries of equality, the world's first elected Communist government came to power.

However, Kerala remains a stronghold of Brahman conservatism, for all its millions of Christians and Communists. The great nineteenth-century Hindu religious leader, Swami Vivekananda – champion of the Vedanta and founder of the Ramakrishna movement – became so confused and annoyed by the intricacies of Kerala's castes and sub-castes that he described the whole region as 'a lunatic asylum'. In his day – before the radical reforms brought about by that saintly Ezhava ascetic known as Shri Narayana Guru – the toddy-tapping Ezhavas had to keep sixty-four feet away from temples, thirty-six feet away from Brahmans, sixteen feet away from Nairs and twelve feet away from untouchables. Even today caste laws operate strongly here, not only among Hindus but among Christians and Jews. Over the centuries most of India's religious minorities have been inexorably – though unofficially – made to fit the Hindu mould. The Malabar Christians are divided into numerous hostile sects and sub-sects and apart from doctrinal and liturgical bones of contention many Christians further complicate the situation by remaining loyal to the hereditary Hindu castes and sub-castes of their remote ancestors. The Roman Catholics have added yet another ludicrous refinement; one sub-sect, claiming direct descent from St Thomas's first Indian converts, regards itself as much superior to the rest and not long ago, when a group of Ezhavas thought to improve, themselves socially by becoming Roman Catholics (or Latin Christians, as they are called here), these 'Christian Brahmans' protested vehemently against their church being polluted by Ezhavas, however thoroughly baptised. So new churches had to be specially built for the new converts, many of whom – seeing that Christianity was not, after all, in favour of the brotherhood of man – relapsed into their former position at the bottom of the Hindu pile. Even today, when an Ezhava convert comes to the home of a 'caste-Christian' he may not enter but must stand outside and shout his message from the garden.

I hated wakening Rachel at 10 a.m. but the alternative – to have her again awake all night – would ultimately have been more upsetting.

We spent the day exploring enjoyably though rather inefficiently. The local climate is not nearly as trying as I had expected, perhaps partly because there is so much water about and one spends half one's time on the motor-launch buses that operate between Ernakulam and the islands of Willingdon, Mattancherry and Mulavukad.

Before lunch we strolled through the Muslim quarter of Mattancherry where men were playing cards on cramped verandas and everybody greeted us cheerfully. The drab little rows of newish, solidly built one- or two-storeyed houses were plastered with slogans in English denouncing local capitalists, yet the worst of Cochin's poverty cannot be compared with what one sees in Bombay. Nor have I noticed here a single dirty person, of any age or condition. Even the inhabitants of the meanest hovels wear clean though often ragged clothes.

On all sides there is water – reeking, shallow canals, thick with slimy mud and crossed by rotting wooden footbridges: or the open, heavily polluted sea, always busy with boat traffic: or those fabled but (from what I have seen of them so far) much overrated backwaters. Little boys swam and played and splashed enthusiastically in the unspeakable canals but usually, I was relieved to notice, they gave themselves a shower, under a wayside fresh-water pump, before going home.

Turning one corner we came on tons of silver sardines being unloaded from long, slim boats into flat wicker baskets which were carried off to be weighed on the heads of sturdy small boys. As we stood watching, an old man sitting on a wooden crate beckoned us to join him and offered us glasses of tea. (In Indian

towns a mobile tea-stall is rarely far away.) He spoke enough
English to tell us that Kerala is India's chief fish-exporting
state, landing more than 30 per cent of the national total of
sea-food: and then he handed me a Communist pamphlet
about the redistribution of wealth. When we were leaving the
water's edge the young driver of a fish-delivery truck, who was
shattering a mini-iceberg with an axe, gave us two huge lumps
off the block and we went on our way through the early afternoon heat appreciatively rubbing our faces and arms to the
intense amusement of the general public.

We next found ourselves in the Jewish Quarter, which consists of a long, narrow cul-de-sac with India's most famous
synagogue at the closed end. A few of the tall, whitewashed,
green-shuttered houses have antique-cum-junk shops at street
level, run by mild, gracious men who would not dream of
pestering the tourist but are happy to talk knowledgeably
about their wares, or about the history of the Malabar Jews.
We chatted for over an hour to a pale, sad character with a
long chestnut beard who was 35 years old but unmarried
because, being a White Jew, he could only marry a White
Jewess and there are few of those left in Cochin. (Thousands of
Indian Jews have migrated to Israel.) I was not in the least
surprised when he explained that White Jews, Black Jews and
Slave Jews (the three 'castes' of Malabar Jewry) cannot intermarry, and that the Slave Jews are regarded as outcasts by the
others and up to a few years ago were forbidden to enter the
synagogues.

The White synagogue was first built in 1568, burned down in
1662 and rebuilt with Dutch help two years later. (The Dutch
had just captured Cochin from the Portuguese.) Our friend
volunteered to give us a conducted tour of the building and I
thought it a good mark for the neighbourhood that he had no
fears about leaving his valuable stock unguarded. Together we
admired the great chandeliers, and the blue and white eighteenth-century Chinese floor tiles, and the ornate golden crown
presented to the community by some past Maharaja of Travancore, and, most precious of all, the ancient scrolls of the Old
Testament. Then I turned to my companion and asked
impulsively, 'Would you – could you – never consider marrying
a Black Jewess? Because otherwise there won't be anyone, soon,

to whom all this matters?' But he only looked at me blankly for
a moment and then silently shook his head; he was unable even
to consider such a shocking idea, preferring racial extinction to
racial pollution. (Not that the Black and White Jews are necessarily dark and fair skinned.)

As we were walking back to our hotel a skinny little boy,
wearing only a loin-cloth, came running after us. In most
Indian cities I would have expected him to beg; here I was not
altogether surprised – though very touched – when he presented
Rachel with an hibiscus blossom, and us both with a lovely
smile, before quickly running away. A tiny incident, but for me
containing the essence of Kerala.

At five-fifteen Rachel heartily agreed that it was her bedtime. And now I must correct myself: this is no tourist hotel, but
the Bharath Tourist Home, which means it is run by Brahmans
for middle-class Indian tourists – conservative, vegetarian
teetotallers who demand clean rooms, good plain cooking and a
non-rowdy atmosphere. The enormous new building is staffed
by charming young men who bound to attention at the touch
of a bell, have at least two university degrees apiece and seem
genuinely to care about the guests' welfare. Incredible value, for
50 pence a night. Admittedly, from the dissolute *mleccha's* point
of view the absence of a bar is a slight disadvantage at the end
of a long, hot day. But this defect is easily remedied by walking
up a pleasant tree-lined road and fetching half a dozen bottles
of excellent Bangalore beer from a liquor-store. Which is what I
did when Rachel was abed, and then I settled down on the wide
terrace-roof outside our fourth-floor room. Beyond the palmy
islands across the bay the sun was sinking in a red-gold sky and
when it had gone – so swiftly – a strange amber sheen lay on the
water and I felt very aware of the *drama* of day and night:
something that passes us by in the twilit north. No wonder
sun-worship has played such a part in the religious history of
man.

Quickly the lights went on, encircling one of the world's
finest natural harbours – for many centuries saluted as Queen
of the Arabian Sea. The beginnings of Cochin's maritime glory
are too distant in time to be seen, but Kerala teak was found
during the excavations at Ur, and the Phoenicians, the Chinese,
the Romans and the Arabs were regular visitors long before the

arrival of the Portuguese, the Dutch, the French and the English. St Thomas the Apostle is said to have landed on the Malabar Coast in A.D. 52 and though much scepticism is expressed about this I see no reason why he should not have chosen to do his bit here. Certainly the first European settlement in India was established in Cochin in 1502 by Vasco da Gama, who died near by on Christmas Day 1524; and on 16 December 1544 St Francis Xavier arrived on foot from the Coromandel Coast and had soon made many converts from amongst the untouchables and unapproachables.

14 December. Cochin.

Food is really scarce in Cochin at present: and an emergency can be said to exist when tourists notice a food shortage. Prices are proportionately high; bananas which elsewhere cost 15 paise here cost 60 and such basics as rice, pulses, onions, tomatoes, potatoes, sugar, eggs and milk cost four or five times as much as in Karnataka and are often not available, at any price, to the ordinary shopper in the bazaar. (Large hotels like ours, which buy in bulk, can still get most of what they need, but yesterday there were no curds – an essential item of Hindu diet and Rachel's substitute for milk.) Today we unsuccessfully tried to get a simple rice meal in four restaurants, and since our return to the coast I have seen none of those piled stalls of fruits, vegetables and grains which are part of the normal Indian street scene. Also tea-house shelves, which elsewhere were laden with piled platters of sweet and savoury tidbits, are empty here at present. Yet the general impression is of a contented, quick-to-laugh people. Kerala's tradition of fish- and tapioca-eating must be responsible for the spectacularly superior mental and physical development of the average Malayali, as compared to his fellow-peasants from mainly vegetarian states. Hunger is not a permanent feature of Malabar life and one hopes this shortage will be temporary. In India one can never be sure such shortages are not contrived by racketeers who bribe or bully the relevant local authorities into submission.

I thought today how appropriate it is that the first book to have been printed in India was published at Cochin in 1577 by the Jesuits. Never have I seen such avid readers as these Malayalis, from the small school-children who bend intently over paperback adventure stories as they travel between islands, to the wizened old rickshaw-wallahs who anywhere else in India would be illiterate but here read substantial, serious-minded daily papers. This afternoon I noticed three coolie-types on our crowded motor-launch who had obviously never worn shoes in their lives but were reading thick Malayalam volumes. These books – dog-eared and carefully jacketed in newspaper – had been borrowed, I discovered on inquiring, from college libraries run by the Shri Narayana Dharma Paripalana Yogam, an Ezhava welfare organisation founded in 1902, long before Gandhi began his campaign to better the Harijans. And on the train the other night, in our third-class compartment, several young men were reading imported Pelican editions of erudite experts which cost Rs.25 each – that is, the price of twelve vegetarian meals with all the trimmings. Kerala State has India's highest rate of literacy: 60·16 per cent. Granted, this need not mean much, but in Kerala millions of those 60·16 really are devoted to learning. A formidable army of secondary school and university students swarms all over Cochin, armed to the teeth with textbooks on everything from Architecture to Zoology. And I mean 'formidable army'. Most of these youngsters cannot hope for even the meanest sort of white-collar job but are unlikely to accept, with traditional Indian fatalism, their share of the subcontinent's misfortunes.

When we got back to our Bharath Home I insisted on Rachel's resting for an hour because tonight she is again going out on the tiles to see a performance of Kerala's unique Katha-kali dance. According to the tourist office bumph, this is a '2,000-year-old Pantomime Kerala Dance'. Maybe it is – what are 2,000 years in India? – but according to the distinguished historian Nilakanta Sastri (who travels in my rucksack), 'Recent research has shown that the first Attakathas were composed towards the close of the fifteenth century.' Kathakali means 'story-play' and is specifically an educational religious dance based on the ancient *puranas*, which recount the adventures and teachings of the gods and heroes of Indian mythology. Traditionally it is performed only by certain families belonging to the *devadasi* community, a sub-caste associated with that temple prostitution which made so many mem-sahibs curl up at the edges. Tonight's performance is being given by the 'See India

Foundation Troupe' which performs every evening, except Thursdays; so I suppose it will be a rather watered-down tourists' version. Yet the lives of the members of the troupe sound extremely gruelling and austere and not in the least commercialised. Training starts at the age of five and throughout the next fifteen years continues for twelve hours daily: two hours a day are devoted simply to exercising the eye-muscles. This Cochin troupe was founded by Guru Gopala Paniker, now 97 years old, who last year received from President Giri the 'India's Greatest Artiste Today' award. His sons Shivaram, the world-famous dancer, and P. K. Devan, the Director, are passing the tradition on – still assisted by their father, who continues daily to massage the student dancers by trampling on them with his bare feet. And now off we go, to see the result for ourselves.

Later. What to say? How to say it? I had read quite a bit about Kathakali – how ancient and awe-inspiring it is, how interesting and skilful and exotic. But no one had told me how exalting and humbling it is, how exhilarating and poignant, how quintessentially Indian, how triumphantly an affirmation of the Immanence of the Divine. I have often seen Indian dancing before and always enjoyed it but this was something quite different: less an entertainment than an escape into another sphere – and at the same time an encounter with an unfamiliar area of oneself.

The theatre is in the garden of a small bungalow up a narrow side-street and consists of a wooden outdoor stage, some ten feet by twelve, under an awning of coconut matting. In front of the stage a handsome brass pedestal lamp, four feet high and filled with coconut oil, burns brightly by way of footlights. Visitors are greeted on arrival by P. K. Devan – quiet, dignified, erudite – a man who at once makes it plain that all this is something more than tourist-bait. Significantly, too, the three musicians begin to play at the back of the stage about an hour before the dancing starts, for this whole ritual has a meaning and a purpose of its own, quite apart from the business of diverting the audience. Two of the musicians are drummers, using the *Chenda* (played with two sticks) and the *Maddalam* (played with the hands); the third is a singer with cymbals who tells the story as the dancers dance.

One hundred chairs had been arranged in rows before the stage, under the starry sky, but this evening the audience consisted only of ourselves and an elderly Danish woman. Normally an audience of three would leave those three feeling too embarrassed on behalf of the performers to enjoy themselves, and the performers too discouraged to give of their best. But one soon realises that ordinary criteria do not apply to Kathakali. Within moments of the dancers' appearing it is evident that to them it does not matter in the least whether three or three hundred people turn up on any given occasion. No one has a sharper nose than I for phoney tourist gimmicks and this Kathakali performance is unquestionably the work of men who feel the religious content of the dance to be of prime importance.

Before the dance began P. K. Devan outlined the story we were about to see enacted and simply explained the 2000-years-old Kathakali technique. The language of gestures has been so developed that by using various combinations of the twenty-four basic hand positions over 800 words may be formed. Also, every movement of the eyes has a specific meaning intelligible to initiates, and the miming and footwork are equally eloquent. The elaborate make-up has to be applied by experts, a process which is gone through slowly and systematically, in solemn silence, and takes two or three hours. Each face is painted all over: green for good characters, black for bad, red for villains and pink for women and saints. These colours must be procured by crushing certain rare local stones or powdering the bark of sacred trees: and when they have been applied the dancer pauses for a moment, to pray with uplifted hands, before moving out of the dressing-room. The fantastic, heavily jewelled brocade costumes are themselves works of art which have passed down from generation to generation. Their weird loveliness is so strange that Rachel exclaimed, 'These must be magic clothes!'

Indeed, magic is perhaps the best word with which to sum up this whole experience. I felt utterly bewitched as time passed and the spell was woven more and more intricately around us. Kathakali dancer/actors make no sound, apart from a few animal-like grunts occasionally emitted by the villain, and in comparison with their slight, exquisitely stylised movements even the most inspired ballet-dancing seems crude. Without having seen them I could never have believed it possible to produce, through the controlled use of eye, face, hand and foot muscles, such an effect of ineffable beauty, adding up to what can only be described as a prayer in movement.

9

Pilgrims at Cape Comorin: Family Life in Tamil Nadu

15 December. Trivandrum.

Statistics mean something to me only when I can see them, as you might say, and I could certainly see them today during our 136-mile bus journey from Cochin to Trivandrum. In area Kerala is one of the smallest Indian states (38,855 square kilometres), but its population of 22 million puts it amongst the most densely populated regions in the world. Moreover, one-third of its area is forest and mountain so some districts have 1,124 people to the square kilometre. Along the coastal strip each village merges into the next and little seems to have changed since Ibn Batuta wrote – some five centuries ago – 'The whole of the way by land lies under the shade of trees, and in the space of two months' journey there is not one span free from cultivation; everybody has his garden and his house is planted in the middle of it.' But in one respect things have been changing for the worse: as the people increase, erosion is diminishing the land area.

Yet Kerala is not depressing; the Malayalis look far better developed than the average crowd to be seen on a European beach and since men and children wear the minimum of clothing (or none) one can fully appreciate their magnificent physiques. (Incidentally, it is only quite recently that Ezhava women have been allowed to cover themselves above the waist in the presence of the Brahman and Nair castes.)

Trivandrum is a hilly, higgledy-piggledy city full of trees and quite attractive, though no urban conglomeration of some 400,000 people can truthfully be said to excite me. Outside the bus stand an ebony-skinned youth – barefooted and extraordinarily handsome – offered to guide us to a good but cheap hotel and led us up a broad street, all the while begging me to hire a coolie to carry my rucksack. He said he hated to see me shouldering it yet could not possibly carry anything himself – not even my water-bottle or canvas bag of books.

Soon we had been installed in a twin-bedded room, with its own primitive shower and latrine, for Rs.5 plus another Rs.5 deposit, which I suppose is intended to ensure the guests don't make off with the bedding. When I handed 50 paise to our guide he waved it aside and smiled and bowed, and said it was his joy to help us, and vanished. No doubt the hotel rewards him, but how often in India does a barefooted boy decline a tip? I could not help reading a certain significance into his use of the word 'joy' where most Indians use 'duty'. It seemed a nice illustration of the average Malayalis' lighthearted approach to life.

We spent the afternoon drifting around talking to people rather than systematically sightseeing. In some respects the southern princely states of Mysore, Cochin and Travancore were far more advanced at Independence than British India – Travancore, especially, had a reputation for being prudently progressive without being pseudo-European. For generations its rulers had treated State revenues as public funds rather than as their own private property and less than 5 per cent was kept for the use of the Maharaja and his mother, through whom (the state being a matriarchy) he had come to the throne. The 'palace' was a simple white house on a hill, and throughout the 1930s one-fifth of the revenue was devoted to education.

The last Dewan of Travancore, Sir C. P. Ramaswami Aiyar, courageously changed the law to allow Harijans into the temples and made possible Kerala's present-day industrial expansion. But he was an autocrat who for years strangled every popular political movement at birth. During the pre-Independence controversy about the fate of the Princely States he announced peremptorily that when power was transferred Travancore would become a sovereign state: whereupon there was a spontaneous revolution and an attempted assassination of the Dewan, followed by his resignation and a hasty announcement from the Maharaja that his *rajyam* would of course become part of the Indian Union.

We spent a couple of hours strolling through the green and pleasant university grounds, talking with students and staff.

Here in the midst of their problems it is easy to sympathise with Kerala's Communists, who of course are not in the least like non-Indian Communists. Their strongly held political beliefs seem to co-exist quite comfortably with a fervent devotion to Harihara, pilgrimages to Guruvayur and Sabarimala, an unquestioning acceptance of made marriages and the pronouncements of astrologers, reunions for joint-family *pujas* – and so on and so forth. In fact I can't think why they don't call themselves something else.

India's two Communist parties (both of which claim to be the One True Party) are known as the Right Communists (Soviet) and the Left Communists (Chinese). The General Secretary of the Left, for all India, is an outstanding political genius called Elamkulam Manakal Sankaran Namboodiripad. (Who must surely say to his friends, 'Call me El'.) This gentleman comes of the highest sub-caste in Kerala, a most rarefied élite of academic aristocrats, and while Chief Minister of the first Communist government he was worshipped by millions as a 'holy man'. This was even before his 1969 Land Reform Act, which prescribed the lowest land ceiling in India, allowing no more than five standard acres for one person, ten for a family of between two and five members, and one acre each extra for every additional member, after five. The young economics lecturer who provided me with these figures insisted on writing them down himself in my notebook. 'You must not forget,' he said. 'Our Communist government really did give "the land to the tiller" – not just *talk* about doing it. Now we have no landless peasants – nobody can be evicted – the cultivator has full ownership. But next it is most important to make him have less children.'

This morning in Cochin we woke to a grey sky and all day the air felt deliciously cool. Then at sunset we heard our first rain since leaving home, exactly a month ago, and it is still slashing down with monsoon-like fury.

16 December. Cape Comorin.

This evening I have come to the conclusion that India – the whole Indian *Dharma* – is peculiarly tourist-proof. By which I mean it is too individual, too absorbent, too fortified by its own curious integrity, to be vulnerable to those slings and arrows of outrageous vulgarity which have killed the loveliness of so many places since tourism became big business. I had expected to find Cape Comorin despoiled, yet it remains first and foremost a place of pilgrimage: a holy place, as it has been for centuries beyond counting. Like so many of Hinduism's less accessible pilgrimage sites, it is marked by an extraordinary atmosphere of quiet excitement, of devout gaiety; and added to this is its own unique flavour. From the bus one suddenly sees the sea – or rather, three seas – and a temple on a rock about half a mile off-shore. And that's it. One has reached the end of India.

Although we arrived on a Sunday afternoon, in the midst of a local Roman Catholic festival, the crowds were not excessive and there was not one other non-Indian to be seen. Having booked into a Rs.5 windowless cell – swarming with ants – we dumped our kit and hastened to the sea. Cape Comorin is emphatically final – a tapering point of rock which is unmistakably farther south than the rest of the coast. Here steps lead down to the confluence of the Gulf of Mannar, the Indian Ocean and the Arabian Sea; and in this water, regarded as most sacred by Hindus, the pilgrims 'take bath' and do *puja*. Fierce cross-currents and occasional sharks make the sea hazardous, so massive boulders have been cleverly rearranged to prevent pilgrims (or Irish swimming fanatics) from being swept away or eaten alive. A memorable bathe is the result, as during the north-east monsoon swimmers are tossed to and fro like corks within this safe area of swirling foam and crashing waves. And while being tossed one inevitably thinks of that other frontier, of rock and eternal snow – the long base of the Indian triangle, 2,000 miles away – and of the 1,138,814 square miles and almost 600 million people in between. And then one marvels at the durability, elusiveness and strange beauty of that mixture of rank superstition and refined metaphysics which unites the shepherds of the snow-bound Himalayan valleys to the fishermen of the sun-flayed Coromandel Coast.

Rachel had a blissful time making castles in a sandy cove just west of the bathing-pool, but to avoid a popular public latrine we had to keep well below the high-water mark. The sand around Cape Comorin is famous throughout India and pilgrims buy tiny bags of it to take home. It is not simply golden, but – in patches – pure white, rose pink, pale yellow, charcoal grey and dark red. Scientists describe these sands as monazite and ilmenite: Hindus say they represent the various dishes once served here at a wedding of the Gods.

Throughout the afternoon I repeatedly plunged back into the bathing-pool since in my estimation the entertainment value of sand is not great, however variegated its hues; and I appreciated the pilgrims not objecting to a *mleccha* using their sacred pool blatantly for fun. In fact no Indian was using it today, because of the storm; instead they were ritually ducking themselves off Rachel's bit of sandy beach. Everyone was welcoming, though to decent Hindus a woman in a bathing-suit is a most shocking sight. Hindu women always enter the water fully dressed and when they emerge, with their thin saris clinging to their bodies, they reveal a great deal more than I do in my black, ultra-decorous, Edwardian-style costume. Most of today's pilgrims seem to belong to the well-off élite and this evening I have spoken to people from Bombay, Ludhiana, Delhi, Lucknow, Calcutta and Madras. All but the Madrassis have to use English as their only possible means of communication with the Tamil or Malayalam-speaking locals; there is considerably more resemblance between Hindi and Irish than between Hindi and Tamil.

Traditionally sunrise and sunset are the most solemn moments at Cape Comorin, as the sun may be seen rising out of one ocean and sinking into another. Therefore at six o'clock we joined the small crowd who had gathered on a huge, smooth black rock against which great green rollers were hurling themselves, sending up curtains of spray thirty feet high. Because of cloud nobody actually saw the sun setting, but the whole western sky became a glory of fast-changing colours – lovelier than it could possibly have been if cloudless. This, however, was no consolation to those for whom it is important to witness the sun touching and being quenched by the ocean.

Having supped in a tiny vegetarian restaurant we stepped out into the darkness and saw, on the east shore of the Cape, a vision seemingly from fairyland. For a moment I was dazzled into incomprehension by the bewildering beauty of the spectacle; then I realised that thousands of brilliant, multi-coloured electric bulbs were outlining the pseudo-Gothic Catholic cathedral against the blackness of the sea. The Indians are very good at this sort of thing and Rachel became quite breathless with excitement. We decided to find our way back to the hotel by the cathedral and went stumbling over piles of excrement, on a pitch-dark *maidan,* before finding a narrow street thronged with excited, jostling, shouting Christians – and their low-caste Hindu neighbours – on the way to the evening's festivities.

Inside the church hundreds of pilgrims, their faces aglow with love, were queuing to touch the feet of a gaudy statue of Our Lady of Mount Carmel, whose feast-day this is. They kissed their finger-tips when they had laid them on the worn plaster feet, and then they touched the feet again and, placing both hands on the tops of their heads, bowed low and retreated backwards from the Virgin's 'presence'. Some had tears trickling down their cheeks as they frantically invoked the statue's help, others laughed joyously as they stroked the toes or caressed the robes of their beloved. These people are amongst the poorest of India's poor, descended from the *sudras* and untouchables baptised by Portuguese missionaries over 400 years ago, and it is plain that they have close personal relationships with their favourite statues – relationships of which some theologians might not approve. But what matter? If the Divine is everywhere it is in chunks of plaster and good luck to those who can find it there.

The general scene within that vast, unfurnished church reminded me of a typical Indian railway-station platform between trains. Many pilgrims were lying asleep on the cool stone floor, their cotton wraps covering their heads; many others were squatting about in family groups, eating meagre suppers out of banana leaves, and some were just sitting cross-legged, staring into space. Our arrival electrified the majority and as usual Rachel was seized and cuddled and tickled and pinched and the pretence of kidnapping her enacted. This is the commonest Indian game with a small child and though Rachel knows it to be a joke she still finds it slightly alarming; obviously the mere thought of being separated from mamma in a foreign land is classic material for 5-year-old nightmares. This evening she kept a stiff upper lip but I could see her peering anxiously at me from amidst a tangle of dark arms and legs and faces, lit by white teeth and flashing, laughing eyes. Indians can be quite rough in their play and sometimes she emerges from this sort of fracas with slight scratches or bruises. During the past few days I have noticed her becoming increasingly irritated by the Indians' obsessive compulsion to handle her – which is an understandable reaction on her part, but I have explained she must try not to hurt their feelings. I suppose her colour fascinates them. By now she is as brown all over as a Punjabi, but that still leaves her a good deal lighter than most South Indians.

17 December. Tirunelveli.

Because of Rachel having been up so late last night we just missed the 6.06 sunrise and got to the bathing-pool as the pilgrims were performing their important morning *pujas*. Against the sombre background – a grape-dark sky, black rocks and a jade ocean – brilliant saris were fluttering like so many silken banners in the gale: or 'cyclone', as they melodramatically call it here. The oceans were churning around the Cape as though being stirred by a thousand giants and a group of pilgrims, having decided discretion is the better part of devotion, were simply pouring water over their heads from brass jars; so again I was alone in the pool. To east and south the sky had become a solid-seeming mass of dark purple and above me I could see towering, bottle-green breakers rushing towards the smooth, glistening rocks to send giant columns of pure white spray leaping into the sky. It is years since I have enjoyed a swim so much; but these clouds were not there for nothing and at nine-fifty the storm broke.

Within seconds everything and everyone in sight had been saturated so I simply put my shirt and shorts over my bathing togs and left Rachel as the good Lord made her. Yesterday's experience taught me that here it is futile to attempt to dress modestly. There are lots of corners, and relatively few people, yet a crowd of men, women and children pursues one to the farthest corner of all and stands staring, with pathological insensitivity, while one attempts, if one is fool enough, to cover one's nakedness. Last evening, being without a towel, I made no such attempt and the sight of my bare bottom provoked cyclones of laughter. It is nice to be able to cause so much innocent amusement by the use of the most basic raw material.

We got a tourists' luxury coach to Tirunelveli (spelt Tinnevelly in British days), where I hoped to find an accumulation of mail from home. This coach cost almost twice as much as our usual peasants' bus but was by no means twice as comfortable. Before we started, a richly dressed lady in the front row (the purdah quarter) raised hell when the conductor tried, most politely, to persuade her to tolerate an equally richly dressed gentleman in the adjacent seat. The conductor then tried to persuade Rachel to sit beside the lady, so that the gentleman could sit beside me. But on the basis of the lady's strident rejection of the gentleman Rachel had already deduced she was not nice to know and refused even to contemplate sitting beside her. So I moved, and Rachel beamed delightedly to find herself with a male companion instead of boring old Ma. The gentleman proved to be a Professor of Sanskrit from Benares University who entertained her with innumerable Rama stories told in immaculate English. But I could discover nothing about the lady, who was plainly appalled to find herself beside a filthy foreigner and resolutely pretended I didn't exist.

In South India one notices many young couples of all castes separating on buses or in restaurants and affecting not to be acquainted until the journey or meal is over. No wonder Indians are so deeply shocked by hippies kissing and petting in public.

Yesterday, coming from Trivandrum, we passed the end of the Western Ghats – extraordinary hills of dark rock, scattered with patches of earth and scrub. They rise sheer from a level plain, creating a most dramatic effect, and the narrow valleys that run between them made my feet itch. We passed them again today, as our road returned to a little junction town some ten miles north of the Cape, and then forked right to run along their eastern flanks. They are superb, rough, chunky mountains, with an atmosphere about them that is still tantalising my wanderlust. If Rachel were a little older we would be sleeping up one of those valleys tonight.

Perhaps, however, it is just as well that we are not doing any such thing, for soon after we left Cape Comorin the heavens opened again, in true monsoon style. Visibility was immediately reduced to thirty or forty yards and the flat land on either side of the road became flooded, as we gazed at it, to a depth of two feet – the water perceptibly creeping up the trunks of the immensely tall palmyra palms. Our bus, despite its exalted status, leaked like a sieve. As water went sloshing around the floor everyone took their bits and pieces on to their laps and several passengers who were sitting under roof-leaks raised umbrellas, to Rachel's huge amusement. The richly dressed lady and myself were sharing a leak but she made sure her most superior umbrella would not become polluted by giving shelter to the *mleccha*. As the drops splashed down my neck the bus trundled hesitantly on through an unnatural twilight, with sheets of water spraying out from the wheels. Then suddenly, half an hour before we got here, the rain stopped, the sun shone and excremental odours arose so strongly from the countryside that one almost expected to see them.

Tirunelveli felt very humid and its streets were mini-lakes. When I asked the way to the post office of an amiable-looking man – tall, slim and dark – he offered to guide us and introduced himself as Mr Luke, a Christian. According to him this is the most Christianised district in India, with a C.M.S. that was established in 1820 and an Anglican Diocese founded in 1896. But I wonder if he is right; the 1971 Census says there are almost 4½ million Christians in Kerala and only about half that number in Tamil Nadu. However, it may be that most Tamil Christians are concentrated in this area.

Mr Luke made consoling noises when the postmaster explained that no air-mail has been coming in from Europe recently, because of a strike, and advised me to call back next week. It seems worth while remaining within reach of Tirunelveli until Christmas Eve, if necessary, since Rachel is expecting all her birthday *and* Christmas cards. But we cannot remain beyond the 24th as she has long since been promised a Christmas visit to Periyar Game Park in lieu of the hectic seasonal excitements she is missing. Actually this delay could have happened in a much worse place; Tirunelveli was put on our itinerary because Ernest Joseph, an old Indian friend of mine, now lives some thirty-five miles away in a village called Ittamozhi.

Amongst the pile of Indian mail awaiting me was a letter from Ernest in which he gave the address of a friend, Mr Mathew, with whom we were to stay the night before catching the morning bus to Ittamozhi. I read this letter in the ironmongery-cum-printing works of Mr Luke, where we had been invited for coffee, and it only slightly surprised me to find that Mr Luke knows both Ernest and Mr Mathew quite well. This sort of thing is always happening in India, despite those teeming millions.

We are now installed in Mr Mathew's home, a decrepit little bungalow on the outskirts of the city. I have never before stayed with an Indian Christian family and it is a most interesting experience; no one would suspect this household of not being Hindu but for the fact that on the walls biblical texts replace oleographs of the gods. Most of the attitudes, routines, prejudices and customs are indistinguishable from those of middle-class, conservative Hindus. Even beef-eating is frowned on, ostensibly because one cannot buy wholesome beef locally. (Possibly this is true, but I get the impression some good excuse would be found for not eating even the best Irish beef.)

At sunset the rain started again and ever since has been coming down in torrents. The roof leaks so badly it is impossible in this tiny parlour to find dry spots for our flea-bags and Rachel's is already sodden, though she continues to sleep peacefully. As the latrine and bathroom are in the garden I got soaked through when nature called me out just now. Most Indian white-collar-workers live in what seem to us slum conditions and amongst this large section of the population there must be a painful degree of frustration: perhaps more than amongst the millions who have less to eat but no ambitions and no special abilities.

There are two children in this family, a 19-year-old son and a 17-year-old daughter. The boy is in his second year at Madras University and was picked last week for Tamil Nadu's State hockey team. He is bitter because the frequent university strikes seriously hinder his work. At present the Madras students are striking to have Tamil Nadu's Chief Minister dismissed and, while it may well be that the gentleman in question deserves dismissal, it does seem absurd to have students involved in politics to this extent.

In the past month I have talked to several so-called graduates who could not possibly pass the eleven-plus in Britain. (Probably I couldn't, either, but we won't go into that.) Many Indian graduates simply bribe their way through and others get by because professors do not wish their own ineptitude to be underlined by a high percentage of failures. The son of this house admits that when he graduates he will almost certainly have to take up some menial job totally unconnected with his studies. I can only suppose the Indian's paranoid determination to acquire worthless degrees is some sort of spin-off from thousands of years of Brahmanical idealisation of learning: a most commendable notion, but unfortunately India has a flair for so radically distorting commendable notions that they breed serious social problems.

I hardly saw the daughter of the house, who is studying hard for her university entrance examination. Her brother told me she will never be allowed to mix with the male students and soon after graduating will be married to the young man of her parents' choice. When I asked what would happen if he himself wished to marry a girl not of his parent's choice he found it difficult even to imagine this situation. After a moment's silence he shrugged and said it would be impossible to do such a thing 'because my mother would cry and put pressure on me until I gave in, and for me the most important thing is not to upset her'. A typical Hindu answer from a Christian boy; what Indian women lose on the wifely swings they gain on the motherly roundabouts. Even when they appear to be demure, timid, characterless or positively down-trodden, their influence within the home is tremendously strong.

Yet the convention of deference to the male has to be carefully preserved and this evening no one ate until Father came home from work at eight-thirty – two hours late because of flooding on the streets. Then, to my embarrassment, I alone was fed in the tiny bed-sitter in which we had been talking, while the family – plus three visiting relatives who had called to meet me – hovered around urging the guest to eat more and more of this and that. Very good it was, too: a typical South Indian meal of rice, dahl, hot vegetable curry, curried fried sardines, omelette, plantain and excellent Coorg coffee.

I suspect the Mathew family treated us as V.I.P.s because we had been introduced by Ernest Joseph. Ernest is a distinctively Indian phenomenon, although brought up in Burma and educated at an English public school. Born of a South Indian Christian father and a Rajput mother famed for her beauty (an elopement, surely, since such a marriage would never be arranged, or even condoned), he has evolved a personal religious synthesis which seems to suit him admirably. His father – a teak millionaire – went bankrupt when Ernest was a young man; there were complicated political overtones and the case caused something of a furore. By then Ernest had already established himself as a painter of widely recognised talent whose pictures give many people an uncanny feeling. To me they seem like messages from another world, rather than human creations, and I am not sure that I could live with them.

Ernest is a bachelor in his early sixties. When I first met him he had long since decided it would be immoral to use his artistic gifts to make money and was living in a one-room shack in a Delhi slum without visible means of support. I myself feel he is wrong not to accept gracefully and use honestly the gift with which providence has endowed him, but that does not lessen my admiration for the steadfastness with which he upholds his curious principles. He is a truly patriotic Indian – of whom there are not a vast number – and his refusal to paint for profit may well be an illogical emotional reaction to the gigantic cesspool of Indian corruption. Also, of course, he is an eccentric of the first order. Every day he shaves his head, he habitually wears a monocle (and in hot weather very little else), he believes firmly in telepathy, astrology, palmistry and graphology and under no circumstances will he speak to anybody about anything on Saturdays – 'my day of silence'. As I have said, he is distinctively Indian.

18 December. Tisaiyanvilai.

At ten o'clock this morning the rain at last stopped and the sun came out as we got on the Ittamozhi bus; there was a strong breeze, instead of yesterday's sticky heat, and water lay refreshingly in sheets all over the level countryside.

The battered bus took us back some fifteen miles along the main road to Cape Comorin, before turning left for the east coast. It was full of peasants with flattish noses, thickish lips, remarkably low foreheads and near-ebony skins. Compared with Kerala, this coastal corner of Tamil Nadu seems to have dourer people, duller scenery and bonier cattle. Hundreds and thousands of palmyra palms grow tall and straight from pastures where the grass is a quarter of an inch high, and patches of thorny scrub support countless goats. The large cattle herds are devoutly decorated with bells and ribbons, and have coloured ropes wound around their carefully painted horns, but they look in miserable condition, as do many of the humans. This has always been one of the poorest areas of South India, scourged by almost intolerable heat for ten months of the year and inhabited mainly by primitive pearl-fishers, toddy-tappers, jaggery-makers and deep-sea fishermen, to whose ancestors St Francis Xavier devoted the best years of his life. Judging by the few villages and people to be seen, it is not over-populated; and yet I suppose it *is*, in relation to what its thin, grey, desiccated soil can produce. We saw only occasional small patches of paddy and it was hard to believe that Tamil Nadu now produces more rice from one hectare than any other rice-growing state and expects soon to have a surplus for export.

It often happens in India that the poorer a region the more jewellery is displayed and on our bus were several women plainly suffering from chronic malnutrition but literally weighed down by their gold ornaments. Rachel was fascinated to see the elaborate tattooing on their necks and arms and the saucer-like ear-rings that hung from their misshapen ears. But then, true to form, she began to fret lest that weight depending from the ears might be causing – or have caused – some pain.

As we approached Ittamozhi lakes of brown floodwater could be seen reflecting the deep blue sky. To reach Ernest's hovel, half a mile from the village, we had to wade and slither through deep pools and sticky mud – an 'adventure' enormously to the liking of my daughter. The hovel was built by Ernest's father as a medical dispensary for the local Harijans but it is many years since any doctor has been willing to work for such people in such a place. Recently, during Ernest's absence, the structure was much depleted by vandals and previously it had lain empty for many years, being adversely affected by wind and weather, so it may not unfairly be described as an uninhabitable ruin.

Ernest nevertheless finds it quite comfortable, though in view of Rachel's age and – compared with her mother – fragility, he has decided we are to spend our nights with friends of his at this little town of Tisaiyanvilai, five miles west of Ittamozhi.

(Incidentally, Ittamozhi is pronounced 'Ittamolly', for some reason best known to the Tamils.) Rachel did not at all approve of this arrangement, having fallen in love with Ernest at first sight. But when he invited her to spend the day painting with him tomorrow, while I explore St Francis Xavier's village of Manapad, she was Ittamollified. (It was Ernest who said that – not me.) Small children seem to have a special affinity with a certain type of unselfconscious eccentric, and with people who are in any way psychic, or genuinely detached from the things of this world. Today, seeing Ernest and Rachel together, I knew that on some plane inaccessible to me they had at once established an exceptionally close relationship. Oddly, they seem to complement each other.

In twenty-five years I am only the second non-related guest to have stayed a night with this Hindu family. Ernest of course is the other, and it is a mark of the family's regard for him that his two wandering *mleccha* friends have been admitted to such an exclusive home. The household consists of a retired doctor and his wife, their eldest son – now the local G.P. – his wife and four shy children, and his equally shy unmarried sister who is his partner in the practice. The large, handsome house was designed by the old man and built only a few years ago on the outskirts of the town. We are in the spacious, never-used-before guest-room, which has been hastily but most adequately furnished for our benefit with two camp-beds and a table and chair. The unglazed, heavily barred windows have splendid teak shutters and the door leads on to a wide roof from which one looks into the sunset over the neat yard with its cattle shed, or into the sunrise across a flat grey-green landscape broken only by straggling lines of palms. It would be impossible to exaggerate the warmth of our welcome here and the anxiety of the whole family to make us happy and comfortable, so I hope not to be misunderstood when I say that this evening I am very aware of having been thrown into the Hindu pool at the deep end.

19 December.   Tisaiyanvilai.

Today a septic mosquito bite on my right ankle immobilised me, but I must be thankful it came to fruition within reach of a good doctor.

I spent most of this cloudy, breezy day sitting out on the

terrace roof with my foot up, savouring the quiet of my daughterless state and reading *A History of South India* by Nilakanta Sastri (O.U.P.). This is probably the best book there is on the subject but it makes no concessions to human weakness and read at home would seem tough going. Read in South India, however, it becomes positively entertaining. I find it a good policy to tackle such tomes while travelling through the country concerned.

Rachel returned at four o'clock, a vision of glory in a Madrassi little girl's costume of ankle-length full skirt and low-cut bodice with short puff sleeves; most attractive, if not very practical for our sort of travelling. She herself had chosen the flowered cotton materials in Ittamozhi bazaar, and then the village tailor's 11-year-old apprentice had most expertly made it up. The total cost of the outfit was Rs.4.

To test my foot, I accompanied Ernest and Rachel to Tisaiyanvilai's bazaar, to buy new sandals, and nowhere else has our advent caused such a sensation. Within moments of our stopping at a shoe-stall I was astonished to see the whole main street become a seething mass of shouting men and boys, pushing and shoving to get closer to us. So fascinated was the populace that the Tirunelveli bus simply had to stop, its strident blaring having been ignored. This over-excited throng was of course entirely good-humoured, but the atmosphere it generated had a perceptibly primitive quality and I found myself wondering how it would behave should something occur to change its mood. I suppose our entertainment-value may be seen partly as a measure of the total monotony of village life and partly as an indication of how few foreigners visit South India. One thinks of India as being an important World Tours attraction but its tourist centres are mere dots on the vastness of the subcontinent and anyway are mainly in the north.

Having failed to find any sandals to fit we went to have tea with Christian friends of Ernest who own the local rice-mill. There are several children in this family so Rachel at once disappeared and as we adults nibbled delicious home-made tidbits, while talking about inflation in relation to wedding ceremonies, it again struck me that the *mleccha* feels not one degree closer to the Indian Christian than to the Hindu. Almost, indeed, one feels further away, since certain aspects of

Hindu-impregnated Christianity seem even less comprehensible than Hinduism itself to outsiders with a Christian background.

Within the past twenty-four hours I have developed a real affection and respect for our host family, despite the formidable and, I fear, insurmountable barriers that divide us. I now feel at home in this household to an extent I would not have believed possible last evening and I long to be able to define the dividing barriers, though I cannot hope to overcome them. They have nothing to do with provincialism, as we understand the term, since the absence of such narrowness is one of the chief distinguishing marks of educated Hindus, however physically circumscribed their lives may be. Perhaps I am especially sensitive to barriers in this family because it is – if one can to any extent compare the two civilisations – almost exactly on my own social, intellectual and material level. Therefore where we do diverge, on what can only be called the spiritual level, our divergence is very evident. It leaves us mutually invisible on opposite sides of that wide chasm which for many foreigners, including myself, is amongst India's main attractions. One suspects that if one could only *see to* the other side – it would be nonsense to think in terms of *getting* there – one might be a lot better off for the experience.

No one could describe the witty and forceful women of this family as docile or down-trodden, yet they adhere strictly to the immemorial Hindu formalities governing the social behaviour of their sex. While Rachel and I eat with the two men, in the dim, cool dining-room beside the kitchen, the two wives stand by the connecting door, poised to replenish our stainless steel platters whenever necessary, joining animatedly in our conversation and affectionately exchanging jokes with their husbands. By now I should be quite accustomed to this business of being treated as an 'honorary male' – it happens in many non-European countries – yet I still find it slightly disconcerting in households where one is surrounded by mod. cons. and educated conversation. In a muddled sort of way I feel guilty and ill-mannered about being waited on by the old lady – who is very much a *grande dame* – and the repression of my urge to leap ups to relieve her of some heavy dish becomes quite a strain. Neither she nor her daughter-in-law ever at any time sits in the presence of their menfolk – this evening they stood conversing happily for an hour and a half – and they eat (in the kitchen) only when the men have finished. The young doctor works very long hours among the poor, for minimal or no fees, and, being deeply religious, will not dine until he has locked up the dispensary, bathed to purify himself after the inevitable polluting contacts of his professional life and gone to the near-by temple to pray. Therefore his wife and mother must often wait until nine or ten o'clock for their evening meal; but presumably such restrictions do not matter to most Indian women, who surely could not appear so serene and relaxed if full of hidden resentment. Incidentally, none of the several servants employed about the place ever appears in the kitchen or dining-room, so I conclude they are of too low a caste to be allowed near the family's food.

In the morning we are going to the little coastal town of Tiruchendur, some thirty-five miles away, to see a famous sea-shore temple dedicated to Subrahmanya, the god of war. We plan to stay overnight in the pilgrims' hostel run by the temple trustees and to return here next day. A leaflet issued by the Board of Trustees reports that the temple also runs 'a free Siddha dispensary for the benefit of the worshipping public' and 'an Orphanage with 67 Orphans'. It owns 444 acres of wet land, 855 acres of dry land and approximately Rs.25,000,000 worth of gold, silver and jewels.

10

On the Coast of Coromandel

20 December.   Tiruchendur.

Not being blessed with either a good ear or a good memory, I
am sorely tried by many South Indian names. But one must
look on the bright side. Things could be worse. For instance,
until the sixteenth-century Tiruchendur was known as Tiru-
bhuvanamadhevi Chandurvedhimangalam.

The landscape *en route* from Tisaiyanvilai was flat and
harsh; gaunt palmyras stood erect in their thousands everywhere and the dusty grey plain was varied only by acres of
thorny scrub, hedges of prickly cactus and occasional fields of
plantains at all stages of development. (I am told the banana
plant is not a tree but a vegetable which in six months grows
from scratch to its full height of eighteen or twenty feet.)

We first saw Tiruchendur's nine-storey temple from many
miles away, over the plain, and by ten-thirty we had booked into
the hostel (Rs.2 for a single room) and been told that non-
Hindus are permitted to enter the temple only between 3.0 and
8.0 p.m. 'Fair enough', I thought; I have always deprecated
hoards of camera-clicking tourists swarming through churches
during services. Then, after paying our respects to the two
sacred temple elephants – an adult and an adolescent – who are
elaborately stabled in the precincts, we went to swim off the
long, smooth, curving beach.

At one-thirty we made our way to the centre of the town
through a mile-long arcaded bazaar that begins in the temple
courtyard and is lined with ancient statues of the gods, their
stone features blunted by the affectionate caresses of generations
of devotees. Tea-shops are interspersed with stalls displaying a
scatter of cheap trinkets or a few bunches of plantains and a
small tray of fly-blown tidbits, and religious oleographs, framed
and unframed, lie on the ground beside shop-soiled bales
of cotton 'going cheap'. According to the temple trustees

Tiruchendur means 'a sacred and prosperous town of Victory' but nowadays one gets no impression of material prosperity. However, the atmosphere is friendly and the citizens seem in no way predatory, possibly because 99 per cent of Tiruchendur's visitors are very poor.

It was difficult to get tea as milk is scarce and Indians refuse to credit the possibility of milkless tea. Eventually we found a cavernous eating-house beneath the arcade where a milk delivery was expected within moments, so we sat down to wait. (This lust for tea was caused by my having forgotten to bring our water-pills from Tisaiyanvilai.) The eating-house seemed without any stock of food and, as he waited for something to occupy him, the slim, barefooted serving-boy went to stand before a wall-niche containing a statue of Ganesh and prayed fervently.

'Indians pray a lot,' observed Rachel. 'Why do they pray more than we do?' To which I replied, rather ambiguously, 'They are at a different stage of development.'

Happily a water-carrier rescued me by stopping his cart beside us at this moment, to deliver the day's supply from the well, and Rachel immediately wanted to know why there was gold paint on the horns of the enormous pure white humped bullock. I explained (if it can be called an explanation) that pure white bullocks are very sacred and therefore merit gold paint, rather than the red or blue or yellow seen on the horns of lesser cattle. Then the milkman arrived, carrying on his head a little brass churn containing a gallon of no doubt heavily watered milk. As this was being boiled in a large copper cauldron over a wood fire we watched the bullock being unharnessed, tied to a pillar of the arcade, stroked reverently on the neck and given a bundle of paddy-straw. Next the water-carrier – a seemingly frail old man – emptied the gigantic wooden barrel on his cart by repeatedly filling a brass jar and carrying it on his head to a row of rusty tar barrels in a corner of the eating-house. And so life goes on, much as it did 2,000 or 3,000 years ago.

At present a most regrettable concrete extension is being added to Tiruchendur's temple but, though materials have changed for the worse since the temple was first built, methods of construction have remained virtually unchanged. On our way back to the beach we saw nine small sweating men, 150 feet above our heads, hauling up a huge concrete roof slab which had been roped by four men on the ground. Three giant bamboo poles leaning against the wall provided support for the slab on its way up and, as a product of the Crane Culture, Rachel was fascinated by this display of muscular Hinduism. Indian physiques are often misleading, especially in the South, where apparent fragility can conceal the strength of an ox. Yet the effects of a vegetarian diet show in the lack of stamina, which is said to be one reason why so few South Indian hockey players are picked for the national team, despite their renowned speed and skill. (Another reason, according to our hockey-playing friend in Tirunelveli, is the deep-rooted anti-South prejudice of North Indians.)

The temple trustees' leaflet, mentioned above, is a good example of the Hindus' attitude – or perhaps one should say 'non-attitude' – to history. It is intended to be factual and informative and in Europe a comparable bit of bumph would concentrate on giving precise dates. But in India we are cheerfully told, 'The date of the temple is hidden in the Puranic past. The nucleus of the structure however has been here for more than 2,000 years as the Tamil classics refer to.' And again, 'The Gopura is said to have been constructed about 100 years ago by Desikamurthi Swami, an Odukkath-Thambiran of the then Maha-Sannithanam of Tiruvavadutharai mutt.' And also, 'Kavirayar belonged to the Mukkhani comunity [*sic*] and lived perhaps in the eighteenth century.'

A people's concept of time lies at the root of their whole philosophy and much incomprehension of India is probably related to the antithetical notions of time held by Hindus and Westerners. We see time as a conveyor-belt, eternally carrying the present moment out of sight for ever. But the Indian sees it as a wheel, eternally revolving, and can believe he will at some stage, in some reincarnation, return to the present moment. For him time is divided into ages (*yugas*) which perpetually recur in cycles. So nothing is new and nothing is old and even Hindus of high intelligence, with trained minds, find it possible to believe that 2,000 years ago their ancestors invented aero-planes which in due course – as that *yuga* declined – ceased to be used.

Since Herodotus, creative minds in the west have been taking an interest in history. But naturally no such interest arose in India, where the most respected human being is the *jivanmukta* – the man who, having freed himself from Time, can perceive the nature of ultimate Reality. Hinduism positively encourages a man to forget his historical situation rather than to look to it, as we do, for guidance in the present, a deeper understanding of human society and some increase in self-knowledge. And of course this attitude is closely linked with what outsiders see as Indian passivity and fatalism. If ages *recur*, instead of *passing*, one obviously only has to wait long enough and the Golden Age will come again; an improvement in social conditions has nothing to do with the efforts of individuals or generations to better the age in which they happen to find themselves.

On the beach this morning I talked to a very articulate young man – a Tamil farmer's son now studying medicine at Madras University – who told me his father has for some years been using the new rice seed, of Green Revolution fame, but has just decided to give it up because it needs too much expensive fertiliser. This snag had been interpreted by both father and son as a sign that, despite the starving millions, India's rice crop *should not* be increased at present. To try to swim against the cosmic current of this *yuga* – to try to outwit Destiny – was *avidya* (ignorance), which might be described as the only form of sin recognised by Hindu ethics. This conversation did nothing to change my long-held opinion that F.A.O. are well and truly up against it in India – especially South India.

On our way up to the temple at three-thirty we were joined by a brisk, elderly little man, covered in *puja* after-effects of ash and coloured powder, who insisted on talking to us volubly in Tamil – which did no one any good that I could see. Tamil is the oldest surviving Dravidian language and has, I am told, a wonderful literature. It is, however, prodigiously difficult. Usually even I can master 'Please' and 'Thank you', or words to that effect, but by Tamil I am totally defeated.

At the temple entrance a notice said 'Admission Rs.1 only' and here our companion held out his hand and indicated that he would get our ticket. At the time I believed he was being disinterestedly helpful and we followed him to the gateway to the Inner Sanctum, where two rough-spoken temple guards in khaki uniforms abusively objected to my entering. They thought I was a man (I was wearing grey slacks and a shapeless grey bush-shirt), and men are allowed in only if stripped to the waist. Our guide quickly signed that they must be given a rupee each, at which point I would have begun to argue˙ had not Rachel's tight grip on my hand told me she was terrified of the guards' aggressiveness. So to spare her I paid up.

Then began a whirlwind tour around many brilliantly lamp-lit shrines through scores of worshippers. It is no exaggeration to say that I have never in my life felt so embarrassed; and I have rarely felt so angry. I had wanted simply to pay my rupee and quietly go wherever *mlecchas* are allowed, leisurely observing all I could. Instead, I was rushed around the entire temple, to the understandable fury of orthodox worshippers, and given no time to observe anything. And when we emerged – both striped on our faces and arms with all sorts of ash and powder – I was less Rs.12 and in that sort of choking bad temper caused by the realisation that one has been taken for a ride.

This was the best-organised exercise in co-operative conmanship I have ever encountered. As our guide took us to various forbidden places the guards or priests (or both) simulated anger and outrage, and the guide then quickly indicated that only by donating another rupee could I appease their alarming (to Rachel) wrath and make amends for having intruded. My puzzled readers may wonder why I did not simply turn around and walk out, but this temple is so vast and complex that we were soon lost and I had no wish to start a riot by inadvertently stumbling into some Holy of Holies. (Remember how the Mutiny was sparked off!) What most upset me was that so many genuinely devout people were distressed by our involuntary gate-crashing and must have been scandalised to see *mlecchas* going through the sacred rituals as – apparently – a tourist stunt. And the intrinsic beauty of those rituals heightened my frustration. If only we had been able to move around slowly, and as unobtrusively as possible, this could have been a wonderful experience.

Outside the temple our guide confidently demanded another Rs.10, as his personal fee. When given a few unprintable home truths instead he became speechless with rage and stood

wordlessly opening and shutting his mouth, making funny
wheezy noises like a toy steam engine. Then he followed us, at a
little distance, up the beach; so I asked Rachel to sit guard over
my clothes and money while I swam far beyond the surf to work
off my ill-temper.

As I swam I thought how right St Francis Xavier had been
when he wrote to his colleagues in Rome, after an encounter
with the Brahman priests of this very same Tiruchendur
temple. 'There is a class of men out here called *Bragmanes*.
They are the mainstay of heathenism, and have charge of the
temples devoted to the idols . . . They do not know what it is to
tell the truth but for ever plot how to lie subtly and deceive their
poor ignorant followers . . . They have little learning, but
abundance of iniquity and malice.'

Not that St Francis could afford to be too critical; he himself
was hopelessly ignorant on the subject of Hinduism and chose
always to remain so. He seems never even to have heard of such
basic concepts as *karma, yoga, bhakti* and *maya* and his years on
the subcontinent were devoted to loving the poor and lambast-
ing idolatry. Yet even in his own century several distinguished
Roman Catholic theologians had agreed with John Capreolus
that idolatry need not be as silly as it looks because 'God of His
absolute power could assume the nature of a stone or other
inanimate object, nor would it be more incongruous to say that
God is a stone than to say that He is a man, because He is
infinitely above both natures.' (The Rev. Capreolus might have
added, 'It would be no more incongruous to say that God is a
stone than to say that He is a piece of bread.')

St Francis seems to have been in some ways singularly
gullible for an ex-Professor of the Sorbonne. This is his own
description of an encounter he had in 1544 with 'more than two
hundred *bragmanes*' in the pillared courtyard (unchanged to
this day) of Tiruchendur's temple. 'I delivered an exhortation
on the subject of Heaven and Hell, and told them who go to the
one place and who to the other. After the sermon, the *bragmanes*
all rose and embraced me warmly, saying that the God of the
Christians was indeed the true God . . . God gave me arguments
suitable to their capacity to prove clearly the immortality of the
soul . . . One must avoid scholastic subtleties in reasoning with
such simple folk . . . Still another of their questions to me was

whether God was black or white ... As all the people of this
land are black and like the colour, they maintain that God too is
black. Most of the idols are black. They anoint them constantly
with oil and they stink abominably. They are also appallingly
ugly. The *bragmanes* seemed satisfied with my answers to all
their questions ...' Poor St Francis! Clearly these 'simple
folk' had a marvellous time pulling his leg, and no doubt they
went to their homes chuckling over the primitive reasoning of
this simple wandering preacher ... Not one of them, I need
hardly say, became a Christian.

As we walked back to the bazaar, in quest of more tea, Rachel
noticed that the young temple elephant was having his make-up
put on. Blue and gold circles were being painted on his ears and
trunk, and white stripes on his forehead, and then (big thrill!) he
was caparisoned in red, blue and gold tasselled brocade – his
Sunday Best, as it were. Next a thick silken rope with heavy
brass bells on both ends was thrown over his back, he was given
a small piece of wood to hold in his trunk and off he went
towards the main temple entrance. 'Let's follow him!' said
Rachel, almost stuttering with excitement – though a quarter of
an hour earlier she had been complaining of acute dehydration.
So we did.

On the way the proprietors of several little food-stalls came
rushing out to present Babar – as I had somewhat irreverently
named him – with bananas, buns or pastries. Before accepting
these he had to hand (not quite the *mot juste*, but never mind)
the piece of wood to his attendant, which meant a check was
kept on what he ate: and I noticed oranges were *verboten*. When
he received coins he carefully handed them to his attendant and
then laid his trunk on the donors' heads to bless them: so he,
poor brute, has also been co-opted. I must say he is beautifully
trained. On arriving at the main temple entrance, where he
was directly opposite the image of Sri Subrahmanya in its
central sanctum, he slowly knelt – giving an uncanny impression
of reverence – then raised his trunk and solemnly trumpeted
three times in greeting to the god. Being a sacred elephant his
touch is greatly valued and Laksmi-alone-knows what he
earned during the next hour as he stood by the main entrance
with his attendant squatting beside him. Many people presented
him with food, which he delightedly popped into his mouth, but

he had been trained to give his blessing only for cash. I handed
him 10 paise, to find out what an elephantine blessing feels like,
and it is quite a pleasant sensation to have that sensitive tip of
trunk laid gently on one's head.

The next excitement started just after sunset, as I was trying
to prise Rachel away from Babar. On the edge of the beach,
near the temple, was a big, ugly concrete shed with padlocked
corrugated iron doors – and suddenly these swung open to
reveal, astonishingly, a glittering golden chariot. To it was
attached a pair of prancing, life-size silver horses and Rachel
stood transfixed, obviously half-expecting the fairy tale to
unfold and the horses to gallop out of the shed. An Indian
crowd gathers incredibly quickly and moments later we were
surrounded by most of the townspeople and hundreds of
pilgrims. A small boy who spoke excellent English (he attends
one of the last outposts of intelligible English in India – a
convent school) told us the chariot-shrine was a new acquisition
costing 2 lakhs (Rs.200,000), and that it was to be used this
evening for the first time to carry the temple's most precious
image of Sri Subrahmanya around the building three times in
procession.

This elaborate example of the work of contemporary Madrassi
goldsmiths proves that their art, at least, is not dying. In its
every delicate detail Subrahmanya's new chariot is truly a thing
of beauty and the countless tiny figures adorning it are not mere
replicas of traditional images but have a life and vigour of their
own. Unfortunately, however, technology has overtaken it, in
the form of electricity. One doesn't actually see any bulbs, these
having been so cleverly arranged that the whole mass of gold
looks as though it were radiating its own light, but when the
procession started four men had to push a clumsy, reeking
generator behind the chariot. (I still have in my nostrils the
warring smells of jasmine and generator fumes.)

It was a most memorable experience to watch the Lord
Subrahmanya, wreathed in blossoms and enthroned in glory,
moving slowly through the blackness of the night. The mile-
long path around the temple is rough and in parts quite steep,
so several torch-bearers held aloft blazing brands of oil-soaked
wood. These gave off an incense-like aroma and both alarmed
and thrilled Rachel by occasionally sending showers of sparks

cascading into the crowd. Three bands of musicians accompanied the procession – but did not mingle with it, being Harijans – and all around us the fervent, unco-ordinated chanting of various pilgrim groups added to the atmosphere of elated devotion.

I was particularly struck by the number of young pilgrims, most of whom were completely absorbed in their worship. Then, observing the whole scene, I felt a sudden conviction that India's civilisation will be the last in the world to capitulate to our sort of materialism. And I saw an analogy between the beauty of the golden chariot, locked away in that ugly concrete shed, and the worth of the Hindu tradition, guarded by a corrupt priesthood.

As the only foreigners present, we were not only permitted but encouraged to walk close to the chariot and when I tired of carrying Rachel piggy-back (at ground level she could have seen nothing) there were many volunteers eager to take her over. From the broad shoulders of a Trivandrum engineer she beamed down at me, her face glowing in the golden light, and said 'Isn't India fun?'

21 December.   Tisaiyanvilai.

Before catching our noon bus we spent a few hours in or near a Parava settlement about a mile down the beach from Tiruchendur's temple. The Paravas are a Coromandel Coast community of pearl-fishers whose ancestors were baptised *en masse* between 1535 and 1537, a few years before St Francis came on the scene. For many previous centuries these gentle, primitive people had been bullied and exploited by both Hindus and Muslims, so they were impressed when an Indian Christian from Calicut argued that conversion would strengthen their position by gaining them the protection of the then powerful Portuguese. But as no available missionary could speak Tamil the original 'converts' received not even the most elementary instruction in their new faith and, despite St Francis's subsequent efforts (he was no great linguist himself), their descendants give the impression of being – shall we say – a unique sub-caste of Christianity.

Those whom we met today seemed not unlike their sixteenth-century ancestors, described by the Portuguese as a simple, humble, handsome race; they quickly made friends with Rachel but were rather shy of me. Their homes are cramped, palm-thatched huts built on the beach, well away from the edge of Tiruchendur, and they keep their antique catamarans – each sporting a pair of rough-hewn wooden horns on its prow – parked outside their front doors, as you might say. The evident ill-health of the little community was a surprise, where every-body must at least have enough fish to eat; but I suppose no unbalanced diet is healthy. This settlement is dominated by an incongruously large, once-white seventeenth-century church of obviously Portuguese provenance which has fallen into a serious state of disrepair. We found all the doors open and it seems to be in daily use, yet the interior was completely un-furnished and undecorated, apart from a few chipped, con-ventional plaster statues. About the whole settlement there was an unmistakable ghetto atmosphere, but I have been warned against generalising from this one example of how the Paravas live. Apparently many of their villages are lively and thriving, and their 'capital' – Manapad – is said to be an exceptionally prosperous and progressive little town with a fine, well-kept church.

As we left Tiruchendur my only regret was that I had seen nothing of Shanamukha, deliciously described in our trustees' leaflet as 'the Bhaktas Idol, the cynosure of all eyes and the Chief attraction of the commonality.'

The paradox inherent in Indian attitudes to animals is at present greatly exercising Rachel; how can a mainly vegetarian race be so callous about suffering animals? On the bus today she was very worried when she saw several pitifully bony cows whose horns had been tied to their legs, securing their heads in the grazing position so that they could not eat the young plantains. And she fretted too – quite unnecessarily – about the many goats we saw with long sticks attached horizontally to their collars to prevent them from breaking through fences of stakes.

To my mind, however, the treatment of small children and babies on pilgrimage beaches is far more disturbing. Both at Cape Comorin and Tiruchendur I saw many infants being carried into the rough sea, kicking and screaming with terror, and being dipped three times under the water, the parents pausing between dips to roar with laughter at the spectacle of their hysterically frightened offspring. Tonight those scenes are haunting me; there is something very disquieting about parents deriving amusement from the deliberate terrorising of small children. One hears a lot about the security enjoyed by the Indian young, who are breast-fed for years, and picked up whenever they cry (because crying is believed to weaken the whole constitution), and who spend so much time close to their mothers' bodies. But how real can this security be if one of the most basic functions of the maternal instinct – to protect a child from fear – remains inoperative? And if some mothers actually *inflict* terror? And, most baffling of all, if they even *enjoy* inflicting it? This behaviour is perhaps connected with the Indians' unawareness of themselves or other people as individuals – or it may be a symptom of acute frustration. Many young couples are still living in joint families, where they must unremittingly defer to their elders; and possibly those who resent this restriction find some release for their tension in bullying the only people with whom they can feel themselves to be independent adults, in control of a situation.

Or am I over-reacting? Most Indians, after all, regard me as a monster of heartless cruelty because Rachel is normally left alone in a bedroom from 6.30 p.m. until 8.30 a.m., without my even once opening the door to make sure she is still alive. In this household, the $3\frac{1}{2}$-year-old – who shrieks with terror every time she sees us – spends much of her day on mamma's hip and the rest of it on grandmamma's lap and all her night in mamma's arms. She is a tiny, dainty little thing, no bigger than Rachel was at two and always immaculately dressed.

When one considers how most Indian children are reared, it is not really surprising that in their company Rachel should sometimes speak and act as though brought up under the personal tuition of Lord Curzon. An alarming number of Indians have an unfortunate way of provoking the mildest Europeans to behave autocratically, and for this the blurred outlines of the average Indian personality are very likely to blame.

22 December. *Tisaiyanvilai.*

This morning we went into Tirunelveli to mail-hunt unsuccessfully – but the postmaster is confident our letters will have

come through by the 24th – and to do a little Christmas
shopping, since Tisaiyanvilai's bazaar offers no toys or gift
articles of any kind. Tirunelveli, being the market centre for a
wide area, was jammed with people, and across the main shopping streets hung banners wishing everybody a Merry Xmas
and a Happy New Year. Christmas is celebrated throughout
this district much as Whitsun is throughout Britain, where little
thought is given over that week-end to the Third Person of the
Trinity.

Rachel is beoming increasingly critical of certain aspects of
Indian life and today her comments on the treatment of Hindu
women got us involved in the whole doctrine of re-birth. I
explained that women are considered inferior because they
would not have been born as women but for sins committed in a
previous life, which means they deserve no better treatment than
they get. Rachel didn't think much of this theory but conceded
grudgingly, 'I suppose it *might* be true.' Then, after a few
moments' silence (an extremely rare occurrence in our joint
lives), she exclaimed, 'Won't it be *interesting* to be dead! Then
we'll know everything. Would you like to be dead?'

'Not particularly,' I said. 'I'm quite happy with my mortal
coil. And there's always the possibility that far from knowing
everything, we'll know nothing!' Which of course led me into still
deeper waters, but these need not concern us here.

Another of Rachel's current grievances – particularly since a
gob of phlegm landed on her bare shoulder the other morning –
is the Indian habit of spitting in the street. This is the sort of
thing I took for granted on previous visits to India but, as I
have already mentioned, my daughter is much more fastidious
than her Ma. And now I come to think of it, it *is* a bit uncivilised
at least not to look before you spit, if spit you must.

I used to assume vaguely that Indian spitting was simply a
consequence of Hindus being inexplicably chesty and peculiarly
devoid of any spark of Civic Spirit. Recently, however, I have
discovered that the habit is closely linked with their pollution
laws, which are complex beyond anything a simple Western
mind could imagine. To us many of them seem outlandish,
though others contain obvious elements of common sense. For
one thing, all bodily discharges are regarded with extreme
horror and fear; and saliva, phlegm and mucus, which are

believed to be 'spoiled semen' (even today semen is popularly supposed to be stored in the head), are thought of as having an especially powerful polluting effect. Therefore the body must be cleared of these ghastly menaces at the first possible moment, and it doesn't matter a damn where the discharge lands or who else is polluted in the process.

23 December. Tisaiyanvilai.

After breakfast we set off to walk the five miles to Ittamozhi. Having spent a week in this little corner of the extremity of India – one of the world's oldest inhabited areas – I now feel quite fond of it. At least during this season, it has a certain muted charm. Mid-December to mid-January is the one enjoyable month, weather-wise; by March nobody ever feels comfortable and by May even the locals regard it as hell on earth. But that was hard to imagine this morning, as we walked under a gay blue sky, strewn with a few high, white clouds, and relished a pleasantly hot sun tempered by a boisterous wind off the sea. After the recent rain the wayside was studded with tiny, brilliant wild flowers and butterflies zig-zagged excitedly from blossom to blossom and the bird-life was so dazzling one almost doubted one's eyes. 'If there were monkeys here it would be perfect,' said Rachel. 'Why are there no monkeys?'

We followed a little road built under the personal supervision of Ernest's remarkable Rajput mother during the heyday of his family but which has fallen into such disrepair that few motor vehicles now use it. It must be fascinating here when the toddy-tappers are at work, shinning up and down all those palmyras every few hours to extract the sap for making jaggery. Much ploughing of the rain-softened paddy-fields is now going on and several men, wearing only ragged *lunghis* and untidy turbans, were driving yokes of small, emaciated oxen along the road while carrying wooden ploughs on their heads: a measure both of the primitiveness of the ploughs and the strength of their neck-muscles. Turning to look back at one such man – young, neatly built, almost black-skinned – we found that he, too, had stopped to stare, and was standing using a hand to balance his plough while gazing at us not with curiosity, amusement or suspicion, but with an expression of the purest astonishment. For a moment we stood thus, on that wide, bright, silent landscape –

Europeans of the twentieth century confronting an Indian of no century, a man whose life is contained in a mould that would be perfectly familiar to his pre-Aryan forbears. And then, wordlessly, we turned away from each other and moved in opposite directions.

Beyond a doubt one has to walk or cycle really to appreciate the flavour of a place. Bus journeys are all very well in their way, but they are not true *travelling*.

Between Tisaiyanvilai and Ittamozhi we counted five little churches or chapels of various Christian denominations and, this being Sunday, all of them were open. In an impoverished toddy-tappers' village most of the children were suffering from malnutrition and/or worms, and many had that rough, dead, brownish-red hair which amongst people naturally black-haired means severe vitamin-deficiency. But even here one of India's heroic malaria-eradication teams had sprayed and meticulously marked each wretched dwelling.

As we were approaching Ittamozhi we heard weird, rapid chanting and rhythmic handclapping coming from a well-built, palm-thatched house a little way off the road. There was no other building in sight and the chanting and clapping, accompanied by frenzied drum-beating and cymbal-clashing, created an hypnotic effect that seemed tribal African rather than Indian. Rachel and I were equally intrigued and decided to enter the compound through a little wooden gate in its high hedge of prickly pear. Then we sat on a rough-hewn chair placed, unexpectedly, just inside the gate, and went on listening in fascinated bewilderment until a young woman in a white ankle-length gown with long sleeves – which look very odd here – came hurrying down the road. She was carrying an armful of Christian prayer-books and I was irresistibly reminded of the White Rabbit as she hastened past us, her pace not slowing for an instant and her eyes fixed on the hut. However, her gestured invitation was quite clear and although her expression had told me that she suffered from some severe emotional disorder we followed her into the building – and none of the rapt congregation appeared to notice our alien presence.

The chapel measured some twenty-five feet by fifteen and neat strips of coconut matting were laid on the polished mud floor. A few biblical texts in Tamil hung on the walls and the only furniture was the preacher's desk, behind which stood a tall, heavily built Tamil of about forty, wearing the sort of simple vestment favoured by Low Church clergymen in all countries. When we entered he was leading the hymn-singing (if you can call it that) in a not too abnormal manner, but I soon realised that the congregation's odd lack of interest in our arrival had a slightly sinister explanation: all those present were in a trance of some sort, having been completely mesmerised by their clergyman.

It was not difficult to count heads. On the males' side were four men – one a hideously deformed idiot – and two youths: on the females' side were twenty-three women – the majority young, and all dressed in white – plus five school-girls and an assortment of sleeping (incredibly) infants. One of the men was beating the drum, one of the women was clashing the cymbals and everybody else was loudly clapping hands and singing while rocking to and fro on their heels. At first glance one might think the whole scene rather touching: simple folk expressing their devotion as best they knew how, and so on ... But it soon became apparent that we were in on something very peculiar indeed.

At a given signal the tempo of the music, chanting, clapping and swaying quickened dramatically. Then, as it reached crescendo point, the preacher suddenly threw back his head, roared like a wounded tiger, thrust his clenched fists into the air and stood shaking them at the ceiling, and sweating and panting and heaving, and screaming in a voice that had become curiously shrill while his congregation went berserk.

Poor Rachel was so terrified by this Scene from Clerical Life (Tamil translation) that I had to take her in my arms. By now the women – shrieking like witches at a Sabbath – were gyrating cross-legged around the slippery floor, working themselves into a frenzy in which sexual excitement was unmistakably inter-woven with religious hysteria. Meanwhile the 'clergyman' (by now I felt he had qualified for inverted commas) continued to scream, tremble, sweat and shake his clenched fists, never once taking his eyes off the ceiling. Several women now began to foam at the mouth and a few soon slumped into unconscious-ness, overcome by the intensity of their emotion. I have twice witnessed Tibetan shamans going into trance, but that was merely uncanny. This morning's session had a nauseating aura and when two women leapt to their feet and began to loosen their robes I decided it was time to go, before Rachel witnessed something not suitable for 5-year-olds.

When I asked Ernest to explain our experience he said we had attended the last half-hour of the regular two-hour Sunday morning service at the local chapel of the Pentecostal Church of Ceylon. I inquired if 'service' could be assumed to have a double meaning in this context, but he would not commit himself. It seems this sect is quite popular, chiefly amongst young women whose husbands belong to other Christian sects in the remoter regions of South India. The Pentecostals wear only white, eschew jewellery of every sort and condemn all fun and games except those involved in their weekly receiving of direct messages from the Holy Ghost, on the hot line described above. No doubt there is a link between the predominantly female attendance and the repression of Indian women. Whatever else may be said about this morning's service, it certainly took the lid off everybody's repressions.

Incidentally, Ernest has been enlightening me about the sexual morals of the local Harijans, Sudras and toddy-tapping Christians. Apparently pre-puberty intercourse is freely indulged in by both boys and girls, and tacitly condoned by their elders. But this means the girls have to be virtually imprisoned between the times of their reaching puberty and being married, since the majority do not revert with ease to chastity. The marriage age is often illegally low in this remote region, yet unmarried mothers do exist. However, contrary to the custom in higher castes they are treated leniently and 'a little error' – even of indeterminate paternity – is not considered a serious obstacle to matrimony.

This morning Rachel produced the Saying of the Week, if not of the Year. Having listened attentively but unprofitably to a breakfast-time discussion on the Bhakti movement in South India, she suddenly announced, during a lull in the conversation, 'I think I'm too young to understand Hinduism. Will you explain it again when I'm eight?'

11

Fever in Madurai:
Wildlife in Periyar

30 December. Madurai.

The seven-day break in this diary is attributable to a nameless fever.

On Christmas Eve morning, when we left Tisaiyanvilai, I felt slightly peculiar but thought nothing of it – until suddenly, as we waited at Tirunelveli Junction for a train to Madurai, I became really ill. We were waiting for a train because we had just missed the bus; and we had missed the bus because we were waiting at the post office for a delivery of foreign mail that again failed to come; and, as a final complication, I had also missed the bank, which on that day closed at noon by way of celebrating Christmas.

This was the first time I have ever been literally penniless – our last paise had gone on the train tickets – and I found the experience interesting. It underlined the extent to which even the poorest of us depends on what little money we have as an essential prop to our personalities; and I began to see the begging type of hippy, who has voluntarily made a vow of poverty, from a new angle. Not for nothing do most religions regard poverty as a pre-requisite for the perfection of sanctity.

Our train, marked EXPRESS in giant lettering up and down its sides, left Tirunelveli at four o'clock and took five-and-a-half hours to cover ninety-five miles. It was almost empty because the railwaymen had been on strike up to that morning and the general public had not yet realised the strike was over.

By the time we arrived here I was too feverish to articulate and Rachel also was sickening fast. However, in the Tirunelveli waiting-room we had met a kindly young Swiss couple – our first foreign fellow-travellers since leaving Goa – and by some means these guardian angels got us installed in Madurai's

Travellers' Bungalow, just beyond the station yard. I dimly recollect stumbling across row after row of railway sleepers in pitch darkness under the noses of gigantic steam engines (*c.* 1910) which hissed menacingly while Rachel vomited over my legs. Then I was on a bed and she was on a couch in a high-ceilinged room well furnished with rosewood pieces – and haunted by generations of I.C.S. officers on tour to inspect their Empire.

I had heard our Swiss friends urging the pudgy, puzzled little caretaker to get us a doctor from somewhere without delay – the irony of it, hours after leaving a doctor's house! – but this man proved more than slightly obtuse and from 10 p.m. on Christmas Eve to 11 a.m. on Stephen's Day no one even put a head around the door to see if we were still alive. Mercifully our gallon water-bottle had been almost full when we arrived and I suppose Rachel helped herself; she tells me she slept most of the time and never had a headache. Meanwhile I dosed myself with fistfuls of codeine which had no effect whatever on any of my symptoms. The worst of these was a headache so excruciating that at times I half-believed myself to be dying of meningitis. And the noise off-stage did nothing to help.

Indians love noise and habitually amplify their degraded cinema pop music to truly diabolical proportions. In this case I have no idea where the original sound came from, but an amplifier had been attached to the roof directly above our window and it is no exaggeration to say that during the first two days and nights in that room I was driven almost insane. Only those who have personally suffered Indian pop music at close range will be able to give me the sympathy I deserve. Occasionally there was a lull in the inferno and I almost wept with relief, but no lull lasted longer than it takes to change a record. Perhaps Richard Lannoy was right when he commented in *The Speaking Tree* – 'Indian pop music . . . pervades the lives of the Indian masses as does no other form of entertainment . . . Here is a people . . . distracted from the human predicament by the highly organised mass media. The pop arts of India merely block individuation, alienate people from personal experience, and intensify their moral isolation from each other, from reality, and from themselves.'

By 11 a.m. on the twenty-sixth I had realised that if I were not to die of neglect some action must be taken. Leaning on the wall I made it to the veranda and tried to persuade three passers-by that I genuinely and urgently needed medical attention; but they all insisted that I must go to a clinic or hospital as no doctor would come to me. However, I knew it would be suicidal to go doctor-hunting in a steady downpour of cold rain with a high temperature, so I tottered despairingly back to my sweat-sodden bed.

Then Rachel appeared beside me, in a rather genie-like way. 'I'm better,' she said, 'and I'm hungry. May I go out to look for food? Why don't you get a doctor? You look terrible. Have you no medicine? Why am I better?'

I mumbled that no doctor was available, whereupon Rachel said, 'Why don't you write a letter to a doctor and get a servant to take it?'

'What doctor? What servant?' I muttered muzzily.

'Any doctor and any servant,' said Rachel, impatiently.

I raised my head and began to take her seriously. She brought me pen and paper and in shaky capitals I appealed to a 'Dear Doctor' while she trotted off to fetch 'a servant'. Moments later she was back with a young cycle-rickshaw-wallah she had found sheltering on the veranda. His English was unintelligible but he seemed to understand when I explained that if he returned with a doctor I would give him Rs.5 before I left Madurai. Pocketing my note he disappeared and less than fifteen minutes later showed an elderly Indian woman doctor into the room. She was from a Christian maternity hospital scarcely five minutes' walk away and she assured me that had we gone there on Christmas Eve we would have been given a very warm welcome and appropriate treatment.

But what was 'appropriate treatment'? Despite heavy doses of fabulously expensive British-made drugs my temperature remained between 101° and 104° for the next few days, while my headache resisted every available pain-killer and I developed a strange racking cough – quite unlike bronchitis – which almost caused me to faint with exhaustion.*

Obviously I could not be moved, but my faithful doctor called four times a day – no doubt she feared further ghastly

---

* Some time later, routine malaria blood-tests incidentally revealed that we had both had brucellosis: so Rachel was lucky to have recovered within three days.

complications – and ordered the caretaker to provide fresh bedding and two-hourly pots of tea. She also brought her senior partner, Dr Kennett, to examine me, which I gathered was a significant measure of her concern. Dr Kennett is an astonishing 80-year-old who has done so much for the poor of this city that a main street has been named after her. Following her visit, the attitude towards us of the caretaker and his staff changed from polite indifference to a respectful eagerness to please.

Apart from all this professional attention, both these doctors were motherly kindness personified. They lent me Rs.100, regularly sent a servant with tempting little delicacies from their own kitchen, and provided Rachel with an abundance of Christmassy snacks, toys, games and balloons. Then yesterday Dr Kennett's car took us to the hospital, where we are now installed in a two-bed cubicle amidst the howls of the newly born. Today my temperature is at last normal, and if it remains so we plan to go to Periyar tomorrow afternoon to convalesce in the depths of the wildlife sanctuary.

31 December.   Kumili.

This morning I rose and shone. Fifteen watt, as you might say, but an improvement on the blackout of the past week.

After breakfast we set off with our cycle-rickshaw friend to see what is perhaps the most impressive of all Hindu temples. The morning was a perfection of clear golden sunshine from an azure sky – after several dark days of non-stop monsoon rain – and the building that came into view in the distance, as we crossed the high railway bridge, seemed almost unreal in its alien loveliness. It is in fact a whole complex of buildings and one could spend days exploring and admiring – though that might overtax Rachel's interest: she was happy enough to leave after five hours. Moreover, since the Madurai temple is one of South India's main tourist attractions *mlecchas* are courteously catered for and racketeers of every sort rigorously suppressed.

On the way back to the hospital we called at the bank – always a long-drawn-out procedure – and by the time we had packed, said grateful good-byes and caught the two-thirty bus I was feeling decidedly feeble. And so – I suspect – was the ever-uncomplaining Rachel, who is still suffering from that odd cough and has not yet regained her appetite. She has had no treatment for our nameless disease because I am very against children being stuffed with antibiotics.

This afternoon's journey took us south-west, through a region where the density of the human population was matched by a staggering number of cattle, mainly the much-revered humped whites. There were also hundreds of buffaloes and several herds of minute donkeys which are commonly used as baggage-animals and too often beaten savagely. Naturally none of these beasts looked well fed, yet even on this rather arid plain I saw no starving animals, as one frequently does in North India. Rachel was distressed on the donkeys' behalf and not consoled when I told her that according to Hindu mythology the ass is the steed or vehicle of Sitala, the goddess of smallpox (one of the ten aspects of Kali), and so is regarded by most Indian peasants with a mixture of fear and contempt. Under the Mughals, no Hindu of the North-West frontier province – now Pakistan – was allowed to ride anything but an ass. I cannot understand why donkeys are universally scorned, despite their being so useful. Perhaps their voice is against them. Luckily Rachel did not notice that many of those we passed today had had their nostrils slit, it being the erroneous belief of Indians that this mutilation modifies the bray.

For miles our narrow road ran between low, grotesquely shaped, rock-strewn hills towards the high blue wall of the Ghats. Then, having crossed the Tamil Nadu–Kerala border at the little town of Cumbum, we drove straight at the apparently sheer mountain barrier that here rises abruptly from the plain. 'There must be a tunnel!' said I to Rachel. But instead there was a dramatic road which I would have immensely enjoyed on foot though I did not greatly relish it from the seat of an overloaded Indian bus.

When we got here just after sunset the air felt cold. Kumili is a single-street village, 3,300 feet above sea-level and four miles from Periyar, and in the larger of its two doss-houses we are occupying a cubicle in which I can only move crabwise between our cots. An icy draught is sneaking through a broken window and I have just come face to face with my first South Indian bed-bug (now deceased). I feel so exhausted the New Year will have to see itself in without me, but I daresay 1974 will be none the worse for my non-attendance at its birth.

1 January, 1974.   Thekkady, Periyar Wildlife Sanctuary.

If the denizens of Kumili celebrated our Western New Year I did not hear their celebrations, or feel their draughts or bed-bugs, or suffer any other interference with my ten-hour sleep.

By seven-thirty this morning we were on the way to Thekkady, which is the administrative and tourist centre for the sanctuary. Near the lake the Wildlife Preservation Officer has his head-quarters in a little bungalow, and an inconspicuous wooden landing-stage has been built for the small motor-launches that take visitors on game-watching expeditions.

'How far is it?' asked Rachel, as we walked away from Kumili through the crisp early morning mountain air.

'Four miles,' I replied.

Rachel looked at me sardonically. 'I thought we were sup-posed to be convalescing,' she said. 'I don't call carrying your big rucksack four miles *convalescing*. Is there no bus?'

'No,' I said firmly – hoping one would not overtake us, for 'The whole area of the Sanctuary abounds in natural scenery,' as my tourist brochure puts it. Soon we saw a troop of Nilgiri langurs, and then that most lovely creature, the Indian Giant Squirrel, and Rachel forgot all about the snags of convalescing with mamma. At the sanctuary border-post an amiable young policeman asked – without getting up from his breakfast – if we were carrying any guns, and then made a sign that we could duck under the barrier and proceed.

The Kerala Tourism Development Corporation owns both Thekkady's hotels. One is the expensive, Western-style Aranya Nivas, where a bottle of beer costs Rs.9, and the other is Periyar House – clean, comfortable, spacious, efficiently staffed, teetotal, vegetarian and only Rs.10 for an airy, well-appointed single room overlooking jungle and lake. Tonight Periyar House is almost full and the guests include half a dozen semi-hippy Euro-pean youngsters and a party of elderly Prussians with thick guide-books and severe sunburn. But the Aranya Nivas, not surprisingly, is empty. I have been told it depends almost entirely on rich Americans and the flashy, hard-drinking type of North Indian who is out to impress his benighted Southern cousins. A pleasing feature of Thekkady is that one can without difficulty avoid one's fellow-tourists; even on the motor-launch this morning there were only four Madrassis and a camera-obsessed Japanese youth.

Periyar Lake is twenty miles long and was formed in 1895 by the construction of a dam across the Periyar river to help irrigate large tracts of Tamil Nadu. Its maximum depth is about 140 feet and, as my brochure explains, 'When the Lake was formed, tree-growth from the water-spread area was not completely removed and therefore a large number of dead tree trunks still exist within the lake. They get submerged or exposed by the fluctuating water-level. These dead trees, though sometimes a hazard to navigation enhances the scenic value of the locality and allows the nesting and roosting of several water birds.' I am not sure that I agree about the enhancing of the scenic value; the cumulative effect of so many dead trees is slightly depressing and they serve as a nagging reminder of the lake's artificiality. However, if they solve the water-birds' housing problems they are well worth keeping.

Our two-hour tour was good value for Rs.4 and the enthusiastic pilot identified many birds for us as we chugged slowly along, enjoying the warm sun sparkling on the water, and the cool breeze, and the faint yet thrilling possibility of seeing some big game. At the edge of the water in the near distance we eventually saw a herd of elephants; but obviously touring by motor-launch is not the most efficient way of animal-watching, though this trip is well worth taking for its own sake.

After lunch I left Rachel playing in the jungle near the hotel – where there were two tame elephants and lots of non-shy langurs to entertain her – while I walked half-way back to Kumili in search of the Wildlife Officer, a pleasant young man who readily agreed to our spending two nights at the Manak-kavala Forest Rest House, six miles away. The Government of India Tourist Office in London had provided me with an excellent sketch-map of the sanctuary, on which all rest houses and footpaths are clearly marked, so I argued that we needed no guide, only the key. But the Officer thought otherwise and in the morning a trainee Wildlife Officer is to meet us outside the hotel at eight o'clock.

2 January.   Manakkavala.

The trek here perfectly illustrated how one should *not* travel with a small convalescing child. All would have been well had we been able to go at our own pace, devoting the whole day to the six-mile walk, but our unwanted guide arrived three hours late, which meant that when we started Rachel had already expended a considerable amount of her at present meagre store of energy and I was in an occidentally bad temper because I detest unpunctuality. On being asked 'Why so late?' the smartly uniformed guide, who was accompanied by a bare-footed 14-year-old, replied that he had been looking for a companion as he would be afraid to return alone to Thekkady – an excuse which did nothing to raise him in my estimation. Then it transpired that our guides were in a hurry, and Rachel was not equal to hurrying over the roughest terrain she had ever encountered. In brief, the whole thing was a disaster, not enjoyed by either of us.

However, to be on our own in this remote rest house compensates for the day's tribulations. It stands near the top of a steep, jungle-covered ridge, overlooking one of the lake's many narrow arms, and about a hundred yards away, across the still water, is a tree-covered peninsula with a long shore of grassland between forest and lake. There, at sunset, I saw seven gaur (the Indian bison) coming to drink and then quickly melting away into the shadows under the trees. These splendid creatures, with their spreading upcurling horns and massive sleek bodies, are aggressively anti-human and by far the most dangerous animals in the sanctuary; but because of their shyness the visitor is extremely unlikely ever to encounter one at close range. There are said to be sixteen tigers and many leopards here though these are rarely seen.

3 January.   Manakkavala.

Today we did some serious convalescing. My original plan had been to trek out from here, but this morning neither of us was up to it. However, as we lay around on the near-by lake shore we probably saw more than if we had been on the move. Scarcely thirty yards away a gaur cow and calf crossed a grassy glade between two patches of jungle: lots of wild pigs and piglets dug vigorously for their lunch during the forenoon: bonnet macaques and lion-tailed macaques swung and screamed in the trees above us: two flying-squirrels played tip and tig for quarter of an hour: a fiercely handsome fish-eagle caught and ate his prey on the opposite shore: darters dived frequently into the water, looking like something out of a fossil museum – and towards sunset eleven elephants, including two young calves, strolled down to bathe in the lake. But alas! – to our great disappointment they turned a corner before submerging, and because of the calves it would have been unwise to follow them.

It feels strange to be the only humans in a world of animals, knowing that every movement and sound is caused not by a member of one's own species. Periyar must be one of the most satisfying game sanctuaries in the world. It is totally uncommercialised – apart from Thekkady on its fringe: and even Thekkady has not yet been spoiled – and when you walk off to a forest hut there are (*pace* that sketch-map!) no discernible paths, no tiresome little signposts, no fussy picnic-sites, no concessions of any sort to mankind, until the hut itself is reached. It is just you and the animals, in a setting of incomparable natural loveliness, blessed by silence. But of course silence is the wrong word; what I mean is the absence of artificial noise. Except during a couple of noon hours there is very little silence, day or night, in an area that teems with bird and animal and insect life. Even when one can see nothing, it is fascinating simply to listen to the complex pattern of jungle sounds being woven against the stillness of a region undisturbed by man.

4 January. Thekkady.

The return trek on our own was an unqualified success and when Rachel said, 'It seems to me you're a better guide than those other two' I felt bound immodestly to agree. Not that it was easy to negotiate either the uncomfortable elephant-bogs or the steep, slippery slopes that in places rise straight up from the lake and had been the main cause of Rachel's alarm on the way out. The latter hazard we avoided today by leaving the lakeside and cautiously following animal paths through the jungle, stopping at intervals for sustenance under a gooseberry tree. The elephant-bogs, however, were another matter. These are swampy stretches of land at lake level, dotted with huge clumps of tough grass which act as stepping-stones, and the penalty for missing one's footing is partial immersion in gluey black mud. To Rachel's delight I soon slipped and, being weighted with a rucksack, sank so fast I lost both shoes. (They were falling to bits anyway, so this was not the economic disaster it might have been.)

It was interesting to observe the impact of animals on the environment in an area where man never interferes. (Though the fact that he deliberately never interferes is itself a form of interference with the balance of nature.) Many of the trees had recently had branches and bark ripped off by elephants, whose gigantic droppings were all over the place, and several grassy ridges looked as though newly ploughed by the wild pigs, of whom we saw dozens today, some quite close and not particularly nervous. We also saw fresh gaur droppings and passed a few of their resting-places, where the undergrowth had been trampled down and shaped. And to Rachel went the glory of noticing a tree from which much of the bark had been scraped by feline claws – a leopard, judging by the height of the marks. But to me – luckily – came the shock of seeing a long, thick snake just in time to arrest my bare foot inches from its back as it crossed our path.

'Why do you look so queer?' asked Rachel, staring up at me. 'Is that why you won't let me go first?'

'Probably it was harmless,' I said briskly. (I notice one always tells oneself this immediately afterwards, doubtless by way of counteracting the shock.)

'How soon would you die if it was harmful?' asked Rachel, indefatigably athirst for scientific data.

'I don't know,' I said shortly.

All day a strong cool breeze sent small white clouds cruising across the sky and stirred the golden elephant grass; and the warm sun sparkled on the lake – from which we never strayed too far – and glistened on the fresh green grass by the water's edge; and all around were powder-blue mountains, rising just beyond the splendour of the forest – a pink-brown-green expanse of noble trees, their colours vivid in the clear air, with the fiery flowers of the Giant Salmalias blazing like distant beacons.

We got back here at two-thirty, having made the six-mile walk last for seven hours, and I shall remember this Periyar interlude as one of the highlights of our journey. The feeling of remoteness, the beauty of jungle, lake and grasslands, and the novel awareness of being a mere visitor in a world of animals, add up to something very special.

After a late lunch I left Rachel playing near the hotel and hitched a lift into Kumili to replace my lost shoes. By the time I had walked back the only available pair were lacerating my feet but as they cost less than Rs.6 I can afford to replace them tomorrow. Trying to shop in a tiny place like Kumili – or even in a bigger town like Tisaiyanvilai – reveals how little cash circulates in rural India.

At supper I got into conversation with a family from Delhi – parents, two adolescent sons and paternal grandmother. Despite their staying in this modest hotel the husband must be a government official of some importance, as they have a State car and a retinue of liveried minions who travel in a jeep. The whole family spoke rather patronisingly about South Indians, as North Indians are wont to do, yet they were charming to me and I found myself talking to them with a freedom one does not normally feel amongst South Indians, however fluent their English.

This takes us into a not very savoury labyrinth. How much thicker is blood than water? Why am I aware of being with my own people – in the most basic sense of that phrase – when I am talking to fair-skinned, Aryan, North Indian Hindus, and aware of being with strangers when I am talking to dark-skinned, Dravidian, South Indian Christians? I suppose the short answer is that blood is indeed a lot thicker than water.

Yet this is not simply a shaming confession of racism: something a good deal more complicated is involved. The expressive cliché 'on the same wavelength' is needed here. One does not always approve of, like or wish to be with those of one's own race, but one understands their emotions and thought-processes by some primitive system that seems not to operate with other races. This lack of instinctive understanding must be at the root of racism, though in itself it is not racism; people fear what they cannot understand, and dislike what they fear.

The Hindu caste laws could be described as an elaborate

contrivance for making colour prejudice look respectable and the immutability of the Aryans' disdain for Dravidians is very striking. Whatever anti-discrimination laws may be passed, and however rapidly India may become a genuinely secular state, I cannot see Indian colour prejudice ever being eradicated. Throughout history it has been a dominant factor here and it does make one question the wisdom of having a single, unwieldy, politically united Republic when a number of smaller independent states would be more manageable from a practical point of view and culturally more realistic. Even in this E.E.C. era no one suggests that Italy and Denmark should be parts of the same nation because they both have a Christian tradition and belong to the same land-mass.

However, I must admit that on the whole I find South Indians far more likeable, outgoing and friendly than North Indians. Just as I find the Tibetans and the Ethiopians far more congenial than certain notoriously pure-blooded European Aryans I could mention.

5 January. Munnar.

In Kumili this morning everybody denied the existence of a Munnar bus so we had to stand shivering for over an hour beside a faded little signpost saying 'Munnar: 110 km.s' and pointing up a steep, rough road not marked on my map.

'Why are we standing here?' asked Rachel, her teeth chattering pathetically. 'The men *said* there was no bus.'

'Don't worry,' I replied confidently. 'There's a bus to everywhere in India if you wait long enough.'

An Indian street-scene is rarely without entertainment-value and to divert us this morning we had the spectacle of some 200 Alleppy pilgrims doing battle for accommodation on three decrepit forty-seater buses. These men had come up from the coast yesterday, to attend a festival at a famous local shrine, and they looked a wild lot. Despite the bitterly cold morning air most were naked from the waist up, with sandalwood ash streaked across their dark torsos, bulky marigold garlands around their necks and bed-rolls slung over their shoulders. On their heads were balanced sacks of Shiva-knows-what, topped by a couple of cooking-pots and another garland. Their struggles to fit the human quart into the pint vehicle were at last successful, as such struggles normally are in India, and with much chanting of prayers, clapping of hands and blaring of horns the three antique buses swayed slowly off to tackle an extremely tricky ghat road.

Our own bus, when eventually it arrived, looked no less decrepit but was not unduly crowded. It was going most of the way to Munnar and took four and a half hours to cover forty miles through the Travancore Hills – Kerala's highest mountains. I was so cold for the first two hours that my numbed hands could not find my handkerchief in my pocket and I was unable fully to appreciate the grandly beautiful ranges we crossed, and the dark, densely forested ravines that sometimes dropped away for 500 feet from the edge of our narrow road.

The surface was so rough and the tyres were so worn that we had two convenient punctures, which allowed us to stretch our legs and admire the view. This is such a thinly populated area (by Kerala standards) that we passed only one town and three large villages – each sporting several pairs of nuns and an array of neatly painted hammers and sickles on the walls of huts and houses.

At one-thirty we were deposited outside a tea-house at a crossroads and told the Munnar bus would come soon. It did, but was so crowded I had to stand and therefore missed the approaches to this enchanting town, which lies in a green bowl of tea-plantations, rimmed by soaring blue mountains – including Anaimudi (8,841 feet), the highest peak in India south of the Himalayas.

As we were extricating ourselves from the bus a slim man about 40 years old, who introduced himself as Joseph Iype, stepped out of the crowd and said we must have tea and biscuits in his electrical equipment shop. Soon we had been invited to spend the night with the Iypes and were being escorted to their bungalow by 11-year-old Chuta, at present on holidays from his Ooty school. We went part of the way by bus, as the Iypes live on a steep, tea-green mountainside some three miles from the town, overlooking the river valley and directly opposite the blue, rounded bulk of Anaimudi. There is a little colony of British-built bungalows here but few British residents remain. Yet the tea-plantations are still British-owned – which is fair enough, as our host remarked, since the British were entirely

responsible for organising the clearing of the jungly mountain-
sides and building the local roads.

English is the Iypes' first language and they are, as our host's
first name indicates, Christians. Their 17-year-old daughter is
in her last year at a Coimbatore boarding-school and Mrs Iype
laughingly admitted it is no coincidence that so many two-child
South Indian families have a five- or six-year gap between children. In this part of the subcontinent there is such a strong
boarding-school tradition that even not-very-well-off middle-
class families send both sons and daughters away at 5 or 6 years
old; and when the adored first-born departs – sometimes to a
distance of several hundred miles – his or her heartbroken
mamma naturally tends to think in terms of a replacement.

Leaving Rachel with Chuta, I set off after tea to walk along
the narrow crest of the 5,000-foot ridge on which these bungalows are built. (Munnar town is at 4,500 feet.) On both sides I
was looking straight down into dizzying depths, with fold after
fold of soft blue mountains fading away into the southern
distance and Anaimudi lying royally against the northern sky,
dominating Munnar's valley – which also holds a swift, tree-
lined river and a cricket-pitch where tiny, darting white dots
were just visible. I wish we could have accepted the Iypes'
generous invitation to spend a few days here, but the Thimmiahs
expect us back on the 10th.

Before dinner the Iypes' closest friend called. He is a most
endearing and prodigiously well-informed Muslim whose wife –
unexpectedly – is an Indian Christian. Recently he started a
toy-factory on the near-by mountainside and to my horror he
presented Rachel with a large, angular, heavy and beautifully
finished wooden truck which will not make life any easier for
the beast of burden over the next few months. Despite our non-
Christmas, Santa somehow managed to function only too
efficiently and I am now carrying, as part of our permanent
equipment, three elephants, two large dolls, one tiger, one
spotted deer, one kangaroo, the dolls' dinner-service and a
sketching-pad accurately described on the cover as 'Monster!'

6 January. Udumalpet.

Today began badly for poor Rachel, who before breakfast
had to have a minute thorn removed from the ball of her right

foot. Overnight it had set up quite a nasty infection and I only hope I got it all out.

I spent the forenoon walking – and climbing a little – in the near-by mountains, while Chuta entertained Rachel. When I set out at eight-thirty an improbable light frost was glittering on the grass but the air soon warmed up and by ten o'clock I was sweating, despite the strong breeze that swept the heights. I hope some day to return to that Idukki District of Kerala, where one could spend weeks happily trekking.

By a pleasing coincidence, Mr Iype and the children were also travelling towards Coimbatore today: otherwise I might never have plumbed the mysteries of the regional bus service. Because of the state of the local roads Munnar is ignored by Kerala's buses and depends on a few privately owned vehicles of infinite whims. Today the Udumalpet bus chose to leave at 2.40 p.m., but tomorrow it may leave at noon, or at dawn. And yesterday it didn't bother to leave at all so its would-be passengers had to hire a truck.

The drive down to the plain, over an 8,000-foot pass, was magnificent – tremendous peaks, densely forested slopes strewn with colossal boulders, deep green valleys noisy with dashing young rivers and a few spectacular waterfalls. Mr Iype had ensured us front seats and as the driver never dared to exceed fifteen miles per hour we had time to appreciate the landscape; yet inevitably I resented being in a motor vehicle.

At the State border we had to endure a forty-minute delay because for some utterly baffling reason an old man was trying to smuggle one live rabbit into Tamil Nadu in a basket of oranges. Having completed our descent to the border by the light of an almost-full moon, the driver went much too quickly for safety over the level road to Udumalpet. It was exactly 8 p.m. when he stopped for our benefit outside the Dak bungalow, so the fifty-four mile journey had taken us five hours and twenty minutes.

We are all sharing the one room that was vacant here, but whereas the Murphys intend to sleep comfortably, stretched out on the floor, the three Iypes have uncomfortably squeezed themselves on to a single bed. I never can understand why most people imagine a bed – some sort of bed: any sort of bed – to be a pre-requisite of sleep.

7 January.   Ootacamund.

On the subject of Ooty I am afraid I disagree with Murray's *Handbook to India*, which observes that 'The astonishing charm of its scenery seems likely to survive modern developments, which include extensive hydro-electric projects, a vast new Government factory for the manufacture of cinema film and a population that now tops 50,000. Its climate has long been famous. As early as 1821, Europeans began to build their homes there.' To my mind, no scenic charm can survive this sort of development.

In 1974 the keynote to the whole Nilgiri region is nostalgia. Around Ooty, in every direction, rise Christian churches of various denominations, and enormous boarding-schools and military barracks, and the innumerable handsome homes of retired Indian Army officers or senior Civil Servants – with neat signposts pointing up steep paths to individual houses and saying 'Col. and Mrs This,' 'Brig. and Mrs That' or 'Mr and Mrs T'other'. During the late afternoon many residents may be seen with the naked eye, wearing heavy overcoats over their saris if female and thick tweeds if male, and carrying shooting-sticks or (inexplicably) umbrellas. Those also carrying dog-eared books are obviously on their way to the palatial Ootacamund Public Library, which stands grandly in its own spacious grounds opposite the main church, St Stephen's. The average age of these senior citizens seems to be eighty and when greeted they usually smile at one a little sadly, a little vaguely. This of course is Ooty's closed season; when the hot weather comes to the plains there will be an enlivening infusion of children and grandchildren.

To me, the library is Ooty's most exciting feature. There are now only ninety-six subscribing members and the wistful, veteran librarian who gave us permission to browse cheered up no end when I went into ecstasies about the fabulous collection of nineteenth-century first editions which just happen to have accumulated on these shelves, where one finds few volumes published after 1939.

Also near St Stephen's are rows of enormous shadowy shops that must have done a roaring trade forty years ago and are still pretending to operate with mainly empty shelves. Their

ancient, dusty owners peer listlessly from unpainted doorways
across the rooftops of the bazaar to the lines of fir-trees on the
highest crest of the Nilgiris. If they lower their eyes to observe a
scruffy white woman and her even scruffier child walking down
the otherwise deserted street they bow obsequiously and I am
overcome by gloom. Then to cheer myself I reflect that, depressing as Ooty is now, it must have been even more so when
infested with mem-sahibs who enjoyed being fawned on by
'niggers'.

Yet I am glad we came here, because of the journey up from
Coimbatore. We left Udumalpet early this morning – still with
the Iypes – and for two-and-a-half hours drove straight across
a densely populated, dull plain where many bullocks were
ploughing poor soil. Then we said good-bye to our friends and
took another bus, heading for the tremendous blue wall of the
Nilgiris. The road soon began to climb gradually through
plantations of palms, which are oddly unattractive when grown
en masse. Then suddenly it was climbing so steeply that within
minutes the air felt chilly and the plain we had just crossed
looked like a view from an aeroplane; no wonder the Nilgiris
were almost deified by the heat-demented British! Again we
had front seats, which gave Rachel a good view of the scores of
half-tame rhesus monkeys who sat by the roadside cheering the
bus on, as it seemed. Every acre of these precipitous slopes is
heavily forested and I have never before seen such an extraordinary variety of gigantic trees.

When at last we emerged on to the grassy, treeless highlands
I could have fancied myself back in the Himalayas had this
whole area not been so built-up. Ooty is at an altitude of 7,440
feet so even at midday, in winter, it is quite cold when one is out
of the sun, and now, at 7 p.m., it is perishing. As we carry no
woollies I have had to wrap both my flea-bag and a blanket
around me. We are staying in what is absurdly called a 'Tourist
Bungalow', run by the Tamil Nadu State Board. In fact it is a
multi-storey hotel, opened in 1963, and it compares very un-
favourably with similar establishments in Kerala. When we
were shown into our Rs.10 single room there was no water
either in the carafe or in the bathroom, the latrine was filthy,
the wardrobe door was broken, the sheets were dirty and there
were revolting stains on the wall over the bed. All these seemed

unnecessary drawbacks in a place that advertises itself far and wide as the 'Ideal Tourist Home', but to give the management its due a brigade of servants appeared within moments of my complaining, to rectify matters.

I am a little worried tonight about Rachel's foot. This afternoon I had to carry her down from Elk Hill – she feels even heavier than usual at over 8,000 feet! – and I don't quite know what to do next. I have a logical distrust of unknown Indian doctors, some of whom buy their degrees without ever opening a medical text-book, so if possible I would prefer to postpone treatment until we get back to Coorg. But at the moment Rachel is tossing and muttering in her sleep, obviously half-conscious of the pain.

8 January.   Gundlipet.

This morning Rachel insisted that her foot felt better, but it looked worse. I was therefore relieved when the bearer who brought our sloppy tray of luke-warm bed-tea told me 'a very smart doctor' was staying in Room 87. Praying that this gentleman's smartness was mental rather than sartorial I carried Rachel to him and he assured me the foot needed only a washing in salted water and a plain gauze dressing. Having given it this treatment I left the patient doing a jig-saw with the doctor's 10-year-old twins and went off on my own to explore.

As one walks through Ooty's less lovely areas a great deal of poverty is evident, and poverty always seems more harrowing in cold weather. Quite apart from the foot complication, I would not have wanted to spend more than twenty-four hours in this tomb of the Raj. But it does have a good Bata shop where I bought strong walking shoes for Rs.25. I also found a small bookshop where imported paperback porn stood shoulder to shoulder with austere tomes on Hindu philosophy and a fat collection of Radhakrishnan essays cost me only Rs.6.

After lunch Rachel limped the two miles to the bus stand without complaining, but despite her cheerfulness I still feel uneasy. Experience has taught me that she is incredibly stoical about personal pain, though she will burst into tears if I accidentally tread on the cat.

The descent to the Mysore plateau was no less beautiful than yesterday's ascent and quite different: India's landscapes are endlessly varied. But by now I really have had a surfeit of just *looking* at the countryside and never coming to grips with it. Beyond Ooty, to the north, stretched mile after mile of open downland with fine plantations of firs and eucalyptus. Then begins the descent, around a series of brilliantly engineered hair-pin bends. As one Indian said to me recently – 'It was worth having the British to stay, if only for the roads they left behind them.' (Had the Indian Empire never existed, who would now be building India's roads? China? Russia? America?) Far below we could see an immense brown plain stretching away to the horizon: Karnataka State's wildlife sanctuary of Bandipur, which is 3,000 feet above sea level.

Bandipur cannot compete with Periyar; most parts are accessible to jeeps and it is a well-organised tourist centre. However, we enjoyed the golden-brown forest and saw a peacock strutting across the road and lots of monkeys, some of whom made Rachel's day by climbing into the cab at octroi posts. We also saw several working elephants going about their Forestry Department business and a mongoose disappearing into the undergrowth.

The sun was setting as we left Bandipur and came to undulating, cultivated land where dark red earth glowed in the hazy golden light and the glossy green of palms, plantains and way-side banyans stood out against a deep blue sky. Then a purple-pink tinge dramatically suffused the whole scene as the sun dropped lower, and its last slanting rays burnished the classical brass water-jars that were being carried across the fields on the heads of slim women in vivid, graceful saris. At such moments the simple, timeless beauty of rural India can be very moving.

It was almost dark when we arrived in this little town and I felt dismayed, though not surprised, to observe Rachel's silent suffering as she hobbled across the road to the nearest doss-house, where there was a vacant cell just inside the street-door. Mercifully, we are due tomorrow at the Hughes's place in Sidapur, to which we were invited when we met Jane and David at Byerley Stud, and I know a good doctor works in the new hospital near Sidapur, which is partly subsidised by South Coorg's coffee-planters.

9 January.   Mylatpur Estate, near Sidapur.

This has been a day I should prefer to forget, though I am
unlikely ever to do so. From midnight neither of us got much
sleep, as poor Rachel tossed and turned and whimpered, and by
dawn her foot was at least twice its normal size. No water was
available in our reeking doss-house wash-room, so I decided it
would be more prudent not to remove the bandage in such
spectacularly unhygienic surroundings but to concentrate on
getting to Sidapur as soon as possible. Accordingly we caught
the seven o'clock bus and arrived at the big village – or tiny
town – of Sidapur at twelve-thirty. The Hughes had explained
that Mylatpur is five miles from the village so I tried to ring
them, but I had no success because the Indian telephone system
is one of the two greatest technological catastrophes of the
twentieth century. (The Irish telephone system is the other one.)
Rachel then volunteered to walk half a mile to a hitch-hiking
point on the outskirts of Sidapur, and though her foot was far
too swollen to fit into her sandal she did just that, hobbling on
her heel. (If V.C.s were awarded to 5-year-old travellers she
would have earned one today.) After standing for only a few
minutes we were picked up by a neighbour of the Hughes, but
we arrived here to find the family gone and my letter announcing the date of our arrival on top of their pile of mail. However,
they were expected back at tea-time and their kindly old bearer
did all he could for us.

I at once put Rachel to soak in a hot bath, boiled a safety-pin
and scissors, punctured the menacing yellow balloon, squeezed
out a mugful of pus, cut away inches of festered dead skin and
was confronted with a truly terrifying mess. Not having the
slightest idea what should be done next, I simply disinfected and
bandaged the wound and at that point Rachel reassured me by
announcing that she was ravenous. She added that her foot
felt fine now, though a bit tender, and having eaten a huge
meal she went to bed at five o'clock and has not stirred since.
(It is now ten-thirty.) But of course she must have medical
attention and Jane has said that first thing in the morning she
will drive us the ten miles to Ammathi Hospital to see Dr Asrani,
a U.S.-trained doctor in whom everybody has complete
confidence.

10 January. Green Hills, near Virajpet.

Everybody is right about the inspired skill of Dr Asrani, but that did not lessen the shock when he said Rachel would have to have a general anaesthetic this afternoon to enable him to probe her foot fully, clean it thoroughly and dress it efficiently. We both still have the residue of our Christmas infection and he admitted he would have preferred not to put her under with a partially stuffed nose: but to do so was the lesser of two evils. At this point my nerve broke, though I regard myself as a reasonably unflappable mother where things medical or surgical are concerned. I hope I maintained an adequately stiff upper-lip, in relation to the general public, but Rachel at once sensed my inner panic and was infected by it. She herself has absolutely no fear of anaesthetics, having twice been operated on in Moorfields Eye Hospital, yet the moment her antennae picked up the maternal fear she went to pieces and a very trying morning was had by all.

As the patient had finished a hearty breakfast at nine o'clock she could not be put under before 2 p.m., so Jane volunteered to take us back to Mylatpur, return us to Ammathi after lunch and arrange to have us collected from there by the Green Hills car. She has been a friend beyond price today and I bless the hour we met her. When she had filled me up with a quick succession of what she called 'Mum's anaesthetic' (rum and lime-juice) I began to feel quite sanguine about Rachel's chances of survival and to marvel at the good fortune that had provided us with such a capable doctor in such an unlikely place.

It is not Dr Asrani's fault that the local anaesthetic techniques are fairly primitive; when it came to the crunch I had to hold Rachel down while a beardless youth clapped a black mask over her face and I begged her to breathe in. No foreign body was found in the wound, nor was it manufacturing any more pus: so I felt secretly rather proud of my do-it-yourself surgery. (Had I not been a writer I would have wished to be a surgeon and I always enjoy opportunities to carve people up in a small way.)

To my relief Dr Asrani did not suggest any form of antibiotic treatment but simply advised me to steep the foot twice a day in very hot salty water, keep it covered with dry gauze and leave the rest to nature. His skill is such that Rachel came to – in an

immensely cheerful and conversational mood – precisely eight
minutes after the bandage had been tied. Half an hour later she
was her normal self again and we set off for Green Hills where
I found, as though to compensate me for the morning's trials, my
first bundle of mail since leaving home. There were ninety-
seven letters, if one includes bills, advertisements, an appeal for
the Lesbians' Liberation Fund and a request for advice about
how to cycle across Antarctica.

12

Ancestor Veneration in Devangeri

11 January. Devangeri.

It is remarkable how easily in Coorg past and present blend together. As we drove this morning to Devangeri, I noticed side by side on the back seat of Dr Chengappa's car a stethoscope and an ancient, heavy dagger for cracking coconuts. Every Friday morning the doctor goes to his Devangeri *Ain Mane* (ancestral home) to honour his forefathers by cracking six coconuts before the sacred brass wall-lamp in the prayer-room and ceremoniously spilling the milk while chanting appropriate *mantras*. Then he returns to his Virajpet clinic to give scores of lucky patients the benefit of his first-rate, up-to-date medical skills: and one is aware of no conflict between his roles as *Karavokara* and as South Coorg's most eminent physician.

Dr Chengappa, one of Tim's oldest friends, is our Devangeri landlord – or rather, our absent host, since no Coorg would accept rent from a stranger. He is tall and handsome, with that air of soldierly authority which marks even those Coorgs who have always been civilians, and he has most generously agreed to let us occupy two rooms in this empty joint-family house four miles north of Virajpet. As soon as I saw the place I knew it was absolutely right for us; Tim has proved himself a man of imaginative understanding by ignoring those who said that foreigners *must* have running water and electricity.

Three miles from Virajpet the narrow road divides beside a small rice mill and, taking the left fork, one continues for another mile until a dirt track branches off to the right. Following this down a slight slope, between low stone walls and tall tamarinds and palm-trees, one soon comes on a wide, neatly swept expanse of pinkish earth in front of an imposing, two-storeyed, brown-tiled house, freshly painted white, with verdigris pillars, balcony-railings and window-surrounds. On the left, as one approaches, are two solidly built granaries; on the right is the well – some eighty feet deep – and beyond it stand three white-washed thatched huts where the Harijan field-labourers live. Moving around to the side entrance, opposite these huts, one sees roomy stone cattle-sheds and two threshing-floors now overlooked by great glowing ricks of rice-straw. And all around, at a little distance, stand majestic trees that must be centuries old – some bearing enormous, cream-coloured waxen blossoms with a powerful scent which fills the air at dusk.

The house faces east, like all Coorg dwellings, so it is quickly warmed after the cool mountain night and never gets too hot during the tropical afternoon. A long paddy-valley stretches away in front – slightly to the left, as one looks out from the main entrance – and is bounded in the distance by high forested ridges. At this season it is a sheet of pale gold stubble on which cattle may unprofitably graze.

Because of the Coorgs' emphasis on ancestor-veneration, their ancestral home is also their main temple. Apart from the compulsory return home for *Huthri* (which applies not only to family members and servants but to any cattle which may be on far-off grazing grounds), the *Ain Mane* is the scene of every important spiritual and social event in the life of a Coorg. Traditional *Ain* houses usually stand on a height, overlooking the family's paddy-fields, and because the majority are invisible from the motor-roads passers-by imagine this countryside to be underpopulated.

The Chengappas' *Ain Mane* was built in 1873 and does not exactly follow the traditional pattern. One steps from the portico into a long, high-ceilinged sitting-room, dominated by portrait photographs of splendidly attired ancestors – all good-looking, proud and keen-eyed. Behind is an even longer but windowless dining-room, containing the sacred wall-lamp, and five doors open out of this room, one of them into the kitchen. At the far end, on the right as one enters from the sitting-room, is a steep double ladder-stair. The right-hand ladder leads to another high-ceilinged room, forty feet by fifteen, which was completely empty when we were escorted upstairs by Dr Chengappa and Tim. It is a most splendid apartment, lit by five tall, wide windows which open inward and have occasional panes of red, green and yellow glass mixed with the 'penny plain' in no particular order. Outside, the slope of the tiled portico roof is directly below and each window is protected by a row of strong perpendicular iron bars. At the far end of the room from the stairs is a most attractive double door, with what looks like a Georgian fanlight imported direct from Dublin. It leads to our bedroom, which has a decrepit bed in one corner, complete with supports for a mosquito-net, and in another corner a pretty little rosewood revolving bookcase containing a complete set of *The Gentleman's Magazine* for 1882. The big arched window also sports several coloured panes – which in Devangeri a century ago must have been the ultimate in status symbols – and the disintegrating cupboard contains numerous bundles of letters addressed to one of the Chengappas and posted in Cambridge in the 1890s. Our ceilings are of wood, our plaster walls have recently been painted a cool shade of turquoise and our earth floors are polished dark red. The whole house is beautifully kept as the family maintains a permanent caretaking staff. At present this consists of a tubercular, pockmarked little man called Subaya, his attractive 18-year-old daughter Shanti and his listless 9-year-old son who is no bigger than Rachel. None of the family speaks English – only Kodagu (the Coorgs' language), Kannada (the Karnataka State language) and some Hindi (which is totally unlike either Kodagu or Kannada and has an entirely different script).

When Tim and Dr Chengappa had departed Subaya furnished our living-room by carrying upstairs a small table, three wooden camp-chairs and two tiny stools (for kitchen furniture). To reach our latrine and wash-room one goes down the ladder, through the kitchen and out to the compound. But fortunately what I have been referring to as 'the kitchen' is really a sort of pantry-cum-dining-room; if it were the true inner sanctum kitchen, where the fire burns and the cooking is done, I could not walk through it without causing a havoc of pollution. The sun-worshipping Coorgs are also, very logically, fire-worshippers, and the kitchen fire is considered sacred. Like the wall-lamp, it is seen as symbolising the power, unity and strength of the family and when a Coorg dies his funeral pyre must be lit with embers from his own kitchen fire.

Here the fire burns in a low mud stove, which has two holes, one behind the other, for saucepans. It is fuelled with long, fairly thin branches which lie on the floor and are pushed farther and farther in as they burn – or are withdrawn, should it be necessary to lower the heat. All this I observed this morning while standing outside the kitchen doorway watching Shanti boiling water to steep Rachel's foot; and since it is not my intention to use the caretakers as servants (even if they would condescend to serve *mlecchas*, which seems doubtful), I immediately realised that because of pollution complications I would have to buy myself a little kerosene stove.

It must be frustrating for Rachel not to be able to race around exploring our new home, but with her usual stoicism she has adjusted uncomplainingly to being a semi-invalid and she did not object to being left alone this morning while I went into Virajpet to shop. Dr Chengappa had given me the local bus times (the bus stop is a mile away, where our road joins the Virajpet road at what is called Mill Point), and I decided to catch the eleven o'clock 'in' and the one o'clock 'out'.

Between our house and Mill Point are two long, low, substantial buildings, standing on their own about a furlong apart. These are Devangeri Middle School and Devangeri High School, the former built about seventy years ago by Dr Chengappa's grandfather, the latter built in 1966 by Dr Chengappa (who paid half the costs) and a group of other Devangeri farmers. The Coorgs have never believed in waiting for some outside authority or central government to provide what they felt they needed; they do it themselves. And you can see this spirit of vigorous independence in the very way they walk and talk and behave.

I did not wait at Mill Point, knowing the bus would stop anywhere to pick me up, but happily no bus appeared. The little road switchbacked through dark green coffee, golden paddy-valleys, grey-brown scrubland and patches of forest. Sometimes I passed a tiled whitewashed house, guarded by plantains and palms, and usually the pale blue mountains were visible, not very far away, against a cobalt sky. Coorg now looks autumnal: the coffee-berries are turning red and in the forest many leaves are tinged pink, yellow, crimson, brown, or orange – though here green always remains the prevailing colour. A fresh breeze blew, a couple of round white clouds drifted south, and the silence was broken only by bird calls and an occasional creaking ox-cart carrying rice to the mill or straw to the market. As I walked along I rejoiced to think that I am no longer merely passing through this glorious region but have become a temporary resident, to whom each curve of the landscape will soon seem familiar.

Virajpet is attractively spread out at the foot of Maletambiran Hill, a prominent mini-mountain visible for miles around. The town's full name is Virajendrapet; it was founded only in 1792, by Dodda Virarajendra, to commemorate the meeting between himself and General Abercromby during the first campaign against Tippu Sultan in 1791.

A disconcerting Gothic-cum-Baroque Roman Catholic church is visible from afar as one approaches Virajpet. Since its foundation the town has had a colony of several thousand Roman Catholics, most of whom speak Tamil, Malayalam or Konkani. At least the Lingarat rajas were not guilty of religious bigotry and when Tippu Sultan began to persecute his Christian subjects these fled to Coorg and were given a free gift of lands. In his correspondence on this subject with Catholic clergy, the Raja always referred to the Bishop of Bombay as 'your High Priest', and under the British the Church lands were registered in the revenue accounts in the name of 'the Chief God of the Christians'.

My kerosene-stove cost me Rs.10; like most Indian factory-made goods it looks very ill-made but may just last for two months. Sugar is rationed and costs the equivalent of 12 pence per kilo, or 22 pence on the black market; this means that only the rich can afford it, even at the legal price. Other prices per kilo are: dahl 15 pence, coffee 45 pence, mutton 60 pence, honey 40 pence, baker's bread 16 pence. Small eggs are 3 pence each (I remember they were half an old penny each in North India ten years ago), ground-nut salad-oil is 45 pence per litre, inferior curds are 4 pence per litre and heavily watered milk is 10 pence per litre – and not always obtainable at this season. Only fresh fruit and vegetables remain relatively cheap – for us, though not for the unfortunate Indians – and a kilo of delicious tomatoes cost me only 2½ pence.

I got home soon after three o'clock feeling very arm-weary: again the expected bus had not appeared. Rachel seemed quite unruffled by having been abandoned for over four hours in strange surroundings; I suspect she becomes so involved in her own affairs of the imagination that she fails to notice time passing. As I scrambled up the ladder she said, 'I like the sounds here' – and I know exactly what she means. Urban sounds merge into a distressing blur of noise, but each rural sound is separate, distinct and comprehensible – the soft trot of cattle-hooves on dust, the tossing of rice on a wicker tray, the crowing of a cock, the squeaking of the pulley as water is raised from the well, the harsh disputes of parakeets, the shouts of men urging oxen around the threshing-floors, the barking of a dog, the grinding of grain in stone hand-mills, the laughter of children, the thud of a coconut falling – and now, as I write this at 8 p.m., the unearthly howling of jackals.

On the way home from Virajpet I met an elderly gentleman with an old-world manner who introduced himself as Mr P. A. Machiah, the husband of a cousin of Dr Chengappa. Later he and his wife called, to make sure we 'lack nothing essential', and I soon realised that we certainly do not lack good neighbours. Mrs Machiah – tall, slim and briskly kind – is such a practised granny that Rachel adored her on sight. She eyed our establishment appraisingly and then said she would lend us a slop-pail, a basin, a jug, a large spoon and two saucepans. I really warmed to this couple, who have invited us to visit them tomorrow. As they were descending the ladder Mr Machiah paused, beamed approvingly up at me and said – 'Anything in excess of what you need is luxury!'

12 January.

I woke at six-thirty to hear an exotic dawn-chorus of jungle-birds and see a silver sky turning blue behind the trees. A thick mist lay on the paddy-valley and moisture was dripping to the ground like slow rain, from the leaves of the immensely tall palms.

Rachel has become much addicted to bed-tea so I got the stove going and for want of a teapot made an excellent brew in a saucepan, tea-house style. At present milk dilution is my only worry. One expects it to be diluted in India, where a variety of desperate governmental anti-dilution measures have merely provided new and better opportunities for bribery and corruption. But if our suppliers, who live on the edge of the compound, are diluting the Murphy half-litre with unboiled water from the well we may soon be in serious trouble because of Rachel's refusal to drink boiled milk. I have assured them I will pay the same for a quarter-litre of neat milk as for a half-litre of milk and water, but I fear the watering habit is too ingrained to be eradicated overnight.

Although I might not choose to live permanently without the modest mod. cons. available in my own home, I do positively enjoy a spell of the simple life; one needs it, to keep in touch with what are still the realities of life for the majority of human beings. It is also worthwhile rediscovering how superfluous, though time-saving, most of our possessions are; and it shocks one to realise how much we waste. Here every banana-skin is eagerly devoured by some bony passing cow, and every discarded sheet of newspaper has a use, and every empty tin, bottle or box is treasured.

Rachel is now able to hobble around our rooms at top speed, but until her wound is healed she must avoid infected dust so she rode piggy-back this morning to visit the Machiahs. We were guided by a little old Harijan woman, with teeth that have been broken and blackened by a lifetime of betel chewing, who lives in our compound. She does errands for anybody who will give her a few paise, and Mrs Machiah had instructed her to show us the way.

Crossing the farmyard behind our house we came to the Devangeri maidan, and then to a rough, dusty, hilly track running west for about two miles through paddy, scrub and forest. It forks at a settlement of substantial Muslim cottages, barns and cattle-shelters – Coorg seems to have no slummy shacks or hovels – and turning right here one descends to a level expanse of stubble, beyond which rises a steep ridge. On this stands the Machiahs' house, surrounded by richly scented rose-bushes, many varieties of flowering shrubs, and papaya, orange and supporta trees draped with black pepper and loofah vines. The Machiahs spent most of their working lives in Bombay, where Mr Machiah was a senior railway official, and I have rarely met a couple who are so zestfully enjoying retirement.

While we sat on the veranda, drinking our *nimbu pane*, Mr Machiah explained the exact significance of the Coorgs' sacred brass wall-lamps. All important family decisions and events must take place before the lamp and agreements made, or loans given or received in its presence, require no signed document or other formality since it is an unforgivable sin to break a promise to which the lamp has been 'witness'. In each household the sacred lamp must be lit morning and evening and it is unlucky to say, 'The lamp has gone out.' Instead, one says 'Make the lamp glow more'. The prayer-room should never be defiled in any way, so when passing through it at Devangeri we must always take off our shoes.

Mrs Machiah invited us to stay for lunch, but I made an excuse about having to go to Virajpet as I hope to establish a casual two-way dropping-in relationship, on the Irish pattern. However, we were sent off laden with sun-warm fruit – a colossal papaya, a hand of bananas and a dozen supportas.

Butter and cheese are virtually unknown here, but we have both become enslaved to the fabulous Coorg honey. It tastes, in truth, like a food of the gods – which is not surprising, given the variety of flowering trees from which the local bees operate.

This afternoon, in Virajpet, an enthusiastic young man in the South Coorg Honey Co-operative told me there are more than 16,000 beekeepers in Coorg, where it is the main cottage industry. But he complained that the average production of honey per hive was only ten to fifteen pounds, compared to almost fifty pounds in the United States. 'Never mind', said I (who knows nothing whatever of sericulture), 'perhaps you can't have both quality and quantity.'

The young man sighed. 'You think not? Then it is better to have quantity and get more money – don't you agree?' And he looked baffled when I replied coldly that I did not.

Already I am being made to feel a part of Devangeri. As I walked home several strangers stopped me to ask how Rachel's foot is today, and how long we are going to stay here, and why I like Coorg so much. The Coorgs seem always ready to stop for a chat, instead of staring suspiciously, as so many Indians do, or turning away to laugh at one behind their hands.

Tonight I have a sore tooth – the penalty for excessive thrift. I bought the cheapest dahl in the bazaar and it was so lavishly adulterated with fine gravel that I am lucky to have any teeth left. Tomorrow I shall present the rest of the dahl to Shanti, who doubtless is more expert than I at the skilled work of unadulterating grain.

13 January.

An uneventful day, full of beauty and contentment. This morning we went for a three-hour walk through the splendidly untouched forest north of Devangeri and – today being Sunday – passed several huntsmen carrying guns and hoping to go home with a deer, a wild boar or at least a rabbit. I had not thought there were any rabbits in India, but the locals assure me there are. Perhaps they were imported to certain regions by the British. As the Coorgs were never bound by the Indian Arms Act they have remained keen *shikaris*, which explains the total absence of monkeys in these forests; unlike most Hindus, the Coorgs do not regard monkeys as sacred animals but as crop-destroying pests and good meals.

The few people we met all wanted to know why I was walking briskly towards nowhere in the heat of the day with a large child on my back. When I explained that I was simply walking for fun, to enjoy the landscape, they plainly either disbelieved me or thought I was at an advanced stage of mental decomposition.

On our way home we came on three *Ain Manes* and, when we investigated these, were of course observed and invited in to drink coffee or *nimbu pane*. A typical *Ain Mane* is approached by a long, narrow, winding lane – an *oni* – cut deep through the reddish soil of a coffee-plantation, with seven-foot-high banks. At the end of this *oni* are substantial red-tiled cattle-sheds and outbuildings – often two centuries old, yet kept in perfect repair – and then comes a paved threshing-yard with a slim stone pillar in the middle and mango and flame-of-the-forest trees around the edge. Half a dozen stone steps lead up from the yard to a long, deep veranda – the *Kayyale* – which is reserved for the elders of the family, who gather there to relax, chat, play cards, confer, drink, arrive at decisions and receive guests. Usually the sturdy wooden veranda pillars are lavishly carved with gods, cows, birds, fish, lizards, snakes, elephants and flowers.

The traditional *Ain Mane* is a handsome, massive, four-winged structure; in far-off days it often served as a fortress, like the Nair houses of Kerala. Half a century ago, before families became so fragmented, it was not uncommon for one

Ain house to shelter seventy or eighty people, perhaps representing five generations, while it was normal to have forty or fifty family members living permanently under one roof. Yet the process of fragmentation began long ago, under the Lingayat Rajas, who feared the power of some of the richer and more enterprising families. These Rajas actively encouraged the establishment of separate homes by Coorgs who had come into property through marriage, or who for some reason had had to leave the ancestral *nad*, and the British presence and the development of coffee plantations accentuated this tendency.

At the first *Ain Mane* we chanced on, our hostess took us indoors to see the general plan of the house. 'Indoors', however, is not quite the right word, for on passing through the heavy, intricately carved main door one is in the *Nadu Mane*, an enormous square hall open to the sky in the centre, where four pillars stand at the corners of a deep depression in the floor – looking not unlike an empty swimming-pool – which is of great importance during wedding ceremonies. Formerly the *Nadu Mane* was used as a dormitory by the young unmarried men of the family, and the kitchen, bedrooms for married couples, guest-rooms, children's rooms and prayer-room all lead off it. Most of the rooms are small, with high, raftered ceilings and beaten earth floors, and though they are kept scrupulously clean their ventilation and lighting are poor.

Each *Ain Mane* has either a *Karona Kala* or a *Kaimata* quite close to the house. The former is a raised earthen platform built around the trunk of a milk-exuding – and therefore revered – tree, and reinforced with stones, rather like the Nepalese porters' resting places. Here, however, such platforms are for ancestor-veneration and the little shrines built on them face east, sun-worship being so closely interwoven with the Coorgs' religious life. The *Kaimatas* seem to be a fairly recent development of these ancient *Karona Kalas*. They are substantial single-roomed 'chapels' dedicated to particular ancestors who died bravely in battle, or otherwise distinguished themselves, and they often contain Islamic-type gravestones though the ancestors in question have usually been cremated and cast upon the waters. Within most *Kaimatas* crudely carved stones represent the ancestors and on all important occasions a little meat curry, rice and Arak are offered to these on a plantain leaf. There is an annual Day of Propitiation, too – known as *Karona Barani* – when special offerings of food and liquor are made. And, not content with all this, some families – like the Chengappas – have evolved their own particular forms of *Karona*-worship, adjusted to the individual characters, noteworthy deeds or possible present needs of their forbears.

We spent the late afternoon sitting in our own backyard, watching the threshers through a haze of golden dust. Nothing could be more primitive than their methods. Each sheaf of paddy is beaten on a long, flat stone, just as a *dhobi* beats clothes, and as the grain falls to the ground it is swept up with a grass broom and shovelled into a sack. Because of the threshing our yard is more populated these days than it normally would be and we are a marvellous added attraction – something like a side-show at a circus. At all hours people wander up to our apartment to observe the odd habits of foreigners: but they never stay long or handle anything – just study us shyly from the top of the ladder.

To add to the charms of Coorg, there are no insects in this house apart from an occasional house-fly. No mosquitoes, no ants, no fleas, bed-bugs, cockroaches, spiders, lice or weird unnameables such as afflicted me in my Nepal home when I wrote – as I do here – by candlelight, near a broken window. Outside, of course, there are various types of large and vicious ants. Probably the red tree-ants inflict the most excruciating bite. I absently sat on some this morning, while resting in the forest, and as a result I now find it very hard to rest anywhere.

14 January.
The fact that I do not recoil from Coorg's curiously anglicised atmosphere must be partly owing to the unusual historical process that brought Coorg under the British. It was never subjected to Government of India laws unless these had been made specifically applicable to it and the Raj, having been invited to stay, wisely adopted a policy of 'Coorg for the Coorgs' and gave most of the subordinate jobs in the Government Service to the scions of old Coorg families. (The senior posts were

of course never open to Indians, however able they might be.)
Thus the local British ghost is quite unlike the spirit that lingers
in Ooty or Simla, though during the second-half of the nine-
teenth century the Coorgs enthusiastically adopted the English
educational system – not to mention hockey, cricket and whisky.

In the November 1922 issue of *Blackwoods*, Hilton Brown, an
I.C.S. officer, wrote: 'There is just one disconcerting feature
about the Coorgs – their ready willingness to be dominated by
the outsider . . . The Coorg's profession is all to the contrary, but
the fact remains . . . It is very puzzling, for it is just what one
would *not* expect . . . The Coorg can think for himself, and he
ought to; but very often he won't.' I wonder, however, if Mr
Brown was altogether right. It is arguable that the Coorgs have
a history of being dominated by outsiders not because of any
innate tendency to submit but because they have never been
able to unite effectively for the good of their country. Up to the
beginning of the seventeenth century this tiny region was never
ruled by any one dynasty but by numerous princelings and
chieftains owing allegiance to bigger outside powers.

My old friend the *Gazetteer* emphasises the benefits conferred
on Coorg by the Raj, yet during the restless 1920s the Coorg
Landholders' Association was formed to demand – unsuccessfully – a greater share in the running of the province. Then in
1940, as part of a Government economy campaign, Coorg
became 'a self-sufficient unit with all the offices located within
its territory and was governed by a full-time Chief Commissioner'.

So the scene was set for much post-Independence political
agitation in a province where the powerful Coorg minority
wished their land to remain 'a self-sufficient unit', while many
of the less influential non-Coorg majority favoured a merger
with Mysore (now Karnataka) State. From March 1952 until
November 1956 the province had what was known as a 'Popular
Government' with a two-man ministry; but 'popular' proved a
very inappropriate adjective and by 1956 many previously
staunch separatists had become so disillusioned by the inefficiency and corruption of their own Coorg politicians that
they, too, advised a merger.

However, most Coorgs still bitterly resent their loss of
independence; walking into Virajpet this morning I met no

less than three men who made a point of telling me what a fine place this once was, when not being manipulated by the bureaucrats of Karnataka for their own ends. One middle-aged man, clad in patched pants and a threadbare shirt, gloomily quoted Abraham Lincoln – 'You cannot strengthen the weak by weakening the strong.' I do not know how real local grievances are, but one does see many signs of a recent decline in the region's traditional level of prosperity. For seventeen years the State government has been siphoning off, through taxation, a considerable proportion of Coorg's income and the Coorgs argue that it is grossly unjust to expect them to prop up the less fortunate areas of Karnataka. At first glance this reluctance to share their wealth seems ungenerous, but at second glance one realises that Lincoln was right. Applied to the vastness of Karnataka State that stream of wealth which would suffice to keep Coorg happy and healthy makes little impression, while its deflection from Coorg has already had perceptible ill-effects.

One is very aware, here in Devangeri, of witnessing a society in transition. This evening Dr Chengappa arrived with his 18-year-old daughter whose duty it was, as the eldest maiden in the family, to initiate the storing of this year's crop by carrying a basket of paddy on her head from the threshing-yard to the granary. She is an extremely sophisticated young woman who speaks faultless English and, as I sat on a window ledge, looking down at that elegant figure ceremoniously crossing the compound with its unaccustomed burden, I wondered if her daughter will in time do likewise, or if she represents the last generation of tradition-observing Coorgs.

15 January.

We lunched with the Machiahs today and on arrival found Mr Machiah sewing up big sacks of paddy to be sent to his three married sons in Bombay. One daughter-in-law is a Cochin Christian, but the Machiahs seem as fond of her as of the two Coorg girls whom they themselves chose. Although the Coorgs are so proud of being a race apart, they are more socially flexible than most Indians. No doubt they are secretly saddened when their children marry non-Coorgs, but the majority warmly welcome outsiders into their little community. Such marriages are now becoming much commoner and there is a danger that eventually the 80,000 or so Coorgs may lose their identity amidst India's hundreds of millions.

We had a delicious lunch, cooked by Mrs Machiah, and everything on the table was home-produced: steamed rice, fried chicken, cabbage so cunningly cooked it bore not the slightest resemblance to what we call boiled cabbage, egg and tomato salad, rice bread, crisp, subtly flavoured potato-cakes (these specially prepared to honour the Irish), fruit salad and coffee. Unlike most South Indians, the meat-eating Coorgs do not care for very hot foods and are such good cooks that I foresee my middle-aged spread getting altogether out of control here.

To my annoyance – and to the great glee of all onlookers – the antique well in the compound utterly defeats me so someone else must fill my bucket and keep the great earthen water-pot in the latrine topped up. Because of caste laws, this is a slightly complicated situation. No Harijan can draw water from our well, and no non-Harijan will enter our latrine. So I myself have to top up the latrine container with water drawn by Subaya or Shanti, poured by them into the large brass wash-room jar, and transferred by me into the latrine container. It would be only too easy unwittingly to do something dreadfully polluting – like borrowing a cooking vessel from the kitchen – which would involve the family in an elaborate and expensive purification ceremony. One is therefore permanently on the alert, watching out for disapproving glances.

16 January.

I realised today that I have not yet adequately described Devangeri. It is a typical Coorg non-village, consisting of our house – the manor, as it were – the two schools already mentioned and a few score homesteads and thatched labourers' cottages, scattered over an area of two or three square miles. Behind our house is a long, two-storeyed building with an outside stairs at one gable-end leading up to the local Co-opera-tive Society's offices and storerooms. The ground floor of this building accommodates the tiny post office – which opens only for brief periods at irregular intervals – and the village tailor's workshop, and a mini tea-house where card-players gather, and a twilit general store too small to hold more than one customer at a time. Anybody who happens to be expecting a letter saunters along to collect it during the forenoon, or sends a servant to fetch it, and so far I have heard no complaints though the battered and rusted metal box to which one entrusts outgoing mail has been *in situ* since the reign of Queen Victoria. I buy my kerosene (a litre in an Arak bottle for 1 rupee) from the store: but nothing else, as village hucksters charge at least 20 per cent more than bazaar merchants, and adulterate even such unlikely things as soap and candles – which have probably been adulterated once already, before leaving their respective factories.

At a little distance from the Co-operative building, on the edge of the forest, stands our 'local', a ramshackle cottage from which Subaya every morning procures my breakfast litre of palm-toddy – in another Arak bottle – for 50 paise. (Where else, nowadays, could one buy a litre of beer for 2½ pence?) This potation is taken from the toddy-palm at dawn, in an earthenware pot that was attached to the top of the tree by a tapper the previous evening, and it arrives in our room fermenting on the wing, as you might say, with numerous dead ants almost blocking the neck of the bottle. If one neglects to drink it within a few hours it is said to do terrible things to the innards, so at last I have an excuse for drinking beer with my breakfast. It is most refreshing, whitish in colour and with a low yet perceptible alcohol content. The Coorgs think it so health-giving that even elderly female pillars of respectability habitually have a glass (but not, admittedly, a litre) before breakfast.

At all hours of the day, Devangeri's alcoholics may be seen sitting on benches outside the local, clutching tumblers of neat, potentially lethal, home-distilled Arak. According to sacred Hindu laws the drinking of alcohol is a most grievous sin, for which the orthodox atonement is suicide by drinking boiling spirits – though it seems unlikely that anyone impious enough deliberately to drink alcohol would afterwards feel remorseful enough to take his own life. At all events, the Coorgs have never heeded this prohibition and excessive drinking is undoubtedly their worst collective fault. Often men stagger home at lunchtime, unable to keep upright without assistance, and local reactions to this spectacle remind me very much of Ireland. People are mildly amused, or affectionately chiding, or ribaldly witty, or occasionally slightly impatient – but never critical. (Except of course for the more responsible members of the community, who think about the drunkard's wife and children.)

I was diverted this evening by the section on Prohibition in the 1965 *Coorg Gazetteer*. Passages are worth quoting: and the reader should bear in mind that the Prohibition Laws have since been allowed to fall into disuse. 'It has been laid down in the Constitution as a directive principle of State policy, that the State shall endeavour to bring about Prohibition of the consumption – except for medical purposes – of intoxicating drinks and drugs which are injurious to health. Drink has generally been responsible for the poverty and misery of man, sinking him lower and lower into depths of danger and despair. There is no gainsaying the fact that prohibition is a social as well as an economic necessity and it acts as the fulcrum and force in our economic programme for social amelioration. ... Though prohibition was formally inaugurated on the 2nd April 1956, effective enforcement began only on 25th April 1956, leaving reasonable time for consumers to adjust themselves to the new circumstances ...' [And to make Other Arrangements] '... Permits for possession and consumption of liquor were issued only in exceptional cases; they were issued to (i) those who were accustomed to take liquor, (ii) non-proprietary clubs for sale to such of their members as held permits and (iii) the church authorities for sacramental purposes ... Government have sustained a loss of about twelve lakhs of rupees annually, consequent on the introduction of prohibition in the district ... As is to be expected, illicit distillation followed in the wake of prohibition ... The incidence of illicit distillery cases was high in the year 1962, 1,846 cases [in tiny Coorg!] having been detected during that year.

'The introduction of prohibition has already brought a change in the social outlook of the people who were once accustomed to drink. It has brought peace to their homes and enabled them to save money, pay old debts, purchase new clothes, eat better food and lead healthier lives ... The general feeling among the public, however, remained that ... the prohibition law was contravened on a large scale and the percentage of convictions was very low ... it has to be admitted that the number of permits issued appears to be large. Action is being taken to restrict the number, only to deserving cases.'

But alas! for the prohibitionists, those 'deserving cases' soon came to form the majority of the population of Coorg, and eventually the whole dotty though well-meaning experiment was tacitly acknowledged to be no more than a breeding ground for bribery and corruption. I daresay something similar would happen if anybody tried to enforce prohibition in Ireland.

Reverting to the Hindu sacred law on alcohol: for years I have wondered why it was so fanatical (by any reckoning, suicide as an atonement is going a bit far), and at Cape Comorin I got a plausible explanation from a splendid old Brahman scholar with whom we watched the sunset. It seems that when the Aryans arrived in India they were confirmed *soma* addicts, and because they assumed their gods must also enjoy this psychedelic drink they decently fixed them a *soma* whenever they made a ritual sacrifice. By the end of the Vedic period *soma* drinking had come to dominate their religious ceremonies and the severity of the anti-alcohol laws was part of a successful attempt to have harmless rhubarb juice substituted for the juice of the extremely dangerous hallucinogenic red-capped mushroom, which is now accepted by most experts as the source of *soma*. Neat *soma* is a deadly poison, but blended with honey, milk and water it becomes palatable. Its addicts were evidently not too fussy about flavour since laymen commonly collected for their own consumption the urine of *soma*-drinking priests.

Virajpet's post office is the oldest such establishment in Coorg – and looks it. This morning, when I patronised it for the first time, a clerk became excessively agitated at the prospect of having to register four air-mail letters to Ireland, and the unruly behaviour of the crowd around me did nothing to help him regain his composure. It had taken me fifteen minutes to establish myself in a position of negotiation, to the forefront of this crowd, and in order to retain my advantage I had to grip the shelf in front of me very firmly: otherwise I would have been pushed beyond reach and sight of the clerk. Meanwhile he, poor man – looking not unlike a harassed rabbit, behind his wire netting – had to thumb through two grimy volumes, and do intricate calculations on blotting-pads, to enable him to arrive at some plausible conclusion about my letters. While he thus did his duty several of the rowdier members of the crowd yelled abuse at him and demanded to be given 15 paise stamps *at once*. It was easy to see how their minds were working. *They* only wanted one stamp each, for which they were clutching the right number of coins in their fists, whereas *I* wanted to transact an infinitely complicated piece of business which might take hours. (In fact it took precisely forty-three minutes.) To placate them the clerk at intervals pushed a few fifteen paise stamps across the shelf, which naturally encouraged another importunate scrum to form around me. There must have been at least fifty jostling, shouting men on that veranda when suddenly one tall, elderly Coorg appeared and said a few sharp words. Intantly the crowd fell back and was silent, not advancing again until I had finished my business. I do not know who this gentleman was, but there could be no more striking example of the Coorg community – minority though it is – or of the enduringly feudal structure of Coorg society.

17 January.

This morning Rachel suddenly announced 'I think I'll be able to walk properly today' – which she was, though wearing only a sock over the thick bandage on her injured foot.

After lunch we went to the Machiahs in quest of eggs, Mrs Machiah having agreed to become our supplier. But today there were none because during the past few nights a mongoose and a jackal have between them decimated the hen population. Early this morning Mr Machiah shot the jackal and gave it to a local outcaste eccentric who relishes jackal flesh – a rare taste, even among outcastes. It is less easy to eliminate a mongoose, and anyway these pretty little creatures kill so many snakes and rats that they deserve an occasional banquet of chicken. We saw one this afternoon, racing across the path near the Machiahs' house. The culprit, no doubt.

Today's domestic excitement was the purchase of twenty large sardines for 1 rupee. I bought them from a ragged youth found sitting on the back doorstep and unmistakably they were fresh, but had I known the wretched things would take an hour and forty minutes to clean I might have felt less enthusiastic. The minute scales proved extremely adhesive, first to their owners and then to everything in the kitchen corner of our living-room. Also, if not gutted very delicately they went to pieces in me 'and, and their multitudinous fins required no less skilful treatment. By the end of that session I had had the simple life and could entirely see the point of buying tinned sardines.

On the whole, however, I am enormously enjoying the rhythm of these Devangeri days. Nothing much happens here, or is ever likely to happen, and if one did not have a lot of reading and writing to do one would no doubt feel bored; but I consider it the ideal life. When I hear Subaya locking up after sunset, and going off to wherever he and his family sleep, I reflect that now it's just the Murphys and the Chengappa ancestors in residence. And if one can go by the 'feeling' of this whole huge silent house, lit only by the two candles flickering on my table, those ancestors are most amiable and welcoming. I am totally unpsychic, and not abnormally suggestible, but in a most curious and pleasing way I am aware of not being quite alone here. The house is companionable: let us leave it at that.

19 January.

This afternoon Mrs Machiah took us to meet cousins of hers who live just up the road but have been away during the past few weeks. The family consists of Lieutenant-Colonel (Rtd., and for some years past a coffee-planter) and Mrs Ayyappa, their 20-year-old daughter Shirley and a 14-year-old son now at school in Ooty. The new Ayyappa bungalow – very handsome, with teak floors and rosewood ceilings – stands beside their old *Ain Mane* but on a lower level, since no dwelling must overshadow the ancestral home. Mrs Ayyappa is a fanatical gardener who has created – starting from bare ground – what can only be described as a mini-Kew. Both she and Shirley are rather shy and very gentle and we are invited to drop in whenever we feel like it.

As we drank our coffee the talk was of inflation, civil disorder, food-adulteration and the oil-crisis. Colonel Ayyappa showed me a paragraph in today's *Deccan Herald*, where India's Defence Minister, Jagjivan Ram, is quoted as having said, 'The Indian

Penal Code provides the death penalty for murder by physical force or weapons, but those who kill people by adulterating medicines or food go practically untouched. Yet the gravity of the crime is far greater in the latter case and warrants a proportionate penalty.' Makes one think, as one goes forth into the bazaar with one's shopping basket. My only real fear is powdered glass in the sugar – a not unusual phenomenon, since some merchants think nothing of poisoning customers if they can thereby rake in a few extra rupees. Several (Hindu) friends have strongly advised me to buy only from Moplah (Muslim) merchants in Virajpet.

This evening, as I read Rachel's bedtime stories – from *The Heroes* and *The Arabian Nights* – it struck me that in future such stories are going to seem much more real to her. Grinding the day's supply of flour, drawing water from the well, going into the forest to collect firewood to cook the evening meal, fetching bales of cloth home from the bazaar on one's head, yoking the oxen, shaping and firing bricks to build a new home, hunting for meat, trimming the lamps at sunset, making offerings to the gods – all these are commonplace activities here, though weirder than space travel to Western children of the Technological Age.

13

Caste in Coorg

21 January.

Last night I came across a remark made in a letter home by a newly arrived ambassador to India. 'No one,' he wrote, 'is allowed to marry outside his own caste or exercise any calling or art except his own.' That ambassador was the famous Megasthenes, whom Seleucus appointed some 2,300 years ago as his envoy to the Mauryan court of Chandragupta, and I thought of him again this afternoon when Rachel appeared at the top of our ladder in bewildered tears, sobbing that Subaya was very angry because she had been trying to persuade her Harijan friends to come upstairs to play with her toys.

Rachel is not easily reduced to tears so I can only suppose she had been frightened by something she could not understand – Subaya's outraged fury at the very thought of Untouchable children putting a foot over this threshold – and hurt by what, from her point of view, was the injustice of his reprimand. She has, after all, been brought up to invite anyone she likes into her own home, and I should have warned her that in India things are different.

In Indian cities, a foreigner might now live for weeks amongst Westernised Hindus without realising there was such a thing as a caste-system; yet one cannot live for twelve hours in rural India without having to accommodate it, and in the cities it has merely been modified – not abolished. Few 'twice-born' Hindus – however Westernised, atheistic, socialistic or liberal they may profess to be – would feel completely at ease sitting in a bus beside a latrine-cleaner.

As aggrieved Sahibs used to point out, when accused of maintaining a colour-bar, the inter-racial barriers in India were first erected by Hindus. (Though it is true the British did eventually become as socially exclusive, in their way, as any Brahman.) What I tried to convey to Rachel today is the strange fact that the majority of Hindus value the caste system just as much as we in the West now value the ideal of social equality. It is not an affliction they helplessly endure but an institution which gives an essential cohesion to their unique and otherwise disparate society. Hence the declaring illegal of Untouchability by the Indian Constitution can at present be little more than a formal salute to an alien concept. Many criticised Gandhi's singling out of Untouchability for abolition, leaving the rest of the caste structure intact, but the Mahatma well knew that the caste system could not exist without a foundation of Untouchables to take upon themselves those impurities which otherwise would pollute the whole of society.

Although Hinduism is renowned for its ability to absorb outside influences, and change them more than it is changed by them, it may now have reached a crisis point at which its genius for assimilation can no longer operate. Richard Lannoy has suggested 'institutionalized inequality' as one definition of the caste system and it is hard to see how the official Indian government policy of social equality can either be absorbed into Hinduism or democratically imposed on hundreds of millions of citizens to whom it is repugnant. Something, it would seem, has to give – and this time it may be Hinduism. But not yet.

At present – especially in South India – a man's caste, rather than his personal talents, determines the degree of political power he can obtain: and this is having a disastrous effect on the national morale. India's parliamentary democracy has of course given the uneducated but numerically more influential sub-castes an unprecedented opportunity to dominate their local scene; yet this opportunity is often wasted because caste still matters more than the interests or opinions of the individual voter.

Gandhi, among many others, argued that those verses from Hindu scripture commonly quoted in support of Untouchability were interpolations or misrepresentations – which is probably true, since one can hardly imagine any religious scriptures, however primitive, prescribing the degradation and exploitation of millions. But it is too late now to oppose the day-to-day working of the caste system with academic arguments. Our neighbours here in Devangeri are not concerned about Vedic authority, or about the compromises that may have been arrived at 3 millennia ago between Aryan kings and Harappan high priests. What matters to them is the magico-religious code they have learnt at their mothers' knees. This includes the lessons that faecal pollution is a spiritual and social calamity of the first magnitude, as is the slightest physical contact with a menstruating woman or an outcaste. And the Harijan child is taught, equally emphatically, to avoid contact with caste Hindus. Many Indian mothers habitually threaten their children with witches, ghosts and demons, or with Kali, the black goddess of destruction – or with pollution by an Untouchable, which is thus equated from infancy with the worst horrors imaginable.

Throughout history a basic fear of pollution has affected many peoples, though none so radically as the Hindus. And, since it is impossible even to try to understand the caste system without taking it into account, I must make the point that Hindu notions of pollution are not bounded by the laws of hygiene. Impurity is naturally associated with physical dirt, but there is much more to it than that – as may be seen from Mary Douglas's comments on the system underlying pollution rules:* 'Defilement is never an isolated event. It cannot occur except in view of a systematic ordering of ideas. Hence any piecemeal interpretation of the pollution rules of another culture is bound to fail. For the only way in which pollution ideas make sense is in reference to a total structure of thought whose keystone, boundaries, margins and internal lines are held in relation by rituals of separation.' I have been fascinated to discover that Mrs Douglas uses the Coorgs as a typical example of 'corporate caste dread', despite their own frequent and vigorous affirmations that caste taboos matter less to them than to most Hindus. Perhaps the gentlemen do protest too much . . .

Hindus agree with Juvenal on the desirability of *mens sana in corpore sano*, but popular Hindu theories about how to keep a body sound range from the comic to the tragic. There is a widespread belief that semen should be conserved because it is the vital essence of the individual man, which is made in the head, from blood, and sustains both physical and spiritual health while it is stored there. This nonsense must have led to even more tension and domestic unhappiness than the Roman Catholic Church's traditional teachings on sexual morality. It has also

* *Purity and Danger*: Routledge and Kegan Paul (1966).

helped to lower the status of women, who are supposed to be much more lustful than men and are regarded as an ever-present threat to their husbands' general well-being. Many Hindus believe that sexually unsatisfied women become witches and revenge themselves in the most horrific ways on the whole male population. So it takes a brave as well as a self-controlled man to practise continence; and the birth-rate figures indicate that such men are scarce.

These curious biological misconceptions are also responsible for the obsessional attitudes of orthodox twice-born Hindus towards what and where they eat. Since the blood from which semen is made is itself manufactured out of the food one eats, any pollution reaching the stomach through the mouth will contaminate a man's vital essence.

All this might seem to indicate that 'institutionalized inequality' could be relatively easily abolished by some elementary scientific education. I have, however, mentioned only one of the caste system's many facets, and it is not hard to find Hindu doctors and scientists of repute who are as rigid about certain fundamental taboos as any unlettered peasant. They will not dread their wives turning into witches, but neither will they admit Untouchables into their homes. Also of course there are by now many educated Hindus who in most respects ignore the caste and pollution laws, but they represent only a tiny minority.

This afternoon, when I had soothed Rachel and done my best to soothe a still furiously muttering Subaya, I sat in the sun outside the back door while trimming beans for our supper. Rachel brought her toys out to the compound, in lieu of her Harijan friends coming upstairs, and after some time one of the little boys approached the back door and called to Subaya's small son, asking for a drink of water. This was at once provided, in a brass drinking vessel, and the little caste boy directed the little outcaste boy to pick half a coconut-shell off the dusty ground and hold it out to be filled. When the water had been drunk the Harijan – who is 6 years old – took the shell to the edge of the compound and carefully threw it into some undergrowth where it could pollute nobody. Clearly these two boys are good friends within the limits imposed by caste – limits which both have recognised and accepted from the age of two or three.

It is when one moves up in the social scale that the contemporary caste situation becomes somewhat confused, because of individuals or families being at various subtly graded stages of 'liberation'. The Machiahs, for instance, after a lifetime in Bombay, are far less pollution-conscious than most stay-at-home Coorgs. They allow their Harijan neighbours to use their well – an enormous concession – and even employ some of them in the house, though not in the kitchen. Yet I found the unpredictability of caste attitudes well illustrated the other day by Mrs Machiah, when she and Rachel and I were walking back from the Ayyappas' house. Ahead of us on the road Rachel saw one of her favourite playmates – an enchanting 5-year-old Harijan girl, who admittedly is always filthy – and immediately she ran to her and slipped an arm through hers. Away they went, skipping together in a continuation of some game started that morning, and I turned to Mrs Machiah, about to remark on the little girl's charm. But my companion's expression silenced me. She called Rachel, and I hesitated, caught between the devil of offending our friend's susceptibilities and the deep blue sea of allowing my daughter to be polluted by caste-consciousness. Then, before I had resolved my dilemma, came the final twist to the situation. Suddenly the little girl's mother appeared out of the forest, with a load of firewood on her head, and shrieked angrily at her child not to touch the *mleccha*. Why? Surely even the most uninformed Harijan is aware that *mlecchas* have no place – do not count, even as outcastes – in the world of caste? (A fact which of itself can give the foreigner in India a strange, underlying feeling of spiritual isolation.)

I longed to ask Mrs Machiah about this but the whole subject of Untouchability is such a delicate one that it has to be approached – if at all – with great tact; and the moment did not seem auspicious. Most educated Indians are now hypersensitive on caste issues, not necessarily because they themselves are ashamed of the institution but because they fancy all foreigners despise it. Often an Indian will – with good reason – accuse a foreigner of over-simplifying and misinterpreting caste, and will then himself add fuel to the fire of misinterpretation by asking defensively 'Don't you have your caste system? But you call it *class*! Where do you send your children to school? Who would you like them to marry? Who do you invite to have meals in your house? What part of your town do you live in?'

At first one is stumped by this, yet the similarity is slight between our constantly changing social classes and the completely segregated units which make up Indian society. The Portuguese saw this at a glance, when they arrived in India in the sixteenth century, and it was they who provided the word *castas* (derived from the Latin *castus*) to describe the intricate network of innumerable *jatis* (sub-castes) into which Hindu society had evolved by about the sixth century B.C.

It is most misleading to refer to 'the four castes'; life in India would be very different if each of its 454 million Hindus belonged to one of only four groups. What really counts is one's *jati* (the word means 'birth'), which is determined by specialised, hereditary occupation, and it does not at all follow that because two people belong to the same main caste or *varna* they can marry, or eat together. *Varna* – the Sanskrit word for caste – literally means 'colour', and even today an ugly, ill-made, fair-skinned Indian will be regarded as incomparably better-looking than someone who is handsome and well-built, but dark-skinned.

There is an obvious parallel between the situation and behaviour of the Aryans, when newly arrived in India, and that of the Europeans in South Africa today. India's Aryan conquerors were divided into three rudimentary, non-hereditary social classes – warriors, priests and common people – and were free of any taboos about intermarriage or eating together. But they were a tiny minority amongst the conquered Dasa, those indigenous, dark-skinned, flat-featured owners and cultivators of the land. (The word *dasa* later came to mean 'slave', which sufficiently explains the fate of these people.) Therefore, the instinct to preserve racial identity being very powerful, they made rigid laws – almost exactly copied by the white South Africans – forbidding inter-racial marriage and enforcing segregation. Much interbreeding of course took place before the caste system was developed enough to make such a thing psychologically impossible. But those of mixed blood were firmly consigned, with the Dasas, to the fourth caste (the *shudras*) who could never take part in Vedic rituals but were left to worship their own primitive, animistic spirits – which they still do, all over India.

22 January.

Today we went by bus to Mercara, to borrow books from the public library, and the twenty-six mile journey took two-and-a-quarter hours. Sitting beside us was a Devangeri neighbour, a slim, trim little man who has recently retired from the Civil Service and come back to his *Ain Mane.* He told me that oranges are the third most important crop in Coorg, after rice and coffee, and that the sweet, loose-skinned Coorg mandarins are famous throughout South India. But it seems the Coorg farmers – whose traditional rice cultivation methods are so scientific – do not make efficient orange growers. The main season is from December to March and most of the crop is transported by truck to Mysore, Bangalore and other cities. Pepper, he said, is another important side-line; it requires a lot of care, and the picking of the pods is a delicate and laborious business, but because of its value as a dollar earner this crop is being officially encouraged. (Coorg's annual output during the 1960s was about 120 tons – a lot of pepper.) Cardamom, too, earns dollars; it grows wild in the evergreen forest along the Ghats and government loans are available to farmers who wish to start plantations.

Mercara, when we first saw it, seemed an enchanting little backwater. But this morning, when we arrived fresh from our forest retreat, I felt myself in a bustling metropolis. To our great delight we met a party of elderly Tibetans from Bylekuppa, who had come up on one of their regular trading trips, and we all lunched together at the bus-stand restaurant. I had intended entertaining them, but to my discomfiture the charming old man who seemed to be their leader was adamant that the *ferenghis* should be his guests.

We returned to Mill Point on the same bus with the same crew and I noticed that as a temporary 'local' I am not being asked to pay for Rachel. This time the journey took three hours because during the threshing season every travelling Coorg is accompanied by sacks of paddy. The rich move it by car or jeep (a distant jeep overloaded with sacks looks strangely like some prehistoric beast lumbering across the landscape), but the less rich move it by bus. And if half a dozen passengers are waiting every few miles with a few sacks each, and if all those sacks have to be carefully secured to the roof, and equally carefully handed down four or five miles farther on – well then naturally it takes three hours to cover twenty-six miles.

26 January.

India's Republic Day – and I think of ten years ago, when I attended the superbly organised triumphal parade in New Delhi, and watched Pandit Nehru and Lord Mountbatten drive down Rajpath four months before the Prime Minister's death. Today felt very different. All over India the celebrations were either cancelled or drastically curtailed, in deference to the world oil-crisis and the domestic economic crisis, which has led to police killing many food shop looters in states where millions are starving, resentful and violence-prone. On Monday next most Kerala schools and colleges are to be given a holiday because organised mass-opposition to the Government's food policy is planned for that day and could lead to further serious rioting – and deaths.

Republic Day has made no impression on Devangeri, apart from the formal ceremony at the local school to which Rachel and I were invited. To my intense alarm I found that I was expected not only to hoist the National flag at the opening of the ceremony but to make a speech. Rachel, however, was thrilled – especially when I at last got hold of the right bit of rope and, as the flag unfurled, she saw a shower of multi-coloured forest blossoms fluttering down to cover my head and shoulders.

I felt quite exhausted after my efforts to communicate with the young teachers, none of whom is fit to teach English. Yet this is one of the three languages which Devangeri school-children have to go through the motions of learning. (The others are Hindi and Kannada.)

India's linguistic problems seem almost as complicated as the caste question and a good deal more controversial. According to the 'Three Language Formula', approved in 1961 by a con-ference of Chief Ministers from India's various states, school-children in non-Hindi-speaking areas have to learn Hindi as well as their mother tongue and English. There are over 133 million Hindi-speakers, so more Indians speak this language than any other. Yet in a population of 560 millions it cannot be described as the language of the majority, as is frequently pointed out by the 37 million Bengali-speakers, the 30 million Tamil-speakers, the 17 million Malayalam-speakers, the 17 million Kannada-speakers, the 15 million Oriya-speakers, the 10 million Punjabi-speakers – and so on, and on, and on, down to the 142,003 Bhumji-speakers and the 109,401 Parji-speakers.

The 1971 Census showed that since 1951 the literacy rate has gone up from 16·6 per cent to 29·45 per cent. However, with only 39·45 per cent of men and 18·70 per cent of women literate at present, in any language, it would seem rather too soon to attempt to teach Indian school-children three languages, each with a different script.

The nineteen-point official programme for the 'propagation, development and enrichment of Hindi' seems utterly artificial – another, self-imposed, cross for India to bear. South Indians naturally wish the funds and energies now being expended on Hindi could be diverted to providing free primary education in those areas where it is not yet available, or to expanding the well-planned Farmers' Functional Literacy Programme, which has already made some 80,000 adult farmers more accessible to advice on how to increase food production.

The status of the English language provokes a more complex set of arguments, though the two controversies overlap when opponents of Hindi affirm that English – or 'Indish', as Indianised English is often called – is the obvious *lingua franca* for India. An increasing number of educated Indians long to reclaim their own culture and do not believe this can be done while India's intellectual life is dominated by an English-speaking, English-reading and therefore English-*thinking* élite. For centuries Indian culture – apart from music and the dance – has been moribund, submerged first by the Mughals and then by that tidal wave of anglicisation which inundated the land as a result of Thomas Babington Macaulay's historic 'Minute' of 2 February 1835.

Macaulay envisaged 'a class of people who can act as inter-mediaries between us and the millions we govern: English in taste, in opinions, in morals, and in intellect' – and quite soon India had got what Macaulay wanted. The then Governor-General, Lord William Bentinck, had himself referred six years earlier to 'the British language, the key to all improvements'; and on 7 March 1835, with the support of Macaulay and Ram

Mohan Roy, leader of the more progressive Bengali intellec-
tuals, he made English the official language of the subcontinent – instead of Persian, the language of the Mughal court.

Since then, speaking English and sending children to English-
medium schools has acquired an absurd snob-value. Those who
have the means and leisure to practise the arts themselves, or
to support creative Indians in practical ways, now too often
feel it necessary to despise their own culture. Also, educational
aims have become confused, with students attaching greater
significance to the English language, as such, than to those
subjects they are supposed to be mastering through the medium
of English. More important still, the fact that so many of the
governing classes live in a cultural world apart means they
tend to take an unreal view of India's basic problems.

In 1971 the Simla Congress of Indian Writers declared, 'The
inescapable reality is that English continues to be the only
expedient language throughout India.' This is very true, but
what does seem necessary is an admission that it must remain a
minority language – though this would involve switching to
Indian languages in the universities. At present 11 million, or
2 per cent of the population, are described as 'English-knowing',
but I have been warned that there is a sinister difference between 'English-knowing' and 'English-speaking'. The former
applies to those who appear in the statistics as having studied
English at school, the latter to the half-million or so who use the
language a good deal more fluently and precisely than the
average Englishman.

The happiest solution would be if English in India came to
have the status of French in England and were regarded as an
asset which, though valuable, is not essential to everybody's
intellectual well-being. Then the lack of it need breed no
inferiority complexes, nor deter creative Indian thinkers and
writers from using their own ancient languages – which were
expressing sophisticated philosophical concepts while Europeans
were still grunting in holes in the ground.

27 January.

Every day I fall more seriously in love with Coorg; it is the
only place, outside of my own little corner of Ireland, where I
could imagine myself happy to live permanently. Several of

our neighbours have wonderingly asked me 'Don't you get bored, walking so much through the paddy and the forest?' And they look equally delighted and puzzled when I assure them that, far from getting bored, I every day derive more pleasure from their lovely land. Wherever one looks there is beauty, none of it spectacular or wild or dramatic but all of it profoundly satisfying. The light has that exhilarating clarity one expects only at a much higher altitude, the colours glow with magical vitality and the very air tastes good. Then there is the warmth of the Coorg welcome, which makes one feel soaked in contentment as the land itself is soaked in golden sunshine.

Coorg women have traditionally led freer and more active lives than most high-caste Hindu ladies, and the secretary/account-ant of Devangeri's Co-operative Society is a competent, elegant young woman named Jagi Chinnappa, who lives about two miles away with her widowed mother, elder brother and 9-year-old sister. This morning, having been invited to spend the day with the Chinnappas, we started out after breakfast and half a mile beyond Mill Point turned into one of those narrow *onis* that seem like paths to some secret paradise as they wind between high red earth embankments, under the shade of mango, peepul, jack-fruit, nellige and palm-trees. When one leaves the motor-road, to approach any of Devangeri's com-ponent villages, there is nothing to indicate that one is living in 1974 instead of 1874.

We first paid our respects to Jagi's mother, who speaks no English and has a great sadness behind her eyes; one feels she is still grieving for her husband, who died six years ago when their youngest child was only three. Then Jagi took us to visit four other near-by homesteads, all occupied by her uncles and aunts. As the coffee-picking season has just started only elderly women or very small children were at home and outside every house was spread a carpet of red berries, which must lie for nine or ten days in the sun, to brown before being marketed. Coorg's main crops dovetail most conveniently, the paddy-threshing ending just when the coffee-picking must begin.

Coorg hospitality seems not merely a social duty but part of

the people's religion. On each veranda – presided over by innumerable ancestral photographs – we had to partake of coffee,
biscuits, savoury scraps with unpronounceable names, papaya
knocked from the tree for us, yellow, red and green bananas,
supportas, and delicious bull's-hearts, which look exactly like
ox-hearts and have sweet, creamy flesh and many large, flat,
shiny black seeds. At the end of all this I wondered where I
was supposed to fit an Indian lunch for an honoured guest, but
when I saw and smelt the meal my appetite revived. There were
two sorts of rice – steamed and fried – curried sardines, salted
raw shark, omelette with onion and exotic spices, pickled
oranges, dahl, dhosies (delicious rice-flour pancakes) and fried
cabbage. Jagi's mother hovered anxiously while we ate,
obviously on tenterhooks lest her efforts proved unpalatable to
the guests, and thus I was compelled, by politeness as well as
greed, to overeat grossly. I was in a semi-coma as I panted
under the midday sun up the steep slope to catch the Virajpet
bus – Jagi having arranged (to my secret dismay) that we should
spend the afternoon at the cinema.

The Technicolor Hindi film began in a packed 'Palas' at two
o'clock. India has one of the four largest film industries in the
world and film-going is by far the most popular form of entertainment for her illiterate 70 per cent. This gives film stars
great power; in Bombay – the centre of the film industry – they
have on occasions significantly influenced election results. They
also raise vast sums through public appeals for flood or famine
relief and they have even been known to calm hysterical mobs
on the brink of violence.

The three-and-a-half hour film was Rachel's first experience
of the cinema and she enjoyed every moment of it. Afterwards I
asked Jagi if India's long-standing nationwide debate about
kissing on the screen has yet been officially resolved: whereupon
she blushed most becomingly, and looked with slightly raised
eyebrows at her small sister and Rachel, and said 'No' in a
very end-of-the-discussion voice. So evidently she herself is not
one of the 'progressives' who favour a change in the law. Some
people think it downright hypocritical that in India, where
many forms of unnatural vice are graphically depicted in and
around places of worship, it is illegal to show an innocent boy-
kisses-girl shot on the screen. However, the unsophisticated

majority do not find this stylised temple sculpture at all erotic; but as they still think it immodest to sit beside their spouses in a bus they would undoubtedly consider any love-making on the screen offensive. In 1968 the government set up a committee under Mr Justice Khosla to inquire into film censorship, and it recommended that kissing should be allowed on the screen where it could be justified for 'aesthetic or social reasons' – whatever these might be. But the traditionalists would not give in and so far the law remains unchanged.

Jagi had arranged that we should be picked up by a jeep which a cousin of hers is able to borrow – every Coorg cousin has multiple uses – and on the way home we overtook Tim and Sita, being driven to call on the Murphys.

It was good to see them again and, although they returned only yesterday from Madras, I was vastly amused to discover how much they already knew about our habits and customs. They had been told of all our movements since we settled here, down to the last particular – when we had lunched with whom, how long we stayed, what we ate most of, how far we walk, what times of the day I read and write, where we shop in the bazaar, what we buy, how often I do my *dhobi*-work, when and how we went to Mercara and who we met there, where my palm-toddy comes from and who has called on us for drinks. What astonishes me is the flawless accuracy of Coorg's bush-telegraph; despite the widespread nature of the gossip we have provoked, not one detail seems to have been distorted or exaggerated. The only thing Tim had been unable to find out was the exact ingredients of an M.C.C. (Murphy's Coorg Cocktail). This blend of Arak, honey and fresh lime juice has deservedly (though I say it myself) become famous throughout the area for its agreeable taste and still more agreeable effects, which Tim and I were both enjoying when Sita broke the party up to get back to Green Hills in time for dinner.

3 February.

This being Friday, Dr Chengappa arrived at seven-fifteen to make his weekly offering to the ancestors. While brushing my teeth I could hear in the room below his murmured *mantras*, and the distinctive, muffled thud of a sharp, heavy knife bisecting hairy coconuts – and then the splash of their milk, which is always followed by the dreamy pungency of incense wafting up the stairs.

The Coorgs' preoccupation with ancestor-veneration, added to their relative independence of the priestly caste, suggests that their religious beliefs have changed less, since the Vedic period, than those of most other Indians. One of the loveliest passages in the *Rig-Veda* is an address to the spirit of a dead man, made while his body is burning on the funeral pyre, and even before those marvellous hymns were composed the veneration felt by the Indo-Aryans for their ancestors was an ancient tradition. They already possessed a vast treasury of myths when they entered India some 3,500 years ago – terrifying the people of the Indus Valley, who were far more civilised but had never heard of horse-drawn chariots. And these myths have ever since been interacting with that more cerebral religion of the Brahmans which was probably just beginning to burgeon in the Indus Valley at the time of the earliest Aryan invasions. Some of the results of this fusion are wildly irrational – notably the failure to eliminate ancestor-worship, despite the evolution of the doctrines of *karma* and *samsara*, and of a hereditary caste system. *Karma* is not hereditary: one's children are not affected by the consequences of one's deeds in this life; and, according to the doctrine of *samsara*, a virtuous man can be born into a higher caste in his next life, or a wicked man into a lower caste. Obviously, belief in a heavenly world full of immortal family ghosts cannot be reconciled with *samsara* by any feat of mental gymnastics – yet for many centuries both beliefs have been held at the same time by millions of Hindus.

This sort of thing drives logical Western minds to the farthest extremes of intellectual discomfort, while leaving Indians apparently quite comfortable, thank you. And such fundamental ambiguities – which are so acceptable a part of Hindu culture that few Indians ever even notice them – contribute quite a lot to the difficulties of Europeans in India. Too often, the mutual understanding one has been working for, and which seems at last within reach, is suddenly swept out of sight by some unexpected, inexplicable eddy that has whirled to the surface of the Indian mind.

14

Forest Funeral

28 January.

Today's social activities took us outside the Coorg community to lunch with a young couple who live about six miles away and spent an evening here last week sampling M.C.C. The husband – a scientist – studied abroad for eight years and belongs to a rich, fairly orthodox Hindu family from another part of South India, but the wife is a European. When first we met, on the street in Virajpet, she said to me by way of greeting, 'I *hate* India!' And looking that day at her husband's strained little smile my heart sank, as a whole familiar situation – which never seems any the less tragic for being familiar – was revealed. Against a European background we have handsome, brilliant Indian boy meeting impressionable, naïve European girl whose ignorance of India is complete. They marry in Europe, and perhaps have their first child there, and then return to India where the dashing, exotic Indian bridegroom is reabsorbed into his family and becomes the peremptory Hindu husband. For most such wives, who may be many miles from their nearest fellow-European and have had no adequate preparation before the transplant to India, it is almost impossible to adjust to this country.

Let us call them Ram and Mary. They live in an amply staffed, very comfortable Coorg-built house which Mary thinks no better than a neolithic dwelling because it lacks electricity. Their two sons, aged three and five, are healthy and attractive: but Mary has her own ideas about child-rearing and these, naturally, do not coincide with Ram's. However, when we first spent an evening together at Green Hills, and again when they came to Devangeri last week, they gave a passable imitation of an affectionate young married couple, Western style. It was only today, seeing them in their own home, that I realised how delicately balanced such relationships are – how permanently

in danger of being pushed, by a word or a glance, into some
lonely chasm of misunderstanding.

Ram is extremely intelligent – already a name to be reckoned
with in his own profession – and he is also a dedicated humanist,
an outspoken opponent of traditional Hinduism in
all its manifestations and an especially fervent crusader against
priestly superstition. Yet on the domestic scene he reverts to
type in an almost eerie way – one feels he has been taken over
by forces too strong for him – and then he orders Mary around
as though she were a not very bright child, showing her none of
the normal courtesies Western women expect. He is, however,
genuinely kind, and I suspect this behaviour may be in part a
reaction to Mary's having as her birthright that freedom which
he, as a liberal, agnostic young scientist, could have voluntarily
conferred on a Hindu girl. He would probably have found it
easier to live up to his ideals with a wife of his own kind – a
well-educated, intelligent young Hindu whom he could have
permitted to lead a liberated life without her ever becoming
that challenge to his masculine authority which a European
woman inevitably is. Mary is far less intelligent than Ram, but
that does not prevent her from voicing strong personal opinions
and the situation must be considerably exacerbated by her
fatuous criticisms of Indian civilisation.

29 January.
Having Rachel here gives me a close-up view of the profound
differences between Indian and Western child-rearing methods;
and this in turn helps me to sympathise more easily with people
like Ram. Many Indians from orthodox backgrounds who try
to grow beyond the static forms of Hinduism find themselves
thwarted by childhood attitudes and ideas which have become
so firmly entwined with the fibres of their personality that they
can never be completely discarded.

This afternoon a neighbour called to present us with a huge
basket of plantains, and Rachel, as is her wont, rushed to show
him the picture of a crocodile she had just completed. He
laughed indulgently and said, 'But crocodiles don't really have
such big teeth. And its legs are too long. And the colour is all
wrong. Come – lend me your crayons and I'll show you how to
draw a crocodile properly.'

Rachel's chin trembled. 'But that's the way I *imagine* a crocodile', she said unhappily. 'That's what he looks like in my *mind*, when I *think* about him.' And later, after our friend's departure, she asked me plaintively, 'Why do the Indians never like my paintings? You said you liked the crocodile. Don't they know I'm only *five*?'

I tried to explain that in this area Europeans and Indians have very different ideas. When Indian children attempt to exercise an adult skill their efforts are rarely judged as those of small children. Instead, they are irrationally expected to perform up to adult standards and are given no praise simply for *trying*. Their drawing or painting or modelling are seen not as forms of creative play but as failures. No doubt this comes of belonging to a society where economic necessity compels most children to perfect adult skills as soon as possible; but, whatever its cause, it has the indisputable effect of delaying development, withering self-confidence and severely discouraging the experimental, exploratory instinct. A child is unlikely to attempt some new achievement if he knows that failure will be derided and success only acknowledged if it is complete. Amidst a group of European 5-year-olds Rachel seems a child of average intelligence: amidst a group of Indian 5-year-olds she seems brilliant.

Rachel had just gone to bed this evening when the Chengappas called – father, mother and younger daugher. Mrs Chengappa, too, is a doctor, and yet another of those youthful-looking Coorg mothers with grown-up families who impress one equally by their brains, beauty, poise, humour and sheer strength of character. But she, especially, recalls one of my grandmother's favourite phrases, which I have not heard used for years: 'There is a woman of great presence'.

Halfway through his M.C.C., Dr Chengappa himself brought up the subject of the local Harijans so I felt free to ask why they have such an aversion to attending school. Since Independence the Indian Government has done everything possible to improve the lot of the 'Scheduled Castes' and Harijan children are issued free uniforms and books, and even hockey sticks, to entice them to school. In some areas both teachers and caste-Hindu parents are strongly opposed to Harijans attending government schools, but I know this is not the case here for I have several times seen teachers trying to convince Harijan parents of the benefits of education.

However, as Dr Chengappa said, the idea of schooling is so novel to this community, and so potentially disruptive to their simple economy, that in Coorg few are influenced by the promise of long-term advantages. They rarely go hungry here, and are accustomed to having children always available to do certain essential jobs while they themselves work to bring in the cash. Moreover, many are probably unable to grasp the magnitude of the change which has officially overtaken their section of the population within the past few decades; and perhaps it is just as well, at this stage of India's development, not to have hordes of unemployed college–educated Harijans added to the millions of young Indians already roaming the cities in search of jobs that do not exist.

31 January.

There is an Irish casualness about Devangeri's social life which naturally appeals to me. When people say 'Call any time' they really mean it: and they do likewise. This morning I was still enjoying my pre-breakfast read – Rachel having not yet been loosed upon the world – when Mr Machiah came bounding up the ladder. (He must be nearly 70 years old but is such a keep-fit enthusiast that he does still bound, even up our ladder.) Rachel of course was thrilled to hear the day's social round beginning so early and came prancing out in the nude, grinning from ear to ear. I made coffee and we discussed the tourist trade in South India, and then Mr Machiah went off to attend to his paddy-business in the compound.

Half an hour later Mrs Ayyappa dropped in for a chat and stayed until eleven, when she had to go home to supervise the cooking of lunch for nine Harijan labourers who are threshing paddy four miles from the house. Every day, for six weeks, nine large lunches of rice and vegetable curry (with trimmings) are wrapped in separate plantain leaves, tied with pepper-vine twine and dispatched in a basket on a servant girl's head to the thresh-ing-ground. Some employers now provide extra money instead of food, but, as Mrs Ayyappa said, 'What use is money to hungry labourers who are seven miles from the nearest eating-house? They would only buy home-made liquor and spend the afternoon asleep instead of working.'

In Coorg, where the only readily available pastimes are reading, card-playing and conversation, one realizes the extent to which, in the West, we have grown independent of our neighbours for entertainment. I suppose this is just one more milestone along mankind's road to a completely dehumanised existence. When I stop to think about it – as I did today, while chopping onions after Mrs Ayyappa's departure – it seems to me intensely alarming that so many of us now have to make an effort to 'fit people in' (even close friends) because of the many 'events' that make up the contemporary social rat race. Increasingly, we tend not to regard each other as capable of providing an evening's – or even an hour's – entertainment. The individual is becoming less and less important in comparison with the occasion that brings people together, whether it be a drinks party, a race meeting, going to the theatre, playing golf, attending a concert, skiing in the Alps – or simply watching television. And one wonders what will be the long-term effect of this changed emphasis on the significance of other people in our lives, this habit of regarding them as companionable accessories to the occasion, instead of as original sources of entertainment, worth being with for their own sakes. Most of our Coorg relationships can only be transitory, but already they have a substance they might never have attained against an urban background.

2 February.

Yesterday morning, on the bus to Mercara, we found ourselves sitting beside the wife of a first cousin of Dr Chengappa, who invited us to a Coorg wedding at the end of the month. It would not be a very big affair, she explained. Owing to inflation, there were unlikely to be more than 1,000 guests.

Because of the oil crisis, one occasionally notices on the local buses richly dressed Coorg women who most certainly have never before boarded a bus. They slowly lever themselves in, holding their saris close to their legs while looking comically martyred. Often they are followed by their young, who regard bus journeys as an amusing glimpse of how the other half travels, and if there is no vacant seat the conductor will deferentially make one available – not, of course, because the newcomers are women, but because they are ladies.

Having changed our books at Mercara's library we set off to walk down the very beautiful mountain road, meaning to stop the bus when it came along; but soon we were picked up by two young cousins of the Andanipura Ayyappas who dropped us off at Mill Point. I had walked only a few steps towards home when an infected ant bite on my right heel – which had been throbbing all the previous night – burst rather hideously and it has been making me feel more than a little sorry for myself ever since.

This morning I longed for daughterless peace, after a second restless night, and when Rachel said wistfully that she wished someone could take her to the Machiahs I impulsively suggested – 'Why don't you go on your own? You should know your way round South Coorg by now.' I felt slightly appalled as I listened to my own words – and a good deal more appalled when Rachel's face lit up and she said, 'Oh, *goody*! May I really go on my own?'

'Of course,' I said, busily stiffening the upper lip. 'Why not? There's no traffic here. But don't stay for lunch. Be back at one o'clock. And stay on the path – don't walk in leaves.'

'Good-bye!' called Rachel, disappearing down the ladder to plunge into the depths of a snake-infested forest.

I immediately remembered an article in a recent issue of *The Illustrated Weekly of India* giving snake-bite death statistics; the annual national average is 3,000. Then I reminded myself that 3,000 is very, very few out of 550 million – and anyway the statistics were probably inaccurate; villagers sometimes poison their enemies and blame snakes. On this consoling thought I settled down to chop cabbage for a salad.

The fact remains, however, that Coorg has more than the national average of snakes per square mile . . . Having finished the salad I lay down to ease my throbbing leg and sought to lose myself in Fraser's *Account of Coorg and the Coorgs under the Vila Rajas* (London: 1796). But I found Mr Fraser downright off-putting, for he chose on page three to inform me that 'there are seven varieties of poisonous snake common in Coorg'. Next I

wrote two rather incoherent letters while drinking my litre of
toddy, which came late today. Then I had a chaser of Arak – at
10.30 a.m., I blush to record. After that I re-read the snake
article and noted that 62 per cent of India's snakes are non-
poisonous. Having made some very strong black coffee I laced
it with rum and told myself how lucky I was to have a non-
clinging, self-sufficient, outgoing child. Drinking the coffee, I
wrote another – even more incoherent – letter which I had just
finished when Subaya appeared to inform me that Thimmiah
Sahib was planning to call at noon. I leaped to my feet. Rachel
dearly loves Tim and would be bitterly disappointed to miss
him; so I must hasten to retrieve her, sore foot or not. It is only
a slight exaggeration to say that you could not have seen me
for dust between here and there.

Rachel was sitting on the veranda, 'helping' Uncle Machiah
to chop betel nuts, and she observed my arrival with a perceptible lack of enthusiasm. 'I thought you were going to rest
your foot,' she said coldly. 'What are you doing here?'

I explained.

'Oh,' said Rachel, 'I do want to see Uncle Tim. But you go
ahead. I'll follow by myself – I know the way.'

As I limped home – painfully aware of my foot, now that the
anaesthetic of anxiety had worn off – I could see my excessive
fussing about snakes as a cover-up for something rather more
complicated. If for five years and three months one has been an
essential prop, it comes as a slight blow to the *amour propre* when
that prop is suddenly discarded. But now I feel we are over the
worst; I cannot imagine myself ever again getting into such a
flap without just cause.

5 February.

Today we caught the noon bus to Virajpet and found it full
of migrant tribal coffee-pickers – filthy, ragged, excessively
uncouth in their habits, covered with crude jewellery and open
sores, almost black-skinned, very small in stature and laden
with babies. (There seemed to be no more than ten months between the countless children in each family: but I daresay this
was an optical illusion.) Before circumstances drove them out
of their jungles these people lived happy, healthy lives; now,
despite all the official benefits and concessions to which they

are entitled, many of them have sunk to the lowest level of
degradation.

In Virajpet we lunched with a retired teacher who lives in a
ramshackle little bungalow half-way up the hill. He had met
us a few times around the town and pleadingly invited us to
his home; his wife died recently and obviously he is still feeling
very lonely.

Like most elderly educated Coorgs, Mr M—— speaks conspicuously good English – precise without being pedantic – and
he greatly deplores the present state of the nation's schools. He
is even sceptical – with good reason, I should think – about the
apparently improved literacy rate. In his view the Indian
government got its priorities wrong at the outset. Thousands of
schools and colleges have been built during the past twenty
years and these make impressive statistics, if one does not know
that most schools are without adequate staff or equipment.
Obviously India's future would be much brighter today if the
money wasted on buildings had been used to attract a better
type of teacher. Nowadays even the most highly qualified and
dedicated teachers cannot give of their best to their school duties
because to feed their families they must overwork as private
tutors. I assured Mr M—— that the quality of education is a
problem all over the world, even in developed Western
countries. To which he replied, 'Every problem is worse in
India than almost anywhere else. And we cannot afford mistakes or vanity or pompous posturing. We have no margin for
error. Our government's slips cannot be minor – they lead
straight to disaster.'

It is odd how many Indians combine hypersensitivity to
criticism from outsiders with an addiction to dwelling on –
almost gloating over – their national defects. They seem to take
a perverted sort of pride in their proneness to corruption, and a
current 'funny story' – I've been told it three times in the past
two days – was printed as a news item in the *Deccan Herald*. It
concerns a young Bombay university lecturer who last week
unsuccessfully attempted suicide because he had become so
depressed by the blatant and universal (in cities) adulteration
of food. When the contents of his stomach were analysed it was
found that he had been sold poison so heavily adulterated it
could not have killed a mouse . . .

7 February.

Today we lunched with the Hughes and while we were waiting for the bus at Mill Point, and chatting to Uncle Machiah
(who was going somewhere on *Aruva* business) Rachel suddenly
said, 'I have a very sore eye.'

I glanced at it and remarked in my callous way, 'It doesn't
look very sore.' But luckily Uncle Machiah was more compas-
sionate and found a tick embedded in the left upper lid, between
the eyelashes.

He is a wonderful person on such occasions – indeed, on every
occasion. 'This happens quite often,' he said calmly, 'but it
must be removed without delay. What could be more convenient? You are passing Ammathi Hospital on the way to
Sidapur. Get off there and Dr Asrani will fix it in ten minutes.
All you need is a drop of glycerine or liquid paraffin on the lid –
when it has been loosened out it comes with a tweezers – no
problem!'

By the time we got to Ammathi the lid had swollen perceptibly
and there was a problem, because Dr Asrani had taken a fortnight's leave and his very young Tamil locum proved hair-
raisingly incompetent. It was plain that within the ten days
since Dr Asrani's departure the whole hospital had nose-dived
into the depths of inefficiency, providing a striking example of
how completely these small rural establishments depend on the
standards of one man.

To begin with Dr P—— diagnosed a sty instead of a tick, and
when I had brusquely put him right – inwardly thanking the
Lord for Uncle Machiah – he looked utterly nonplussed until I
suggested glycerine or liquid paraffin. A search revealed that
neither was available so we settled for vaseline, applied with
cotton wool, and proceeded to the treatment room where
Rachel lay obediently on the couch. Then Dr P—— turned to
me and said briskly, 'You must please wait outside. You can
come in when I have finished. Parents are never allowed in here.'

'They are, by Dr Asrani,' I retorted, feeling my blood temperature rising by several degrees. 'And I can assure you that
I am not leaving this room until my daughter does.'

Dr P—— looked considerably taken aback. 'You have been
here before?' he asked.

'Yes,' I replied, 'I have.'

During this exchange Rachel had been lying calmly on the couch with her hand in mine, knowing quite well I would never desert her and obviously rather enjoying the adults' battle. She now asked, 'When is the doctor going to remove the tick?' and I looked questioningly at Dr P——.

In retrospect I can see the funny side of what followed, but at the time it left me shaking with rage. The nurse couldn't find the cottonwool, or tweezers, or any forceps smaller than a jack – and finally a forceps of more practical dimensions was produced by a sweeper who was carrying it in her bare hands. By this stage Dr P—— was looking thoroughly demoralised. He sulkily obeyed when I ordered him to sterilise the forceps in my presence before putting it near Rachel's eyelid – a delay which may have done good by giving the vaseline longer to work. When the 'operation' at last began the 'surgeon' made mighty heavy weather of it, though his patient, on maternal instructions, remained more unflinching than I could have believed possible. However, since the tick was extracted intact at the fifth attempt I suppose I should count my blessings and complain no more. As usual, Rachel rapidly recovered from her ordeal – though the eyelid is still very sore – and we arrived at Mylatpur in time for several *iced* beers (forgotten luxury!) before lunch.

At three-thirty Jane drove us to Ammathi to catch the bus but it had made extra good time from Mercara and left ten minutes early; so we decided to hitch-hike. Often, in Coorg, drivers stop to offer unwanted lifts, but on the whole traffic is very light and this afternoon we saw not even a motor bicycle during our seven-mile walk from Ammathi to Devangeri.

Approaching Vontiangadi, poor Rachel became quite exhausted – she had already walked over three miles this morning – and as I was carrying fifty eggs, bought cheap from a mass-producer at Mylatpur, I was unable to provide a piggy-back. But when the air began to cool at six o'clock she suddenly revived and finished the course at a gallop. It was a memorable walk, through the loveliest of this lovely region, and our road climbed high at just the right time to allow an unimpeded view of a vast fiery sunset behind the dark blue splendour of the Ghats. Then came an unearthly pink glow, over our whole silent world of forest and paddy-valley, and Rachel was moved to lyricism – 'It looks as if a giant spilled his pink paint over everything!'

8 February.

This being Friday, Dr Chengappa arrived at seven-thirty and brought the sad news that last evening our tailor's 36-year-old wife died in Virajpet hospital. The eldest of their three children, a clever girl in her first year at Bangalore University, will now have to give up her studies to look after her brothers, aged nine and thirteen.

We know the tailor, Ponappa, quite well – Rachel often visits his workroom and returns with great bunches of finger-bananas – so we accompanied Dr Chengappa and Uncle Machiah on their visit to the house of mourning. Outside a neat, solid, typically Coorg home half a dozen musicians were playing mournfully – as they had been all night – under the plantain and papaya trees. Many neighbours were chatting quietly in groups, at a little distance from the house, and Ponappa himself stood on the veranda, clad all in white, receiving condolences. When I offered our sympathy he said expressionlessly, 'It is my fate.' There was a certain moving dignity about him: yet those four syllables unconsciously put Indian womanhood in its place. *Her* death at thirty-six was *his* fate . . .

The corpse had been brought from Virajpet during the night and was reclining on a wicker chaise-longue under a canopy of white cloth in the room just off the veranda – robed in a fine sari, with crudely painted scarlet lips. Rachel had been inclined to regard the occasion as a 'treat' and I had had to warn her to suppress her light-hearted interest in corpses; but when she saw the devastated daughter bending weeping over her mother, stroking the dead woman's cheeks, she suddenly clutched my hand very tightly and said, 'I feel sad. I hope you won't die until I'm married.' The two sons were sitting cross-legged on a wall bench opposite their mother, looking completely dazed as they whimpered and moaned and rocked to and fro; and beside the chaise-longue sat the dead woman's elder sister, wielding a fan of sago-palm leaves to deter flies and tending a dish-lamp. When Dr Chengappa entered the room he touched the corpse's chest with the back of his hand and then his own chest with the palm, to indicate that the bereavement has left him feeling heartbroken. But, because dead bodies are regarded as one of the most potent polluting agents, Uncle Machiah had to remain on the veranda, postponing his ritual gesture of grief until later. He was due to meet somebody in Virajpet at ten o'clock, as part of his apparently ceaseless round of *Aruva* duties, and so he could not return home for the purifying bath and change of clothes that would have been essential had he crossed the threshold of the death-chamber.

As we left, I told Ponappa I would be at the funeral this afternoon and when we were back in the doctor's car Rachel said that she, too, would like to attend. But Uncle Machiah explained that it is not the custom for children – other than close relatives – to witness cremations. Poor Rachel was ravaged by disappointment. 'I wanted', she wailed, 'to find out if burning humans smelt like cooking meat.'

A few days ago we were invited to accompany Uncle Machiah to this morning's *Aruva* session – it apparently included some sort of 'brunch' meal – and, as we drove towards Virajpet, I noticed an unprecedented awkwardness in his manner which momentarily baffled me; luckily I recollected our polluted state in time to back out before our unfortunate friend was forced explicitly to cancel the invitation.

We had walked home and I was preparing lunch when one of Dr Chengappa's sisters-in-law (a widow who lives some six miles away, towards Vontiangadi) appeared in the compound to collect her share of this year's paddy. She shouted a greeting to us, and I went to a window and asked her upstairs for coffee or a drink. But she declined. 'I can't come into the house', she explained, 'I've just been to Ponappa's.'

It is impossible to estimate how seriously each individual takes the pollution taboos, so I made some coffee and took it out to the compound, hoping Mrs Chengappa would drink it there. But no: she would neither eat nor drink until she had performed her purifying ceremonies.

At three o'clock I set off for the cremation with Rachel's instructions ringing in my ears: 'Tell me what it smells like!' In fact I was destined not to discover this, as women have to leave before the pyre is lit – a custom originating in the tendency of women mourners to become so unbalanced by grief (or fear of widowhood) that they impulsively throw themselves on the fire, even if they have not planned to become *satis*. However, this rule is not always enforced strictly enough to protect widows from self-immolation. In Rajasthan, during the past six months, at least four women have voluntarily joined their husband's corpse on the pyre and been burned to death. Moreover, in one case there were some 70,000 witnesses, none of whom felt it necessary to intervene.

Mrs Ponappa's cremation was to take place not far from the Muslim settlement on the way to the Machiahs, under one of those extraordinary 'double trees' often seen in Coorg. It is an ancient local custom to plant two sacred trees together, encourage them to entwine as saplings and then 'marry' them, with much pomp and lavish entertainment, to symbolise the union of Eshwara and his consort Parvathi. This particular Devangeri couple must have been married centuries ago, for each partner has attained a prodigious height and girth and the red and green canopy of their mingled leaves shades an enormous area, including the spot chosen for the cremation.

When I arrived there were only two young village men under the trees, tending the bonfire from which the pyre would be lit, but the usually so silent forest afternoon was throbbing with the slow beat of distant drums, accompanied by the melancholy wailing of Coorg horns, and when I peered through a tangle of scrub I could see, far away, the little funeral procession advancing across the pale gold stubble of a paddy-valley. No more beautiful setting for a poignant ceremony would it be possible to find, with royal blue mountains visible between the slender silver-grey trunks of areca palms, and the high poinsettia hedges around the Muslim settlement forming cascades of colour, and the dense burgundy-red leaves of the incense trees glistening above the countless shades of green in the undergrowth, and the purple-red earth, and the leafless, angular cotton trees bearing their blood-red blossoms like chalices against a cobalt sky.

Many Coorg customs have been abandoned during the past fifty years, or made obsolete by Progress, yet most of those connected with the anthropologists' 'rites of passage' are being maintained. Last night, just as I was falling asleep, I heard two distant gun shots and wondered if Uncle Machiah was still trying to pot that mongoose. But I have since learned that this was the announcement to the village of a bereavement; if those shots had been fired during the day, even at the height of the ploughing or reaping seasons, every Coorg would at once have stopped work and hastened to the house of mourning to offer not only sympathy but practical help. Also their servants would have been sent running to the other homesteads of the *nad* that were out of earshot, to spread the news and rally support. All the food needed in Ponappa's house for the next eleven days will be provided and cooked by neighbouring women, all his farm work will be done by neighbouring men and all the valuable firewood for the pyre was presented to him today – a little from each village family – as an expression of sympathy and solidarity. On this point, however, discretion must be the better part of generosity; every branch specially cut for a cremation has to be used because, it is believed, the Gods would regard any surplus as an invitation to take another life from the family of the deceased.

By four o'clock quite a crowd had gathered in the shade of the double tree, including Uncle Machiah and Colonel Ayyappa, and at last the funeral band appeared through the thick scrub. It was followed by two men bearing a split bamboo stick designed to serve as a holder for half a coconut shell; this had been filled with oil to form a lamp which had to be kept alight throughout the ceremony. Next came the bier – that same wicker chaise-longue – carried by Ponappa and three other male relatives. The chief mourners included about a dozen women, clad in that unrelieved white which is the equivalent of our unrelieved black. One of them, who belonged to the family of the Ponappas' *Aruva*, was carrying on a section of plantain leaf the *Sameya*, a mixture of coconut, puffed rice, rice with mutton or egg curry, rice seasoned with turmeric and vegetables fried in oil. This meal has to be provided by a deceased woman's natal family, or by a deceased man's mother's family, and before the ashes are left alone to cool during the night the *Sameya* is placed beside them, to sustain the spirit on its journey.

When the corpse had been borne three times around the framework for the pyre – a square construction of rough-hewn, leaf-decorated logs — it was laid on the ground near by, with the head pointing to the south, and Ponappa stripped himself to the waist. The white cotton robe in which he had been clad was now used as a canopy, under which he and his father's brother's wife led the chief mourners three times around the pyre, the elderly women scattering rice and small coins from a flat wicker basket. Next the widower and his daughter and elder son again thrice circled the pyre in single file, each wearing a finger ring of sacred *Kusha* grass. Ponappa was carrying on his head an earthen vessel of water from which he sprinkled the ground, his daughter was carrying a small brass pot with a spout, a *kindi*, which would have been carried by her husband had she been married, and the boy was holding a coconut on his head. After the first circuit their family *Aruva* stepped forward and with the sharp point of his heavy knife punctured Ponappa's vessel so that the water trickled down his face as he continued to walk, symbolising that inexorable flow of time which is every moment bringing each of us closer to death. It might be thought that these elaborate rituals impose an unnecessary strain on a grief-stricken family, but the therapeutic effect of having to concentrate on so much activity and detail is considerable.

Next Ponappa stood at the corpse's head, his son at its feet and his daughter by its right side. Then Ponappa took the pot off his head and twice made as though to break it against the leg of the chair. The third time he did break it, and pushed the pieces under the chair, and then his son cracked the coconut and pushed the two halves under the chair, and his daughter emptied her *kindi* and pushed it under the chair. Meanwhile the dead woman lay looking quite beautiful and very young, with a small mirror on her folded hands, many fresh forest blossoms tossed on her shroud and an elderly aunt devotedly fanning to keep the flies off.

Next Ponappa put a coin in a tiny bag and tied it to a corner of his wife's sari, which was the signal for everybody present to pay their last respects to the deceased and leave a little money on a near-by plate to help with the funeral expenses. Most people moistened the dead woman's lips with water before touching her breast in a last gesture of grief and farewell. Then the women mourners began to withdraw, as all jewellery, and every garment apart from a flimsy sari, were removed from the corpse. The clothes and the bloodied shroud were given to the Harijan bandsmen, who would not consider them polluting. Finally, a new white cotton sheet was spread over the body, covering even the face, and was smeared by Ponappa with the juice of mango leaves.

Thus far the ceremony had been conducted with great dignity, in a silence broken only by the traditional music. But when the face was covered, by which time the women had all withdrawn to a little distance, the unfortunate daughter suddenly broke down, burst into loud lamentations and shook off her restraining relatives to rush back to the corpse and pull down the sheet that she might look once more upon her mother.

Immediately, as though some lever had been touched, all the women, and quite a number of the men, gave way to their emotion and the ensuing harrowing scene could not possibly be mistaken for a ritual 'funeral display'. However, order was at last restored, the women withdrew again – out of sight, this time – and the macabre business of the day began. For some extraordinary reason custom requires the corpse to recline straight-legged up to this point, when it has to be made to sit cross-legged on the pyre. Almost twenty-four hours after death, this naturally presents a problem. Then the corpse is held in a sitting position while the pyre is built up around it until only the head is visible, at which point the chief male mourner has to come forward to add the final lengths of wood that obscure the head. The eldest son then carries a burning brand from the bonfire, which itself has been lit from the domestic hearth of the deceased, and inserts it into the space left between the bottom of the pyre and the ground. At this moment I, as a woman, had to withdraw, to avoid seriously offending local susceptibilities.

For hours pale blue smoke was visible all over Devangeri, rising through the majestic branches of that double tree, and I knew that at least one representative of each village family was sitting by the pyre to make sure the body was completely burned before the night. Tomorrow, at dawn, the ashes will be removed for immersion in the sacred Cauvery river, and the site of the cremation will be lavishly watered and planted with paddy. If these seeds germinate, it is believed the departed spirit is happy and at peace.

I have always been pro-burial (without a coffin) but this afternoon's ceremony has almost converted me to cremation – if one could arrange to be cremated in a Coorg forest. Aesthetically, being consumed by flames is certainly preferable to being consumed by worms. Fire is so beautiful, and fierce, and final.

15

A Naming Ceremony and a Wedding

7 February.

Today we lunched with Aunty Machiah's sister-in-law, whose elder daughter had her first baby three weeks ago in Dr Chengappa's Virajpet maternity home. Like all Hindu brides, Coorg girls return to their parental home, however long the journey may be, for what is regarded as the ordeal of their first confinement – a custom based on the reasonable assumption that a baby will arrive before the bride has had time to settle into an unfamiliar household.

In Coorg, however, the new mother is excessively pampered. She remains with her own family for the sixty days of birth-pollution, following delivery, and during that time is confined to one room with her baby and is not allowed out of bed. Carefully chosen strength-restoring foods are provided and she is given a vigorous daily oil massage and hot bath by specially trained servants – which Uncle assures me has the same effect as normal exercise. But I still feel that such paranoid cosseting must be dreadfully deleterious. We last visited this young mother in hospital, within hours of her confinement, and I thought she looked a lot healthier then than she does today. Yet she seemed perfectly content just to lie there being entertained by her mother, younger sister, servants and a stream of callers. Most of the household's entertaining is now done in the new mother's room, to alleviate her boredom, which means that the baby, throughout each of its waking moments, is being cuddled and fussed over and talked to. In this family the infant's aunt – whose marriage Uncle was arranging today, following her graduation from Madras University with First-Class Honours in economics and political science – is the Spoiler-in-Chief. She also set about spoiling Rachel and when we were leaving presented her with a magnificent hand-embroidered dress and a silver necklace.

10 February.

I woke this morning feeling more than slightly peculiar, having lunched yesterday with a gentleman whose hospitality far outstrips his judgement. Our party began at 11 a.m., with beer, and continued through whisky and Arak to a long after-noon spent on the veranda absorbing small coffees and large (genuine) cognacs. At 5 p.m., when my host and I could no longer convince even ourselves that it was 'just after lunch', and when an hour remained to sun-downer time, the Murphys got up to go. I therefore deserved no sympathy this morning, nor was any available. Rachel took one look at me when I became perpendicular and asked shrewdly, 'Are you hung-over?'

'Of course not,' I said crossly, groping for the Alka-Seltzer.

'Then why do you look so ghastly and dopey?' challenged Rachel – a combination of adjectives which so took my fancy that I was at once restored to cheerfulness. Daughters have their uses.

My restoration needed to be pretty rapid this morning as we were invited to a Naming Ceremony at Byrambada, about six miles away, quite close to the scene of yesterday's debauchery.

About one hundred guests had already assembled when we arrived at nine-thirty – seventy or so women within the house, and twenty-five or thirty men on the outer veranda. Naming Ceremonies are not normally attended by many males, apart from close relatives, and only women participate in the *Ganga Puja* (water worshipping). Formerly children were named and cradled twelve days after birth, at the end of the first stage of the birth-pollution period, during which family members are debarred from taking part in village festivals or *pujas*. Now, however, it is more usual to combine the Naming Ceremony with the *Ganga Puja*, which takes place sixty days after a birth to mark the mother's resumption of normal life. Having bathed, she dresses as a bride, and the enormous vessel in which her bath water has been heated for the past two months is removed from the wash-room and filled with cold water by a woman who intones 'May your stomach be cool like this copper pot'.

Our first duty, privilege and pleasure was to admire the cause of today's excitement – a dainty baby girl who, since she had not yet been cradled, lay asleep on a double bed under a muslin net in a wicker basket. She cared nothing for the procession of proudly beaming female relatives, ranging in age from two to eighty-eight, who were passing through the room. Under the cradle I glimpsed the knife that had cut the umbilical cord, a formidable weapon on which all Coorg babies sleep until they have been named. Soon after our arrival the child had to be roused, but she retained her oriental calm even when Rachel helped to change her nappy with more zeal than skill. (The nappy was of course dry, since nicely brought-up Indian babies, however young, seem to perform only on their pots.)

The brief naming and cradling ceremony – attended only by women – took place in the main room of the house. Her paternal grandmother held the infant over a vessel of burning incense while Aunty Machiah, acting on behalf of her dead maternal grandmother, tied black threads around her wrists and ankles. (Had she been a boy, a thread would also have been tied round the waist.) Then, before cradling her, Aunty and two other women three times placed a grinding stone in the cradle and lifted it out again while chanting, 'Live long like a stone!' – for the first time addressing the child by name. This little girl was simply named Cauvery, after Coorg's most sacred river. But many Coorg names are more colourful: Belliappa (Silver Father), Ponappa (Gold Father), Maiddanna (Brother of the Village Green), Puvakka (Flower Sister), Muttakka (Pearl Sister), Chinnava (Gold Mother) – and so on in this rather ornate vein.

Next the paternal grandmother called, 'Cauvery, get up and eat rice mixed with milk!' And, to Cauvery's very evident distaste, a minute particle of curds, rice and honey was forcibly fed to her off the edge of a gold coin. She at once spat this mixture out with the well-known decisiveness of Coorg females, yet she did not disgrace her warrior ancestors by crying or even whimpering.

When the men had joined us everybody formally saluted Cauvery and dropped an envelope containing a few rupees into the cradle. Then, to drink her health, the women were given glasses of extremely potent home-made wine and every woman emptied her glass in one, as is the custom here. I noticed, too, that not all were averse to a refill, though in most regions a high-caste Hindu woman would as soon go out naked as drink alcohol.

At noon, for the *Ganga Puja*, Chinnava – the baby's mother – appeared in a shimmering, pale pink, gold-spangled sari, wearing glittering gold and silver ornaments. She beckoned me to follow her to the well, where Aunty again had a central rôle to play, she and the paternal grandmother handing Chinnava the ritual coconut, three betel leaves, three pieces of areca nut and some rice. First Chinnava offered prayers while breaking the coconut over the well and throwing it into the water, followed by the leaves and nuts. Then she drew a vessel of water and drank three gulps out of the palm of her hand before filling two small, antique silver pitchers. These she placed one above the other on her head, and meanwhile Aunty had filled two other pitchers which were carried by a couple of Chinnava's nieces, aged six and ten. Very slowly, in an atmosphere of joyful solemnity, the little procession moved back to the house through a garden brilliant with saris and flowers – yellow, scarlet, deep blue, white, pale pink. When the water had been left in the kitchen Chinnava went to the central hall, where the sacred wall-lamp had been lit, and quietly offered prayers while sprinkling rice on the flame. Finally, she turned to take the blessings of the older women, bowing low before them and touching their feet three times while they gently laid their hands on her glossy raven hair. And an old lady beside me exclaimed – 'What a wonderful girl! Did you know she is one of India's best nuclear scientists?' Of such shocks is life in modern Coorg compounded.

The banquet was served in the garden, under a temporary roof of freshly cut branches, on long trestle tables draped with snowy lengths of cotton. Chinnava's immediate family waited on us, bearing great cauldrons of delicious food: steamed rice, fried rice, curried mutton, chicken and pork, fluffy *idlis*, soft rice flour pancakes, fresh coconut chutney, *sambhar* deliciously tangy with tamarind, fresh curds, spiced cabbage with grated coconut, curried potatoes and beans with hard-boiled eggs. For pudding there were large tumblers of a delectable liquid made from ground rice, jaggery and milk, flavoured with fragrant cardamom and laced with crunchy cashew-nuts; and for dessert there were bananas, oranges, grapes and fresh pineapple chunks. At last we all rose, washed our hands and moved slowly indoors to chew pan and betel-nuts while a swarm of servants descended on the tables to lay them with fresh plantain leaves for the men.

Betel-leaves and areca-nuts are believed by the Coorgs to be very auspicious and the mixture certainly aids digestion. At all important religious ceremonies and social functions chewing is considered essential and it is so closely associated with happiness and contentment that abstinence from betel is required during mourning periods. The ceremonial giving of a betel-leaf is accepted as an adequate receipt for money or goods, and an exchange of betel leaves, in the course of an agreement involving mutual trust, is regarded as more binding than any signed and witnessed legal document. Obviously this is a relic of the days when most Coorgs, whose own language has no script, were illiterate.

At four-thirty the party began to break up and, after a prolonged hunt, I found Rachel in the nearby forest with about twenty other junior guests who had been prompted by my daughter to indulge in nefarious activities which did their party clothes no good. On the way home I asked Rachel what game they had been playing: 'Oh,' she said unconcernedly, 'we threw a coconut into the well and fished it up again'; which reply I found not a little unnerving, as many wells are over eighty feet deep.

Incidentally, Aunty wordlessly registered disapproval today when she saw Rachel dressed for the occasion in that Madrassi outfit made for her by the Ittamozhi tailor's apprentice. This baffled me, until I realised that the outfit is typical of what little Harijan and low-caste girls wear, not only in Tamil Nadu but here in Coorg. Little high-caste girls, before they graduate to saris at puberty, wear European-style clothes, usually beautifully tailored by mother, aunt or grandmother but modelled exactly on Marks and Spencer's children's garments. So poor Rachel's glad rags – of which she is so proud, and in which she looks so attractive – were today a *faux pas* of the first order.

18 February.

In every Coorg home, from the grandest to the humblest, one notices a photograph or oleograph of Tala Cauvery – the source of Coorg's sacred river – and Coorgs treat these pictures with as much reverence as though they were statues of a god. So I was very pleased today when invited to visit Tala Cauvery with Tim and Sita.

Inevitably I felt restless during the twenty-mile drive, which took us almost to the top of a steep, forested mountain, but when we got out of the car our journey seemed well worth while. From this lonely height we were overlooking the whole of South Coorg, stretching away in three directions.

Unhappily, Tala Cauvery itself is well on the way to being modernised. Crude concrete walls surround the ancient, sacred stone tank beside the even more sacred spring, surmounted by a small shrine, which is the source of Mother Cauvery. Another very old and beautiful shrine, not far away, has been enclosed in a corrugated-iron-roofed cube that looks like a temporary public lavatory hastily erected on an earthquake site. (This is the first piece of corrugated iron I have seen in Coorg.) Beside the temple another 'lavatory' is in the process of construction, as are various larger buildings of indeterminate purpose and shocking ugliness; and nothing can be done to halt this despoiling process. As Tim said, 'In the old days you had thousands of penniless pilgrims walking from all over South and Central India to Tala Cauvery. Now you also have black marketeers and venal government officials sweeping up the new road in their illegally imported Mercedes to try to save their rotten souls by paying lakhs of rupees to the Brahmans. Which is how the temple authorities can afford to ruin the place with all this nonsense.'

Soon after our arrival an elderly priest, stripped to the waist, came panting up the hill, having been summoned by Tim's ringing of the handsome bronze temple bell. Unlike most temple priests, he was not obese – possibly because of these frequent sprints up a steep slope. However, had he known who was there this morning he might not have bothered to hurry himself because Tim, following in the footsteps of his ancestors, holds strong views on the part money should play in religious ceremonies. He is a man who in his time has given lavishly to schools and hospitals, but today he only spent 5 rupees on his *puja*.

The fact that Tim goes to Tala Cauvery as a simple pilgrim made our visit memorable for me. While Sita wandered around nearby, taking photographs, Rachel and I stood beside the little shrine over the spring, watching the pilgrim and the priest. And, as we watched, all the confusion that Hinduism creates in Western minds suddenly cleared away, like our morning mists at Devangeri when the sun has climbed above the palms. A good man was worshipping, with faith. I looked down into the clear, fresh water of the spring-well, where rose petals and coconut shells and red powder and mango leaves floated on the surface, and it all seemed wonderfully simple. Then, as though he could sense my mood, Tim quickly looked up and signed that if I wished I might join him. So Rachel and I received some of the purifying well-water from the priest, drank it, held our hands over the sacred camphor flame of the dish-lamp, and thrice followed Tim as he walked clockwise round the little shrine. And I knew he knew I was not doing this *puja* to be polite, or for a stunt, any more than I was affecting to be a Hindu.

We took another road back to Green Hills – a narrow track, inches deep in red dust, which switchbacked through miles of forest before coming to a vast coffee estate surrounding Tim's *Ain Mane*. This magnificent house was built towards the end of the eighteenth century and is the most impressive of the many *Ain Manes* I have seen; its wood carvings are of a fantastic delicacy and intricacy. Three young men greeted us: all were comparatively poor relations who have been enabled to get started on good careers (law, army, university lecturer) because Tim uses some of the income from this estate to support a whole tribe of relatives. The rest goes on maintaining the structure of the *Ain Mane*, which is at present being discreetly modernised.

Although our arrival was completely unexpected, Coorg law forbade us to leave without partaking of food and drink; so while the womenfolk put their emergency plans into operation we walked down a long *oni*, under the shade of gigantic ebony and sandalwood trees, to gaze respectfully at the elaborate tombs of some of Tim's more illustrious eighteenth-century ancestors. Sita explained that not all Coorgs are cremated: burial is also quite common and children and young unmarried people are always buried, usually on the family estate.

Here the veranda wall was – as usual – covered in family photographs, some obviously contemporaneous with the invention of photography, and as we enjoyed our thick squares of sweet omelette I found my eye being repeatedly drawn to an enlarged and surprisingly clear portrait of Tim's grandmother. This splendid but evidently formidable old lady was successfully organising girls' schools here when Suffragettes were a novelty in Britain. She is largely responsible for the fact that about 73 per cent of Coorg women are literate and have been for a few generations, though the all-India women's average is 18 per cent – rising to 54 per cent in Kerala and falling to 8 per cent in the densely populated states of U.P. and Bihar.

Tomorrow we must be at the Machiahs by 8 a.m., when I will be robed in a Coorg sari before we all set off together for the *Kodava Samaj* – a large, rather dreary edifice on the outskirts of Virajpet. It was specially built some years ago for the holding of marriage ceremonies-cum-wedding parties and has already acquired that shoddy look which marks most newish Indian public buildings. To have such a building available for the complicated and lavish entertaining of one thousand or more guests is obviously labour-saving, but the older generation complain that the abandoning of private homes for the occasion has meant regrettable changes to the traditional rituals.

In the arranging of marriages a very important role is played by the family *Aruvas*. When both sets of parents have come to an informal agreement the girl's *Aruva* asks for the boy's horoscope – or, if there is none, both *Aruvas*, accompanied by members of both families, go to the temple to ask for God's blessing on the union. An idol is decorated with white and red flowers, and if a white flower falls during the ceremony this is considered most auspicious, especially if it falls from the idol's right side. But if a red flower falls some families, even today, will abandon a match simply on the strength of this inauspicious indication. Other families consult an astrologer instead of doing the temple *puja* and are greatly influenced by his findings; and an astrologer is in every case consulted, during the betrothal party at the girl's home, to determine the most auspicious date and time for the *Muhurtham* (marriage). During betrothal parties the *Aruvas* play leading parts, the girl's *Aruva* guaranteeing to keep her safe until the wedding day and receiving from the boy's *Aruva* a jewel to mark the betrothal. On the day before the wedding the *Aruvas* complete all the arrangements for the *Muhurtham*, supervise dress rehearsals of the ceremony (which rehearsals are part of the ritual), and organise feasts for the neighbouring villagers.

On several points, Coorg marriage laws and traditions diverge from those of most Hindus. Divorce has always been easy to obtain if loss of caste, incompatibility of temperament or a wife's unfaithfulness could be proved before the village *panchayat*; but of course a wife can take no action because of her husband's unfaithfulness, nor can she leave him without his consent. A divorced wife may not keep any of her children over the age of three, and babies or toddlers who accompany her when she leaves home must normally be returned to their father on their third birthday. Should the mother in an exceptional case be able to obtain permanent custody, the children's links with their father are formally severed and they forfeit their right to any share of his family property. Divorce, however, has always been rare amongst Coorgs, as has polygamy, though a man without a son by his first wife is free to take a second. Alternatively, he can adopt his eldest daughter's husband (as was also the custom in Tibet), if the young man is willing to forfeit his share of his own family property.

Child-marriages were never customary here and widows and divorced women have always been permitted to remarry – the former one year after their husband's death, the latter six months after their divorce. In pre-British days, polyandry was sometimes practised: but the strangest of the six forms of marriage available to a Coorg woman is the *Pachchadak Nadapad*. This is a temporary marriage, now uncommon though still occasionally resorted to when for some reason no suitable husband can be found to wed an heiress. The young man's only duty is to beget a child so he retains his right to his own family property, receives no share of his wife's – apart from food and clothing while he remains with her – and is free to marry another girl whenever he chooses. The children of such marriages can claim maternal property only. Another odd form of 'marriage' is the *Paithandek Alepa Mangala*, a special ceremony to honour a woman who has borne ten healthy children. (Formerly Coorgs considered five sons and five daughters the ideal family: now one of each is the aim.)

Many university-educated Coorg women continue to work after marriage, if they have already been leading independent professional lives, and many others return to work as teachers, doctors – or whatever – when their children go away to school. Moreover, the women of less well-off families are often on their local *panchayat* committee, where they take a vigorous part in debates on every aspect of rural development.

19 February.

We arrived at the *Kodava Samaj* in a hired jeep at nine-thirty, Rachel wearing a smartly tailored skirt and blouse, specially made for her by Aunty, and myself gorgeously attired in borrowed plumes and laden with borrowed jewellery. The bridegroom was not due until ten-fifteen, so we had time to study the scene before the crowd gathered.

The open space in front of the *Kodava Samaj* had been covered by an awning of bamboo mats and dried plantain fronds, under which 500 metal folding chairs awaited the male guests; within the building, another 500 awaited the female guests. At the far end of the long main hall, on the right as one entered by the central door, was a small carpeted platform under a canopy of white and red cloth, supported by four tall plantain stumps decorated with coconuts, mango garlands, jasmine and various other richly scented cream-coloured blossoms. In the centre of the platform stood two low, three-legged teak stools with a large, shallow, circular wicker basket beside each, and to the left of these stools, as one faced the hall, was a rosewood and brass pedestal lamp, three feet high, which would soon be lit with a flame from the sacred wall-lamp in the bridegroom's *Ain Mane*. Near the platform was a door leading to a small room, simply furnished with two single beds and two chairs, where the bridegroom and his closest friends could lunch in private and rest during the afternoon; and at the far end of the hall was a similar room for the bride and her attendants. Opposite the main entrance another door led to the dining hall, which seats 400, and behind that we found the enormous kitchen shed where, at ten o'clock, mountains of chopped vegetables and raw meat loomed in every direction, and rows of colossal cauldrons, attended by battalions of servants, were simmering on gigantic mud stoves.

'It's like the witches brewing in my book!' exclaimed Rachel, goggle-eyed. 'Are the bride and bridegroom very rich?'

I had wondered the same thing, but in fact neither family is particularly well off, the bride's father being a retired army major and the bridegroom's a retired secondary school teacher. For this reason, no alcohol was served: a most sensible decision since drinks for 1,000 guests could have run these families into lifelong debt. And those who wished to have a self-supplied drink before lunch were free to do so without giving offence.

Coming back from the kitchen we stood in the doorway and looked around the huge hall, brilliantly lit by clear golden sunshine. I have already described the simple splendour of the *Kupya* – the Coorg man's costume – but we had not previously seen a gathering of women in all their traditional glory and this was such an overwhelming vision that even Rachel remained speechless for half a minute. Here were hundreds of glossy raven heads and golden-skinned arms and faces, and shimmering gowns and fluttering veils, and glittering, gleaming, glowing gold and silver ornaments – studded with rubies, emeralds or diamonds – and, standing in that doorway, I was mesmerised by the ever-changing pattern of saris and jewels, blending and contrasting, as little groups strolled up and down the hall, or stood animatedly chatting. There were so many rich materials, their colours and shades beyond counting – pale blue, rosy pink, old gold, turquoise, silver-grey, lime green, primrose yellow, sapphire, crimson, smoky blue, russet, dove-grey, flame red, deep purple – and here and there the pure white of a widow's sari, adding an effective touch of elegant austerity.

I failed to recognise several elderly neighbours who were wearing the Coorg veil, now no longer in everyday use. This is a large kerchief, of which one end encircles the forehead with those two corners tied at the nape of the neck, so that the rest gracefully drapes the shoulders. The fine features with which Providence – or Mother Cauvery – has endowed most Coorgs are thus emphasised, and one wonders why such a simple aid to beauty has fallen out of fashion.

At ten-fifteen a distant throbbing of drums announced the imminent arrival of Ponnappa, the bridegroom. (Here Ponnappas are as thick on the ground as Murphys in Ireland.) I hurried out to watch the procession and found that Rachel, quite beside herself with excitement, had joined a group of

Ponnappa's small nieces and was enthusiastically dancing in the middle of the road, to the huge amusement of the watching crowd. And indeed the bridegroom presented a spectacle romantic enough to make any Irish girl lose her head. He wore a dazzling white *Kupya*, a broad crimson silk sash, a flat-topped white and gold turban, a short ivory-handled dagger in a silver and gold ornamental scabbard, a heavy golden-sheathed sword, a solid gold bangle and a necklace of alternate gold and coral beads. In his right hand he carried a long staff of intricately carved rosewood, decorated with silver rings and bells and known as the *Gejje Thandu*. Formerly, if the bridegroom fell ill at the eleventh hour, this staff was accepted as his substitute and the ceremony was performed without him. To complete the picture, as Ponnappa walked slowly up the road his best man held a crimson-and-gold-tasselled white umbrella over his head.

A chair draped with crimson cloth had been placed in the centre of the road – weddings take precedence over traffic – and along the verge a dozen four-foot-high plantain stumps, each decorated with a flower, had been embedded in the ground. When the bridegroom had seated himself, and been surrounded by merrily playing musicians, his *Aruva* offered clear water from a pitcher, and a betel-nut, to a small group of relatives and close friends who in times past would have brought with them meat, rice, plantains, and their own drummers and trumpeters. Then the *Aruva* handed the bridegroom's sword to one of this group, who was supposed to cut each plantain stump with a single stroke while praying to the village God. (He succeeded in cleanly cutting only four; obviously Coorgs are not what they were.) This custom is said to be of *Kshatria* origin and to symbolise the winning of a bride through superior physical strength, skill and courage.

When we returned to the hall for the *Dampathi Muhurtham* the pedestal lamp and several dish-lamps had been lit on the platform and a large basket of rice stood ready near the stools for the giving of blessings. First the groom was led to the right-hand stool and then Nalini, the bride, who had arrived by a side entrance while we were watching the plantain cutting, took her place beside him. Dressed all in red, she looked, poor girl, very pale and tense. It was now time for each guest to ascend the platform individually, sprinkle rice on the couple, bless them, and drop a few rupees into one of the baskets. This part of the ceremony is initiated by the bride's mother. Standing before the groom, she tosses a handful of auspicious rice over his head and shoulders while invoking the blessings of God, gives him milk to drink from a spouted silver vessel and presents him with the *Pombana* – a gold coin which, being a mother's gift, is considered most precious and treasured throughout the couple's life. The women guests ascend the platform first and then, when the men form their long queue – the only orderly queue I have ever seen in India – the women move into the dining hall for lunch.

I was advised to eat with the first sitting lest I might miss the *Sambanda Kodupa* ritual, which follows immediately after the *Dampathi Muhurtham*. From my seat near the door I watched many members of the bride's family moving up and down the long lines of white-draped trestle tables, serving food with an unhurried air that belied their speed and efficiency. When each guest had a heaped leaf-platter before her someone called out, '*Ungana?*' (Shall we eat?) and the feast began; it is considered very bad form to eat before everybody has been served. As always at a Coorg banquet, the main dish was curried pork, accompanied today by a lavish variety of irresistibly delicious foods.

It is also considered bad form to get up before everybody has finished but an exception was made for me when Uncle Machiah beckoned from the door, calling that the *Dampathi Muhurtham* was almost over. As I hurried back to the hall the headman of the bridegroom's party – always the last to ascend the platform – was giving his blessings and gifts. The groom then stood up to be led three times around the sacred lamp by his best man, who next presented him to the still-sitting bride. Having sprinkled Nalini with rice, Ponnappa gave her a gold coin which she received in both hands and then, holding it in her left hand, she put her right hand in the outstretched right hand of the groom and stood up. Next her bridesmaid tied the coin presented by the groom into the corner of her sari, and the young couple stepped off the platform for the *Sambanda Kodupa* ritual.

This ceremony might be described as the legally binding part of the marriage – according to traditional law – since it involves the formal transference of the bride to the groom's family and the granting to her of all that family's rights and responsibilities. During the *Sambanda* the young couple stand at a little distance from the *Muhurtham* platform, with the bride's *Aruva* and two of her kinsmen beside the groom, and the groom's *Aruva* and two of his kinsmen beside the bride, while relatives and friends of both families gather near by to listen. According to a translation I obtained later in the afternoon, the main part of the *Aruvas'* dialogue goes as follows:

Bride's *Aruva*: The people of both *nads*, men of the houses, relatives and family friends, are they standing in rows?

Groom's *Aruva*: Yes, they are standing.

Bride's *Aruva*: Will you give to our child Nalini of Ponnappa family, whom we are about to give in marriage to your child Ponnappa of Subbiah family, the *Sambanda* of the groom's *Okka*? (Paddy-valleys.) Will you give her rights in the ten plots of pasture, in the cattle stand, in the ten pairs of bullocks, in the house, in the garden, in the ten milch cows, in the bamboo receptacle used for milking, in the cattle shed, in the manure heaps, in the axes, swords and knives, in the paddy in the granary, in the bellmetal dish leaning against the wall, in the wall-lamp, in the stock of salt in the kitchen store, in the buried treasure, in the stock of threads and needles and in all from one to hundreds of things?

Groom's *Aruva*: We give.

Bride's *Aruva*: On the marriage of our child into your family, our servants will carry on their heads goods and valuable things and cash in a box. If this is lost who is to be held responsible for the loss?

Groom's *Aruva*: I am.

Bride's *Aruva*: Then take these twelve pieces of gold (in fact eleven small pebbles are handed to the groom's *Aruva* at this point).

Groom's *Aruva*: I have received the pieces of gold. If your innocent child, who is given in marriage to our boy, complains at the groom's house that the cooked rice is too hot, the curry too pungent, the father-in-law too abusive, the mother-in-law mean, the husband incompetent and that she is not willing to stay with him, or complains that his people are too poor and goes back to her natal family and sits there, who is the person to be held responsible to advise her properly and send her back to us providing servants for company and torches to light the way?

Bride's *Aruva*: I am.

Groom's *Aruva*: Then take this witness money (he hands over a token coin).

Bride's *Aruva*: If our child were to suffer unforeseen misfortune (by this is meant the loss of her husband before she has conceived), who is responsible for sending her to her natal family with servants for company and torches for the road?

Groom's *Aruva*: I am.

Bride's *Aruva*: Then take this witness money (and he hands over a token coin).

So ends the *Sambanda* ritual, and when I inquired about the rather mystifying presentation of eleven pebbles I was told that twelve pebbles (representing pieces of gold) symbolise the sum total of an individual's rights within a joint family; and so when the bride's *Aruva* gives eleven to the groom's *Aruva* this signifies that the girl has forfeited most of her rights in her natal family, in exchange for those granted by her conjugal family. But one pebble is retained because she has a right to return to her natal family if divorced or prematurely widowed.

By this time it was two-thirty and most people were departing, leaving only one hundred or so relatives to attend the *Ganga Puja* and subsequent 'dance ordeal' at four-thirty. Nalini and Ponnappa, both looking utterly exhausted, had retired to their rooms and I assumed their doors would remain firmly closed all afternoon. But when I got back to the hall after a shopping trip into Virajpet – where my appearance in a Coorg sari occasioned much delighted comment – I saw people constantly trooping in and out of both rooms and was warmly invited to do likewise. From the door of Ponnappa's room I observed the poor fellow lying full length on a bed under a heap of tumbling small children – one of whom, need I say, had fair hair ... In an effort slightly to alleviate his torment I urged Rachel to come with me to admire the bride's ancient ornaments, but my daughter merely abated her gymnastics for long enough to say –

'I prefer the bridegroom'. Tactful prevarications have never been her forte.

In Nalini's room, the money collected during the *Dampathi Muhurtham* was being carefully counted by the bride's brother, tied in bundles and packed in a tin trunk. It looked a lot but most of the notes represented only a rupee or two and the total would scarcely cover one-quarter the cost of the banquet. Nalini was talking to three Indian nuns from Ammathi Convent School – one of them was the only Coorg ever to have become a Christian – and I sat on the bed beside her to study the bridal ornaments. I particularly liked her silver *Kausara* – a ring on each finger connected by silver chains over the back of the hand to a heavy silver wrist bracelet. No less beautiful was her *Kasara* – a similar ornament of toe rings, connected to an ankle bracelet. Most Coorg married women habitually wear a silver ring – a *Kamoira* – on the second toe of their left foot, as well as a plain solid gold wedding ring on the third finger of the left hand. Loveliest of all, however, was her *Kakkethathi*, a necklace of golden beads from which hung a large, crescent-shaped golden pendant, studded with rubies and edged with many small pearls.

The next ceremony – the *Ganga Puja* – took place soon after four-thirty at the well behind the *Kodava Samaj*. For this Nalini was attended by two maidens (her first cousins) and a little group of older relatives. On the wall of the well were laid out a towel, a coconut, a hand of plantains, a bowl of rice, a lime, betel-leaves and nuts, *vibhuthi* (a coloured powder for anointing the forehead) and the bridegroom's ornamental knife. Having washed her face, hands and feet, and prayed while anointing her forehead, the bride thrice sprinkled auspicious rice into the well as a salute to Ganga, the goddess of water. Then she placed three pieces of areca-nut on three betel-leaves and dropped them carefully into the water, so that they would not overturn. Next she half peeled the bananas and left them on the well wall while she cracked the coconut with her husband's *peechekathi* and spilled all its water into the well. She chewed betel – an indulgence not permitted to unmarried women – while filling two brass pitchers with water and placing them one above the other on her head: and then her ordeal began.

The ordeal called *Battethadpa* (obstructing the path) is another of those Coorg marriage customs said to be of *Kshatria* origin. When the bride, followed by her attendants, leaves the well to carry the pitchers around the house and into the kitchen, she finds her way blocked by energetically dancing menfolk of the groom's family. This gambol sometimes continues all night and a four- or five-hour session is common. Obviously it imposes a severe strain on the already exhausted bride, who is being closely studied by scores of her new relatives as she stands immobile, balancing two heavy pitchers of water on her head and only occasionally being allowed to move a few steps forward. Perhaps it is appropriate that a martial race should thus treat its young women, testing their fitness as mothers of the next generation of warriors, but I did feel very sorry for Nalini this afternoon.

The moment the bandsmen began to play dance music Rachel came bounding along from I don't know where, and seizing Major Ponnappa's hand (they seemed by now to be intimate friends) proceeded to execute a most complicated *pas de deux* with him. At its conclusion she continued to dance in front of the bride, without ceasing, for an hour and forty minutes; and, though only males are supposed to take part in the *Battethadpa*, she was constantly egged on by her fellow dancers.

The Coorgs are a strange and delightful mixture of traditionalist and what you might call 'unconventionalist'. They seem always ready to make allowances for the customs, whims and eccentricities of others and, much as they value their own ancient ceremonies, they are not fanatically rigid about detail if for any reason it seems desirable to improvise or permit modifications.

When we left the *Kodava Samaj* at six-thirty, as the bride was entering the kitchen, I had misgivings about Rachel's ability to walk three miles after so vigorous a dancing session; but she went leaping ahead of me, over-excitedly recalling the day's highlights. These included being allowed to play with the bridegroom's sword – which brought me out in a cold sweat, as Coorg swords are kept in good working order.

On our way home the sunset seemed like an echo of those saris in the *Kodava Samaj*. At first the western sky was spread with pinkish-gold clouds, against which the ever-present Ghats were sharply outlined, their shadows a delicate mauve, while beyond a burnished paddy-valley stood the dark silhouettes of palm and plantain fronds, and all the noble trees of the forest. But soon the clouds deepened to crimson, as the clear sky above changed from pale blue to blue-green – and then to that incomparable royal blue of dusk in the tropics. Now the clouds were a rare, pink-tinged brown, above purple mountains, and moments later the first stars – chips of gold – were glinting overhead, and jungle bats bigger than crows came swooping and squeaking from the trees, and in the distance a jackal began his forlorn, eerie solo.

16

Praying and Dancing

20 February.
Today six *banjaras* – known to generations of British as 'brin-jarries' – arrived in Devangeri with three covered wagons and set up shop on the maidan behind this house. These traders criss-cross South India with huge covered wagons drawn by pairs of magnificent Mysore whites, which, according to Hydar Ali, are 'to all other bullocks as the horses of Arabia are to all other horses'. (In Coorg, where there are no representatives of the equine species, one begins to develop an eye for a good bullock.) Most brinjarries look exceedingly wild, ragged and unkempt but are cheerful, friendly and scrupulously honest. They spend five or six days in each village, exchanging the produce of their land near Mysore for surplus paddy which is eventually transported to areas where it is scarce and dear. When I asked why the Coorgs do not keep their surplus grain, and sell it themselves later on, I was told the cost of arranging transport for small quantities would make the profits not worth while. It is more economic to barter it now for a supply of potatoes, onions and pulses, which will rocket in price during the monsoon.

It does one good to see such institutions still flourishing in 1974. This afternoon I bartered our surplus rice – Tim had presented us with enough to feed twenty Irish people – for potatoes and onions, which have recently become very expensive in the bazaar; and as I watched my little bag being carefully weighed on an antique scales, I remembered a letter written to Bombay by Arthur Wellesley before the Battle of Assaye: 'The brinjarries are a species of dealers who attend the army with grain and other supplies which they sell in the bazaars. In general, they seek for these supplies which are sold for the cheapest rate and they bring them on their bullocks to the armies . . . Captain Barclay wrote by my orders to the brinjarry *gomashta* (agent) . . . to inform him that all the brinjarries of the Carnatic, Mysore and the ceded districts would be immediately wanted and that they were to load and join the army.' That was in 1803 and already the brinjarries had become the mainspring of Britain's military campaigns throughout South and Central India. There was then no issue of army rations and no army service corps; the Maratha and French troops simply lived off the land, looting their way through various regions and naturally not endearing themselves to the inhabitants. So when the British bought their supplies from the brinjarries at current market rates they made a good impression which has lasted to this day in South India.

This evening, as I was reading Rachel's bedtime story, Ponappa the tailor called – he whose wife died a few weeks ago. I did not at once realise that the poor man had been on the batter and an M.C.C. reduced him to an hour and a half of maudlin lamentations. His main obsession was the humiliating fact that the drugs given to his wife during her last illness had darkened her skin, previously 'as fair as a European's', so that I never saw her 'looking beautiful like a flowering jasmine'. He anxiously asked if I believed him, and repeatedly asserted that he could never have married a girl 'with so much darkness on her'. Having given him three mugs of strong black coffee I at last succeeded in gently but firmly guiding him down the ladder – no easy task, by candlelight – and setting him on his homeward path. But I suspect he will have stumbled back to our 'local' as soon as my back was turned.

As I write, a group of men and boys are making merry in the courtyard by torchlight: dancing, leaping, singing, shouting, drumming, fluting, horn-blowing – and exhaling such powerful Arak fumes that I shall scarcely need another M.C.C. this evening. They are celebrating, as I suppose Ponappa was, an annual Hindu festival which, being very light-hearted, particularly appeals to Coorgs. The Lord Krishna is supposed to be fast asleep tonight, so petty thieving is allowed by tradition and householders are meant to admit these roving bands who may help themselves to food, drink and small coins. They also play practical jokes on the community, such as throwing something unpalatable (but not polluting) down public wells, felling trees to block roads and filling with water the petrol tanks of buses

or motor cars. Subaya very properly says they must not be
admitted to this house because the owners are absent, but I
suppose I had better go down now to tip them before they
waken Rachel. They certainly make a cheerful scene, by the
wavering light of unsteadily held plantain-stump torches, but
their musicians are rather too far gone to be melodious.

24 February.

Today we were invited to a farewell lunch with the Chengappas in Virajpet and, it being Sunday, I decided to attend
Mass in the Roman Catholic church. The large building was
packed, mostly with women and children, and everyone sang
hymns lustily if untunefully. By far the best feature of the
interior was a simple Face-the-People altar of polished teak.

As we left the church we were stopped by a skinny, frail-
looking little man of perhaps thirty-five, who had collected the
offerings. He asked Rachel her name and then exclaimed,
'Rachel! That is nice bit of chance! This minute my daughter is
to be christened Rachel also, so you must come to watch how
she gets her name!'

Turning to follow the proud father into the church, I
marvelled that such a fragile creature should have begotten a
child. Then we took our place beside the font, where a
40-day-old infant was being held by an elderly woman whom I
assumed to be a godmother of granny's generation. By now most
of the congregation had left, though I noticed that one long
pew near the font was full of school-children of mixed ages who
seemed to be taking a lively interest in the proceedings.

At the end of the twenty-minute ceremony, Rachel II's father
turned to the elderly 'godmother' and introduced her as his
wife; then he turned to the pewful and introduced it collectively
as 'my other children'.

'How many?' I asked weakly, feeling too pole-axed to do my
own counting.

'Thirteen, with Rachel,' said the skinny little man happily.
'So now we quickly have another, because thirteen is a bad and
misfortunate number.' He beamed at his haggard wife. 'Perhaps we shall have the full score, the round twenty – my wife is
aged only thirty-four – there is time.'

·   ·   ·   ·   ·

At the Chengappas Rachel for once said the right thing by remarking that she would like to live here always; and I can quite see why. There is never any fuss about the dangers of motor-traffic, or about getting too hot, too cold or too wet – she can run naked all day through the forest and over the paddy-valleys and in and out of as many streams and ponds as come her way. This morning she was out with friends from eight o'clock until ten-thirty and returned mud to the ears, having obviously had a whale of a time in some buffalo hole. I had to take her to the well and pour several buckets of water over her before she was fit to go out to lunch.

During the meal we discussed the problems of recruiting well-educated Indian girls to the nursing profession, which because of pollution complications is still regarded as fit only for the lowest caste. Mrs Chengappa explained that until living conditions for the student nurses are improved there is little hope of the situation changing. The younger Chengappa daughter's ambition to be a nurse is supported in theory by her parents; but in practice they feel bound to discourage it because student nurses are not allowed to rent flats and conditions in the hospital hostels would prove intolerable for such a girl. Yet nursing will only become socially acceptable *after* a pioneering corps of high-caste girls has led the way, so here India has yet another vicious circle.

25 February.

On the third of March we leave Coorg for North India, so we have only six more nights in Devangeri. Coincidentally, on our last evening a torchlight display of Coorg folk-dancing is being staged on the maidan here, as part of the annual Mercara-Darien (Connecticut) get-together, and those jollifications may perhaps lighten that gloom which has already settled on me at the thought of leaving Devangeri. We have been invited to spend the night of the second at the Machiahs, and next morning we catch the Bangalore bus.

Now the midday hours are noticeably hotter – though never uncomfortable, as there is an increasing amount of cloud and breeze. Soon the heavy 'blossom showers' of March will come; how I wish we could have stayed to see the plantations being transformed into white oceans of heavily scented blossom, and

the grey-brown maidans turning green! These March showers
are vitally important for next year's coffee; if they are inade-
quate the crop is ruined, however good the later monsoon rains
may be. And it is not always easy to get the ripe berries harvested
before the showers, which would destroy them, so during the
past week we have observed tremendous activity in the plantations.

Rachel had just gone to sleep this evening when an unfamiliar
car appeared in the compound and I saw emerging from it one
of our Virajpet merchant friends, coming with his wife and two
small sons to say good-bye and present us with farewell gifts of
sandalwood and expensive Cadbury's chocolate. Mr Kusum's
father wrote a history of Coorg in Kannada, and in addition to
his flourishing general store in Virajpet he owns a printing
press in Mercara and is therefore, by Indian reckoning, a
publisher.

When I first asked Mr Kusum, 'To which community do you
belong?' he proudly replied, 'I am of Indira Gandhi's community – a Kashmiri Brahman.' But the family moved from
Goa to Coorg eighty years ago and it is many generations since
they left Kashmir. They remain, however, strict vegetarians,
teetotallers and non-smokers – not easy people to entertain *chez*
Murphy.

Mr Kusum's account of the status of Indian authors made my
hair stand on end. He assured me that an author can hope to
make no more than fifteen or twenty pounds sterling on a book
that sells 2,000 or 3,000 copies. Moreover, reviewers are paid
nothing by the newspapers – the free review copy is their fee –
and are therefore open to bribes from authors or the enemies of
authors. Probably – added Mr Kusum – the enemies, because
by the time the author has paid for the printing of his book, and
the paper on which it is printed, he is unlikely to be able to
afford a bribe. My professional blood ran cold as the Indian
literary scene was thus revealed in all its ghastly detail. No
wonder Indians are incredulous when their persistent question-
ing reveals that I am, (a) a writer and, (b) not given a grant to
travel by the Irish Government, a university, a business firm or
anyone else. They simply cannot imagine a lowly *writer* being
able to afford to travel abroad.

26 February.

At last week's wedding the Good Shepherd nuns who were our fellow-guests invited us to their Ammathi school to meet its ancient English founder. This school has over 300 pupils, between the ages of four and thirteen, and it was built and is being run without the government support that was hoped for – which lack of support is interpreted by some as a symptom of official anti-Christian bias. However, the Good Shepherd Order is extremely wealthy in India, where it has been established for over 130 years, and the Coorg families for whom the school caters are well able to pay high fees. The tiny minority of non-fee-paying pupils are 'deserving cases' from poor Ammathi families and are presumably admitted as a token gesture, since the Order was founded not to educate the rich but to tend the poor – and especially to reclaim the souls of unmarried mothers and prostitutes.

After touring the well-equipped classrooms I was taken to meet Mother Christine, the 79-year-old English woman who founded the school. Sixty years ago she became a Roman Catholic, to the horror of her peppery old colonel father, and a year later she joined the Good Shepherd Order in Bangalore. Her forefathers had been soldiers in India for almost two centuries and I enjoyed her account of coming to Ammathi at 70 years old, with only one 73-year-old companion, and briskly building a new school of which the local Indian authorities did not really approve. It is beautifully ironical that this archaic flare-up of British Imperialism was in a cause which Mother Christine's forbears would have abhorred.

By any standards Mother Christine is a memorable personality: a tiny wisp of a woman, hardly up to my shoulder, but still vibrant with energy, intelligence, good humour and determination – and having, at the core of all this, great gentleness, sympathy and wisdom. As we sat drinking endless cups of tea, in a small, sunlit, freshly painted parlour, I again became aware of the difference between Roman Catholic and Protestant missionary attitudes to non-Christians. In theory the Roman Catholic church is one of the most inflexible: in practice the majority of its representatives are conspicuously tolerant and considerate in their relationships with non-Christians.

At noon, when we stood up to leave Mother Christine, she accompanied us on to the balcony, looked at the children erupting from their classrooms and suddenly exclaimed, 'I love India!' Then she turned to me and said, 'Perhaps the hippies are right – perhaps in the future mankind's spiritual salvation will flow from here. Have you ever thought that this is the most prayerful country in the world?'

27 February.

In the forest near Jagi's village is an ancient temple to which, for certain festivals, pilgrims come from all over South-West India. I find its special character most attractive; so discreetly does it merge into the landscape that one could walk by without noticing it, but for a massive black Nandi facing the entrance. The oblong structure is crudely built of dark grey stone blocks, unskilfully dressed, and the façade has only a few clumsy carvings of mythological figures, almost erased by time. Such a temple could well be 1,000 years old, or more; no one has the least idea when it was erected, though all agree that it is of extraordinary antiquity. The door is kept locked and only the local Brahman priest, who lives near by, may actually enter the shrine, but yesterday Jagi suggested that I should attend this morning's *puja* and then have a farewell breakfast at her house; she added that I would most likely find myself alone with the Brahman, Coorg villagers not being great temple-goers.

We set out early this morning, before the sun had lifted the night mist from the face of Coorg, and walked enchanted through a world all silver and green and filled with bird song – until suddenly, as we approached Jagi's house, a warm golden light came sliding through the trees to catch the richly blooming poinsettias that line this *oni*.

I left Rachel with Jagi and continued alone, removing my shoes at the little opening in the low stone wall around the grassy temple compound. As the priest had not yet arrived, Nandi and I were on our own in the shade of giant nellige, peepul, jack-fruit, mango and palm-trees. The sky above those lofty, mingling branches was a clear, fresh, morning blue, criss-crossed by the emerald flashes of parakeets, and the peace of that place was immense.

Then the Brahman appeared: a tall, thin, stooping elderly

man, wearing only a *lunghi* and a forbidding expression. Probably he disapproves of *mlecchas* within the temple compound – but this, I must stress, is sheer conjecture. Nothing was said or done to make me feel unwelcome. Indeed, so completely was I ignored that at the end of an hour I had begun to doubt the reality of my own existence. Yet I could sympathise with his attitude: in a remote, impersonal way I even found him congenial. Plainly he was a devout man of the gods.

Amidst the hubbub of a big temple, or even of a small temple in a town, all is bewilderment and confusion for the uninitiated, and one cannot quite grasp what is going on. But this morning, alone with the Brahman in the stillness of the forest, I could observe every detail from the moment the sacrificial fire was roused in the little stone hut beside the temple. As I stood by the open door, watching the small flames jumping and lengthening in the half-darkness, I saw them – not too fancifully – as links with the *garhapatya* fires of the earliest Aryans in India, who had no temples or holy precincts of any kind but lit their sacred fires on some level grassy spot and worshipped joyously under the sky.

All the time murmuring Sanskrit verses – for in the beginning was the Word – the priest took his brass pitcher to the well near Nandi, and fetched water in which to cook his sacrificial rice. While it was simmering he stripped a coconut, half-peeled a few plantains, prepared his camphor dish-lamp and incense-burner, strung a few aromatic garlands of forest flowers, and ground antimony between two stones to make a red paste – symbol of happiness – with which to anoint Shiva, Ganesh, Nandi and the *lingam* stone that stands under a sacred tree behind the temple.

When he approached the hut door with his laden brass tray I stepped aside, and then followed him to the temple door, which he had opened on his way to the well. Two ancient images loomed within, close to the entrance – the four-armed Shiva, dancing on the prostrate body of the demon of delusion, and Rachel's beloved elephant-headed, pot-bellied Ganesh, who is Shiva's son by his consort Parvati, the mountain goddess. Standing at the foot of the half-dozen worn stone steps that led up to the shrine, I was hardly six feet away from the Brahman as he sat cross-legged before his gods and began to perform those rituals that already were old when Christ was born.

Occasionally, in India, the sheer weight of tradition over-whelms and our Western concept of time becomes meaning-less – a disturbing and yet exhilarating experience, offering a glimpse of possibilities discounted by logic and modern science, but not by the immemorial intuitions of mankind. And so it was this morning, as I watched the Brahman making his oblations, ringing his bell, wafting incense, presenting garlands, cupping his hands over the flame of the dish-lamp and gravely reciting Sanskrit formulas the exact words of which he may or may not have understood.

I despair of conveying, to those who have never seen it, the eloquent gracefulness of a Hindu priest's hand-movements as he worships. All his oblations and recitations are accompanied by these intricate, stylised, flowing gestures which symbolically unite him to the object of his worship and are of surpassing beauty. At the end of this morning's *puja*, as the Brahman withdrew from the temple – moving past the *mleccha* with down-cast eyes – I could not at once emerge from the state of exalta-tion into which he had unwittingly drawn me.

2 March.

The Ayyappas had nobly offered to entertain Rachel today, while I got on with sorting and packing and cleaning, but early in the afternoon I heard at the foot of the ladder that choked kind of sobbing which means a child is deeply upset. During a romp with her Harijan friends she had fallen on to a pile of broken stones off a five-foot wall and she is lucky only to have minor cuts on her left upper arm and what looks like a badly sprained right wrist. When I had washed her cuts and read three chapters of *Alice* as an anaesthetic she said chirpily, 'Aunty Ayyappa has asked us both to tea so I think we'd better go now'. Which we did, and she skipped ahead of me like a spring lamb. But by the time Dr Chengappa and his family arrived at six o'clock, to supervise the final arrangements for the dance display, her right forearm was perceptibly swollen and the doctor said she should wear a sling.

By sunset all Devangeri had assembled on the maidan. A row of chairs stood ready for the dozen or so Darien guests, who were being driven down from Mercara, and Tim beckoned me to sit beside him; predictably, he is President of the Mercara-Darien Association. He told me that Devangeri is among the few villages in which women's dancing is being revived. During the pre-Lingayat era Coorg women participated in all community events, dancing at village festivals and joining their menfolk in those lengthy songs which form an important part of the ceremonies at funerals, weddings and *Huthri* celebrations.

In the centre of the maidan stood the *Kuthimbolicha* – a tall brass pedestal lamp, around which the dancers circle – and by seven-fifteen the guests had arrived, the lamp had been lit and Rachel was well established on the lap of the most famous of all Coorgs, General K. M. Cariappa, retired Commander-in-Chief of the Indian Army. Clearly they had fallen in love at first sight, which then astonished me; later I discovered that the General is famous on three continents as a child-magnet.

There were three groups of dancers and the programme was opened by a score of slim, shy, graceful schoolgirls who performed with great assurance and skill. Next came the women, who have several times been invited to participate in New Delhi's annual Republic Day celebrations. They dance to the music of a cymbal, chanting gravely as they circle around the flaring lamp – bending, swaying, twisting – and rhythmically they raise and lower their arms while their ornaments tinkle and flash and their silken saris ripple in the torchlight like cascades of colour.

Then appeared the turbanned, barefooted men in their immaculate *Kupyas*, each armed with his shining sword, ready to dance the renowned and exhausting *Balakata* – a Coorg war-dance of incalculable antiquity. I was stirred to the depths by these handsome sons of warriors who invoked the war gods while running and pirouetting and flourishing their swords as though about to behead the next man. As the dance progressed everyone became increasingly caught up in the emotion it generated and the circle whirled faster and faster, while swords were flourished more and more boldly, and the dust rose from proudly stamping feet, and dark eyes gleamed beneath gilded turbans. Then the excitement spread and, with typical Coorg spontaneity, many of the crowd surged on to the maidan to give their own performances – including General Cariappa and

Rachel, who went stamping and leaping through clouds of dust, hand in hand, beaming at each other and waving gaily in response to the cheers of the delighted crowd. I shall not quickly forget the tall, slim, military figure of the General, contrasting with the small, sturdy, sun-tanned figure of my daughter as they cavorted improbably together by the light of mighty plantain-stump torches – held high, with rosy sparks streaming off them in the night breeze, by a dozen laughing youths on the periphery of the crowd.

An hour later, as we walked with the Machiahs through the silver and black silence of a brilliantly moonlit forest, we could hear behind us the chanting, cheering and cymbal-clashing of the Devangeri villagers who had settled down to an impromptu dancing session that was unlikely to end before dawn.

Epilogue

Our train journey from Bangalore to Delhi took forty-nine hours. Luckily, however, a kind attendant – who never looked for a tip, much less a bribe – went to a lot of trouble and was eventually able to provide us with sleeping-berths. (These were narrow slatted wooden shelves and during the heat of the day they were too close to the roof for comfort; but we both had good nights.) Only when travelling by rail is it an unqualified advantage to be a woman in India; the third-class ladies' coaches are usually less crowded and filthy than the rest, although men accompanying women relatives also use them.

We changed trains at Madras, where I had only forty minutes to find our reserved seats. The anxiously hurrying crowds were so dense I had to use force to make progress and Rachel understandably found the scene a little frightening. As she was in some danger of being injured by the mob I bundled her into a convenient ladies' coach and left her guarding our kit, sitting beside an amiable European nun for company. Then I resumed my search, but because of the startling metamorphosis that had overtaken the name MURPHY at the pen of some railway clerk it was too late to move Rachel by the time I had found the right coach.

The nun was an Italian who had spent twenty years in India as a medical missionary. She mentioned that she now practises as a gynaecologist in Kerala and this reminded me of a name given me in London by Jill Buxton, before we left for Bombay.

'Do you know a Sister Dr Alberoni?' I asked. 'She works in the Nirmala Hospital near Caldicot.'

The nun looked at me strangely for a moment and then said – '*I* am Sister Alberoni!'

One long, unbroken rail journey is an almost essential ingredient of travel in India, for it enables the traveller to *feel* that country's vastness. North of Madras city we passed through mile after endless mile of flat, desiccated, unpeopled landscape, where one remembered that India is not at all overpopulated in relation to her area. The earth was cracked and grey and worn, and the grey-brown, dusty, ragged leaves, dangling from stunted trees in the still heat, looked like the grey-brown, dusty, ragged garments of the peasants who crowded every station, staring impassively at the train. Although many outsiders, including myself, may romanticise about the beautiful simplicity of life in rural India, there is nothing either beautiful or simple about life as it is now lived by the majority in Maharashtra, Gujerat, U.P. or Bihar.

The very poor are rarely met on a train, for obvious reasons – though my ticket from Bangalore to Delhi cost only Rs.62 – but near Wardha one conscience-smiting family did get aboard for a few hours. It consisted of a mother and five small children and they had their lunch wrapped in a leaf: two thin chapattis and a little chilli sauce at the bottom of a tin mug. They sat opposite us in a row, like an Oxfam advertisement, and when the two chapattis had been divided between six each had only two or three mouthfuls. It was plain that never in their lives had they eaten a full meal and this is the fate of hundreds of millions of Indians – the grim reality which we had evaded in Coorg. When I handed a banana to each of them they stared at me for a moment with a dreadful incomprehension, then hastily peeled the fruit and stuffed it into their mouths as though afraid I might change my mind and take it back. There was no attempt at a smile or nod of thanks; these people are so unused even to the minimal generosity involved that they received it with incredulity rather than gratitude.

Several attempts were made to board our train by 'ticketless persons', who are always suspect though they may genuinely only want a free ride. One nasty incident involved a youngish, ragged man with a tangled beard and a not unpleasant expression. He tried to jump on as we were moving out of a small station and I happened to be sitting by an open window beside the locked door with which he was struggling. Then a guard came along and, instead of merely forcing him to drop off, opened the door, dragged him on board and beat him up so savagely with a truncheon that he fell unconscious outside the lavatory door – and lay there for three hours, with a bleeding head. He had not long come to when the train stopped in the middle of nowhere (as it not infrequently did, for reasons of its own) and the guard again unlocked the door and thrust the man out into a hot, barren, rocky wilderness.

In Delhi we were invited to spend the night at Crystal Rogers' Animals' Shelter. This institution consists of an enormous, dusty compound, containing many comfortable enclosures for animals and one acutely uncomfortable bungalow for humans – or at least that is the theory. In practice the bungalow might belong to Dr Dolittle; it is so full of dogs, cats, guinea-pigs, rabbits, monkeys, mice, parrots and mynahs that we had to sleep in the compound on charpoys. Rachel was ecstatic to find herself having supper in a room where two tame monkeys were playing ball and within moments of our arrival a pack of puppies had eaten through three of the most vital straps on my rucksack. Half an hour later, as I straightened up after trying to wash myself with a quart of water in a hip bath, I almost split my skull on the sharp end of a cage that hung over the bath and contained two foul-mouthed parrots. At meal times ravening cats attempted to intercept one's food between plate and mouth, and in the compound were countless other cats and dogs, and several injured bulls, bullocks and horses lying around looking contented. Spacious wired-in enclosures are provided for badly maimed or seriously ill large animals, whose eyes would otherwise be picked out by carrion crows. Some patients have to be put down every week, but any with a chance of recovery are given the best treatment. Moreover, each animal, from a colossal white humped bull to a diminutive white mouse is loved individually and reacts accordingly; and the whole of this extraordinary institution is run on funds raised through Miss Rogers' own efforts.*

On 13 March, a few hours before we were due to catch our train to Bombay, I discovered that our return air tickets were missing: perhaps a monkey or a mouse had devoured them. This looked like being a major disaster, since our cheap-rate concession expired on 15 March. Most appropriately, however,

---

* Many question the ethics of expensive animal relief work in a country ravaged by human suffering and I myself cannot see the point of saving the lives of unwanted animals who could be painlessly put down. However, some of my readers may feel otherwise, so here is the address to which subscriptions to the Animals' Shelter should be sent: Mrs P. M. Skeate, 50 Pensford Avenue, Kew Gardens, Surrey TW9 4HP.

we were rescued by a Coorg – P. M. Ayyappa, one of the Machiahs' three sons, who is an Air India pilot and was then living in Bombay. His parents had arranged for us to spend our last Indian night in his flat and when he drove us to the airport, to catch a plane for which we had no tickets, he took enormous trouble to contact London and use his influence to get confirmation of our right to board the 9.30 a.m. British Airways flight from Bombay.

As we took off I glanced at Rachel, who was peering down at the 'shattered' environs of Bombay, and it struck me that 5-year-olds are scarcely less enigmatic than Hindus. What had the past months meant to her I only knew that from my point of view she had been the best of travelling companions – interested, adaptable and uncomplaining. Then suddenly she turned to me and said sorrowfully, 'I don't really like leaving India!' And with that comment I was content.

39 - 53 - 61 - 72 - 3 - 5 - 7 -

Select Bibliography

Beast and Man in India. J. G. Kipling (Macmillan: 1891).
Mother India. Katherine Mayo (Cape: 1927).
Father India. C. S. Ranga Jyer (Selwyn & Blount: 1927).
An Indian Journey. Waldemar Bonsels (Allen & Unwin: 1929).
The Myth of the Mystic East. R. H. Elliot (Blackwoods: 1934).
The Legacy of India. G. T. Garratt (O.U.P.: 1937).
India of the Princes. Rosita Forbes (The Book Club: 1939).
The Discovery of India. Jawaharlal Nehru (London: 1946).
Religion and Society Among the Coorgs of South India. M. N. Srinivas (O.U.P.: 1952).
The Other Mind: A Study of Dance in South India. Beryl de Zoete (Gollancz: 1953).
Just Half a World Away. Jean Lyon (Hutchinson: 1955).
A History of South India. Nilakanta Sastri (O.U.P.: 1955).
India. Madeleine Biardeau (Vista Books: 1960).
Hinduism. K. M. Sen (Penguin Books: 1961).
Caste in India. J. H. Hutton (O.U.P.: 1963).
Marriage and Family in India. K. M. Kapadia (O.U.P.: 1963).
India. Taya Zinkin (Thames & Hudson: 1965).
The Continent of Circe. N. C. Chaudhuri (Chatto & Windus: 1965).
The Crisis of India. Ronald Segal (Cape: 1965).
Purity and Danger. Mary Douglas (Routledge & Kegan Paul: 1966).
A History of India (2 vols.). Romila Thapar and Percival Spear (Pelican Books: 1966).
The Kodavas. B. D. Ganapathy (Privately published, Mangalore 1967).
A Special India. James Halliday (Chatto & Windus: 1968).
India from Curzon to Nehru and After. Durga Das (Collins: 1969).
The British Image of India. Allen Greenberger (O.U.P.: 1969).
Life Without Birth. Stanley Johnson (Heinemann: 1970).
Basic Writings of S. Radhakrishnan (E. P. Dutton: 1970).
Portrait of India. Ved Mehta (Weidenfeld & Nicolson: 1970).
The Speaking Tree. Richard Lannoy (O.U.P.: 1971).
Delusions and Discoveries. Benita Parry (Allen Lane: 1972).
Witness to an Era. Frank Moraes (Weidenfeld & Nicolson: 1973).
Journey to Gorakhpur. John Moffit (Sheldon Press: 1973).
Into India. John Keay (John Murray: 1973).
India 1973 (Published by Ministry of Information, Government of India).
Murray's Handbook to India, Pakistan, Burma, Ceylon (21st Edition).
The Penguin Bhagavad Gita, translated by Juan Mascaro.

Index

Index

261

pollution, 195ff., 217–18. *See also* caste system
Ponappa, 217–22, 226, 243
population problem, 29–30
Prajapita Brahma Kumaris, 75–6
princely states, 68, 69, 70
Puranas, 84

Radhakrishnan, Dr 6, 9, 70
Ram, 7, 8
Rashtriya Swayamasevak Sang, 79–80
Ratnagiri, 15–16
Rolling Thunder, 250

Sastri Nilakanta, 132
Shanti, 175, 176
Shivaram, 114
Shri Narayana Guru, 109
Sidapur, 169, 170, 215
spitting and pollution, 146–7
sterilisation, *see* birth control
Subaya, 175, 186, 187, 193, 196, 244

Tala Cauvery, 228–30
Tamil Nadu, 126–68 *passim*
Tellicherry, 104, 107
Tethong, T. C. and Judy, 31, 34–5, 36–9, 43, 44, 64
Thekkady, 156–7, 159
Thimmiah, A. C. and Mrs, 57, 59, 62, 81, 83, 87, 91, 94, 97–9,

100, 174, 205, 213, 229–30, 242, 251
Thimmiah, Sita, 57, 92, 95, 98, 99, 205, 229, 230
Thomas the Apostle, St, 113
Tibetans, *see* Mundgod, Bylekuppa
Tippu Sultan, 67, 177
Tiruchendur, 134, 135, 136, 140, 144
Tirunelveli, 124, 145
Tisaiyanvilai, 129–34, 143–7
Travancore, 119
  Hills, 163
Trivandrum, 118–20
Tucci, Prof., 43

Udipi, 45–9
Udumalpet, 165–6
untouchability, *see* caste system, Harijans

Virajpet, 91–103, 171–2, 173, 177, 180, 213–14, 230–1, 244
Vira Raja, 55–6, 58
Visvesvaraya, Dr M., 67
Vivekananda, Swami, 109

Wadeyars, 67, 68
Webb, Kay, 62, 65, 80
Western Ghats, 125
Willingdon, islands of, 110
women, rights of, 87–8

Xavier, St Francis, 113, 130, 140–1, 143

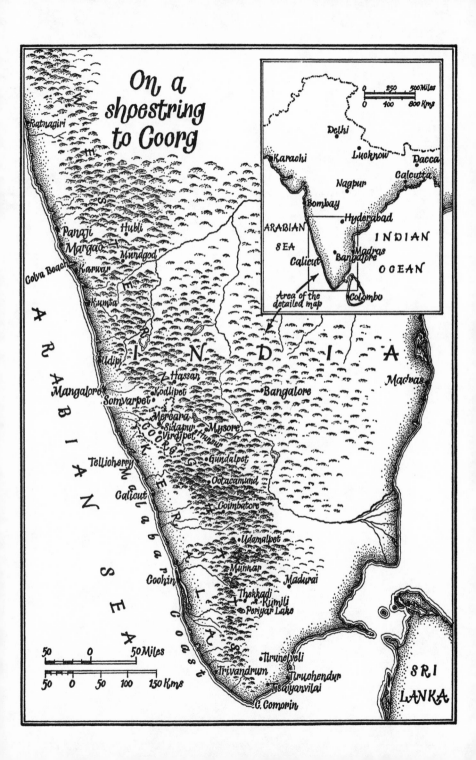